# WHAT THE BEST
# COLLEGE STUDENTS DO

# WHAT THE BEST COLLEGE STUDENTS DO

Ken Bain

THE BELKNAP PRESS OF
HARVARD UNIVERSITY PRESS

Cambridge, Massachusetts, and London, England

2012

*Library of Congress Cataloging-in-Publication Data*
Bain, Ken, author.
What the best college students do / Ken Bain.
pages    cm
Includes bibliographical references and index.
ISBN 978-0-674-06664-9 (alk. paper)
1. College students—United States.
2. Academic achievement—United States.
I. Title.
LA229.B24    2012
378.1′98—dc23        2012015548

*To two future college students,*
*Adam Bain and Nathan Bain,*
*to all future grandchildren,*
*and to Andra Looper,*
*the little girl who was so fascinated with astronomy*

# Contents

# WHAT THE BEST
# COLLEGE STUDENTS DO

# I

## THE ROOTS OF SUCCESS

Sherry Kafka came from a small town in the Arkansas Ozarks. Her little community in the backwoods of that largely rural state had none of the artistic trappings that would later define her life and make her one of the most celebrated designers and planners in the country. In fact, she later reported, her town didn't even have a movie theater. Once a week, "a gentleman" would come to town with a tent, set it up in the square, and show a movie "if he didn't get drunk that week."

Her family didn't have much money, and they moved around a lot trying to make ends meet. She went to sixteen schools in twelve years, and midway through her senior year she transferred from a fairly large school in Hot Springs to a tiny hamlet that had only six graduating students. "I think only five of us actually made it," she later reported. "I even went to schools that don't exist anymore because they were so small and could barely scrape together enough teachers." Yet all that moving didn't daunt her. "It made me forge my own methods of using what the schools offered me," she concluded. "I figured out very early that all schools are cultures, and my job was to go into that school and understand how that culture works."

No one in her family had ever gone to college right out of high school, although her father did attend a Baptist seminary later on.

They seldom read anything but the Bible, and except for the Holy Word, they had no books in the houses where she grew up—only stories. When she was four and five, her great-grandfather would tell her stories he had heard from his parents, or ones he had just made up along the way. After spinning a yarn that would fascinate the little girl, he would point at her and say, "Now you tell me a story." And so she would begin. The old man would ask her questions about the characters and animals wandering through her tales, forcing her to invent more details about them. When Sherry was in the eighth grade, a few years after her great-grandfather passed away, she decided she was a "person of the story" and that she wanted to be a writer. To become a writer, she realized that she needed to learn more, and that meant eventually going to college.

Because her family was poor, she knew it wouldn't be easy, and thus she began to fish around for some means to pay for her higher education. In her senior year of high school, she entered and won a national writing contest that promised to pay all expenses for her first year in college. When she asked her parents where she could go to school on the scholarship, they told her she could go to a university in Texas because they knew a dorm director there who could keep an eye on her if she got sick.

That fall she arrived on campus, full of excitement about her new adventure in this faraway city, and was presented with a list of mandatory courses. Before she left home, however, she had promised herself that every semester, she would take at least one course "just for me," something she would enjoy. When she looked at the list of requirements, she spotted a happy coincidence, a course that looked interesting but also fulfilled a fine arts requirement.

It was a course in the Drama Department called "Integration of Abilities." The title itself spoke to a childhood memory. When she was a little girl, her father had told her that the most successful people, "the most interesting" people, the people "who got the most out of life," were the "people who were the best integrated." He had told her that she should make a connection between every course she took and find ways that they overlapped. "When I studied," she concluded, "I should think about what happened in biology and how that applied to English, or music."

She decided to enroll. It would change her life.

Her class met in a strange theater with stages on four sides and chairs that you could spin around to face any direction. As she sat in one of those high-backed chairs the first day, a man with dark, wavy hair came into the room and sat on the edge of one of the stages. He began speaking about creativity and people. "This is a class in discovering your own creative ability," he told the students, "and all you will have to help you with your discovery is yourself and getting acquainted with the way you work."[1]

Sherry later reported that she'd never encountered anything quite like this strange man who sat on the edge of the stage in his suit and tie. "We're going to give you some problems," he said, "and some of them are pretty crazy, but they all work." As Sherry twisted a bit in her revolving chair, he continued. "What you bring to this class is yourself and your desire to participate, and what you do in here depends finally upon that."

Over that first meeting and in the days to come, her professor, Paul Baker, invited Sherry and the other students to participate in a new kind of learning. "To some," he said, "growth is almost all" just improving your memory. To others, "it lies in learning how gadgets work—how to put motors together, how to attach pipes, mix formulas, solve problems." The purpose of that type of growth, he said, "is never to develop a new method but to become extremely adept at the old ones." To a third group, growth means you develop "cults" and "systems" in which you can estimate "how far below your own standards other people have fallen." You "join, dictate, slap backs, smoke cigars in backrooms, belong to important committees, become a pseudo artist, musician, actor, prophet, preacher, politician. You drop names and surround yourself with position."

To only a few, Baker concluded, "growth is the discovery of the dynamic power of the mind." It is discovering yourself, and who you are, and how you can use yourself. That's all you have. Baker emphasized that in all of human history, no one has ever had your set of body chemistries and life experiences. No one has ever had a brain exactly like yours. You are one of a kind. You can look at problems from an angle no one else can see. But you must find out who you are and how you work if you expect to unleash the powers of your own mind.

As Sherry Kafka sat in that revolving chair, now listening intently, her professor invited her into that highest level of growth. "Everybody is unique," he kept saying, and you have much to contribute to the world. "Each of you has your own philosophy, your own viewpoint, your own physical tensions and background," he emphasized. "You come from a certain soil, a certain family with or without religious background. You were born in a certain house to a certain family at a certain time. Nobody else in the world has done so." You can, Baker argued, create in ways that no one else can.

This is a book about creative people and how they became that way. These creative people went to college and emerged from that experience as dynamic and innovative men and women who changed the world in which they lived. How did their college experiences, particularly their interactions with professors, change their patterns of thinking? Although current and future college students may find this question most compelling, teachers or parents will also find solutions here for fostering creative development and deep learning.

## Who We Studied and Why

I begin with the story of Sherry Kafka because her experience in that course with Paul Baker reflects many of the major concepts and approaches we will encounter repeatedly, and because that course transformed the lives of hundreds of people who became scientists, musicians, physicians, carpenters, historians, painters, hairdressers, philanthropists, editors, political leaders, teachers, philosophers, writers, designers, engineers, and a raft of other creative folks. What those "best students" did was take a phenomenal class, often far afield from their major area of study, and use their experiences in that course to change their lives.

They pursued the development of the dynamic power of the mind, and that end—not academic honors or simply surviving college—became their primary goal. In Baker's course, they learned a new language of creativity that centered on what you do with space, time, motion, sound, and silhouette. Sherry and her classmates came to understand themselves better and out of those insights to appreciate the unique qualities and experience that they could bring to any project. In turn, the more they understood about themselves, the greater confidence they had, and the more they appreciated the special qualities and achievements of everyone else. They became students of other people's histories—in the sciences, humanities, and arts. Most important, they found a way to motivate themselves to work.

I should say right now that this is not about people who made the highest grades in college. Most books and articles on being the "best student" concentrate only on making the grade. But my fellow interviewer, Marsha Bain, and I were after bigger game. We wanted to know how people did *after* they left school, and we selected people to follow only if they obviously learned deeply and subsequently became those highly productive individuals who continued to grow and create. We wanted to find interesting people who are aware of the world, difficult to fool, curious, compassionate, critical thinkers, creative, and happy. We sought men and women who enjoyed a challenge, whether in learning a new language or solving a problem, people who recognized when old ways would not work, who were comfortable with the strange and challenging, who had fun finding new solutions, and who were at ease with themselves.

We wanted to know how they got to be that way. How did they find their passion? How did they make the most of their education? How can we learn from them? In some cases, these highly confident, creative problem solvers learned despite college; in others, they flourished through their wonderful experiences there. Some of them have always been successful. Others spent most of their high school years barely scraping by before finally breaking out of the pack in college, or even later.

We looked for people who have distinguished themselves with great discoveries or new ways of thinking, who make good decisions and have the self-confidence to explore, to invent, to question. A physician who established a path-breaking practice, a teacher who made a huge difference in students' lives, a comedian who changed the way people laugh, a writer who captivated readers, a musician who redefined music, an innovative bricklayer or dress designer—all these are examples of people who adapt easily to new situations and can solve problems they have never encountered before.

Did they make tons of money? In some cases, yes, but that wasn't part of our criteria. If any of the people we interviewed had accumulated considerable wealth, we were interested in what they did with it, how creative they became. In other cases where the financial reward had accumulated slowly, we wanted to know how they spent their lives, and what they produced.

Did they also make good grades in college? For the most part, yes, but so did lots of other people who didn't really benefit from their education in the same way. High marks, by themselves, don't tell us much. Consider for a moment the history of grades. They haven't always been a part of formal schooling. About two hundred years ago, society began asking educators to tell them how much students had learned. Somebody somewhere—probably at Oxford or Cambridge in the late 1700s—came up with the system of giving the best learners A's, the next best B's, and so forth. It was just a system of shorthand that was supposed to describe how well people think. Through most of the 1800s, schools in England and the United States used only two grades. You either got credit for taking a certain course or you didn't. But by the late 1800s, schools had adopted a range of grades from A to F, from one to ten, or some other scale. In the twentieth century they added pluses and minuses.

What did all those letters and symbols tell you? Quite often, not much. As Neil deGrasse Tyson, the astrophysicist who directs the Hayden Planetarium, put it, "As an adult, no one ever asks you what your grades were. Grades become irrelevant." And with good reason. It's pretty difficult to get inside someone's head and discover what they understand, let alone anticipate what they will be able to do with that understanding. As a result, grades have often been lousy predictors of future success or failure. Martin Luther King Jr., for example, received a C in public speaking.[2]

A few years ago, two physicists at an American university conducted an experiment that shows how meaningless grades and test scores can become.[3] They wanted to know whether an introductory physics class in college changes the way students understand how motion works. To find out, they devised a test called the Force Concept Inventory. That examination measured how students understand motion, but it was not the kind of exam normally used to grade students in physics, and for all sorts of reasons I won't discuss here, it really can't be used for that purpose on a regular basis.

They gave that quiz to 600 people entering an introductory physics course. Most of them did poorly on it because they didn't understand motion. Without going into a lot of details, let's just say they could never put a satellite in orbit based on how they thought motion worked. But that's before they took the course. The students then took the class, and some received A's, others B's, some C's, a few D's, and several flunked.

Several months after the course ended, the students retook the same test. A few demonstrated that they had gained a better understanding of motion. Most students, however, clung to their old ideas. More important, the students' grades in the course did not predict which ones really understood Newtonian concepts of motion. The A students and the C students were just as likely—or unlikely—to have changed their understanding. Thus, some of those A students got no more out of the course than the students who flunked. The top students were simply better at memorizing formulas, plugging the right number into the equation, and calculating the correct answer on the exam, but that performance reflected nothing about how well they really understood how motion works. That doesn't mean that low grades produced better results. It just means that grades often tell us little about a student's learning.

Recently, I had lunch with a prominent chemical engineer who told me about a subject he had actually taken twice, once as an undergraduate and again in graduate school. "To this day," he said, "I don't understand that material, but I made A's in both of those classes. I learned to study in the right way and pass the examinations with flying colors, but I never really learned anything." He had learned deeply from other courses and had become quite successful in his field. But imagine for a moment that his experience in that one subject had been more typical, that he had gone through school playing the strategic grade game in all of his courses. He could have made high grades without really learning anything.

Maybe you don't care about chemical engineering, physics, or putting satellites in orbit. That's not the point. No matter what ambitions you may have, good grades don't necessarily tell us what you know or what you will be able to do with that understanding. Later in the book, we'll explore how someone could get an A and still not understand motion, but for now, just bear in mind that good grades don't necessarily mean you really comprehend anything. In school, we are often asked to memorize lots of stuff that has no influence on our subsequent lives.

Imagine for a moment a different world, a place in which students find deep meaning in everything they learn. In that universe, learning changes who people are and how they view the world. It makes them into better problem solvers, more creative and compassionate individuals, more responsible and self-confident people. Students are able to think about the implications and applications of what they learn. Not afraid to make mistakes and full of questions and ideas, the citizens of this place easily and happily explore new areas with ease while possessing a deep humility about how complex their world can be. Learning remains an adventure. Someone may forget a few facts but still know how to find them when needed.

Such a world does exist for some people. But everyone faces increasing pressures in college and life to learn only for the test or for someone else. Straight A's in high school or college are great, but—and this is a big qualification—they say little about who you are, what you are likely to do in life, how creative you are likely to be, or about how much you understand. Of course, even if you didn't get good grades, we still don't know much about you.

We have seen five types of students in college:

1. Those who receive good grades but become no more productive than their friends who receive C's and D's;
2. Those who receive good grades and who become deep learners, adaptive experts, great problem solvers, and highly creative and compassionate individuals;
3. Those who receive mediocre grades but someday achieve phenomenal success because they did learn deeply, despite their transcripts;
4. Those who receive poor marks, give up, and live a life that is largely dependent on others;
5. Those who receive poor grades but tell themselves (without much evidence) that someday they will shine.

Sure, high marks have their rewards. An excellent academic record can serve anyone well in our society. Later in this book, I'll spend some time helping anyone learn how to achieve an A, but if we had to choose between good grades or deep learning, I'd pick the latter every time.

Fundamentally, we want to promote deep, passionate, joyous, and creative learning. Grades are important, but anyone who concentrates just on making straight A's will probably not become a deep learner. Anyone who concentrates on deep learning, however, can make high marks. We will show you how that can be done.

We have two major sources for our advice. First, we pored over the research and theoretical literature on good students. Thirty to forty years of research have told us a great deal. We paid attention to some of those studies but not all of them. Some of that literature measures good students by their grade point average, and as we've already seen, that doesn't tell us much. Another group of researchers, however, has looked primarily at students who became deep learners. You will see their studies and ideas reflected here.

Second, we interviewed several dozen people who have become highly successful and creative people, good problem solvers, and compassionate individuals: physicians, lawyers, business and political leaders, computer scientists and artists, musicians, mothers, fathers, neighbors, Nobel Laureates, MacArthur "Genius Grant" recipients, Emmy winners, and a few current college students. We share some of their stories: some funny, some sad, but all inspiring.

## Integrating Your Abilities and Finding Your Passion

"This is a class," Paul Baker kept saying, "that assumes you are interested in the work of the mind." Sherry hardly noticed the guy sitting next to her—a future pro football player—as they both listened intently. Creativity can come in any area, Baker explained, not just the arts. "It could be a sermon, a scientific formula, or a book, but it could also be something you build, a well-planned street system, a beautiful meal, or a well-run gas station." Engineers, scientists, physicians, musicians, real-estate brokers, lawyers, historians, hairstylists, and others can all become creative people in their own field. A work of the mind, Baker concluded, could be anything fresh and innovative.

Her professor said something that day that startled most of the class, but Sherry found it intriguing. "A lot of people I know died when they were juniors in high school," Baker declared. "They've got the same concepts, the same ways of looking at conditions about them, the same answers, the same emotional and visual images and pictures that they've always had; there has been practically no change in them."

He invited Sherry and her classmates into a different kind of future, one in which they came to know themselves, and out of that knowledge learned to create and grow. "I hope everyone in this class will decide to take control of their lives, to reach inside themselves, to explore who they are and what they have, and learn to use those inner powers." He paused and looked at the people sitting in the back row. "Not for success, not to be seen; that's not important. What is important is that you fulfill your own personal need to keep growing."

To be creative, he emphasized again and again, you must understand yourself, including your strengths and your weaknesses. You must learn to integrate your abilities, to train them to support each other. To do that, you must open up a dialogue with your inner self. Baker asked the students to keep a notebook handy to record their reactions to the exercises. "Write out your life story up to now, and write your reactions to everything we do." Write in pencil, he told them, "or with crayons. Whatever suits you." Most important, examine yourself and how you work. "Get used to the pattern by which things come up in your mind and in your imagination. Find out when and at what times of the day you work best and what motivates you." Is it anger or serenity? Do you want to prove someone else wrong? "What sort of inner needs do you fulfill?" he asked.

Everything you create, he told the class, will come from inside you, so you must know yourself. That's the reason you must write your life story and learn to talk to yourself, to find out what's inside you, and to discard the parts that are old and stale, and enhance and use the elements of yourself that are unique, beautiful, and useful.

Every day thereafter the class began with physical exercises "to get the blood flowing," Baker told them. "I cannot work with you if you are tired and listless," he said. "I want the blood flowing and your mind sharp."

Years later, long after she had helped redesign cities, published a novel, made television documentaries, and worked on projects around the world, Sherry recalled how this phenomenal learning experience began to unfold. Baker talked about work and told the students they had to find out what kept them from working. Write a paper, he said, on your resistance to work. Explore your habits. Think about some really creative work you did in the past, and ask yourself what you had to do before you did that work. What conditions? What mood? Did you put your feet up? Walk around? Look out the window? Did you need a closed space with no distractions? An open area? Where did you go? Visualize yourself working and then go do it. "I have to eat ice cream first," he confessed.

"Faulkner," he told the class, "climbed up a tree quite often. He also spent hours with his shoes off, sitting down by the magazine counter of the local drugstore listening to people come and go. And it is said that he wrote all of *As I Lay Dying* while perched on the back of a wheelbarrow stoking a furnace at the University of Mississippi."

The goal is not to do what Faulkner did, but to understand yourself: to explore who you are, how your mind works, and what keeps it from working. This course, he told the students, is fundamentally about you. It will explore the ways you react to work and acquaint you with yourself so that you will know what you can bring to the table. "Many times you may wake up at three o'clock in the morning, and you should get up then and work. If your mind is alive and vital, get up and work. What's the loss of a few hours of sleep if you can do something?"

Maybe you have to scare yourself into working, Baker mused. Think about what it will be like when you are old, when you approach death. Will you have already died inside or will your mind be alive with new ideas that are unmistakably your own?

First, you must learn about yourself. Next, find a great creative work of the mind that excites you: see its reflection in others and in yourself, probe behind that work, seek its inner nature, and explore the possibilities it suggests. Then find your own passion and let it drive you. "If you are not capable of excitement, you will never produce anything," Baker warned.

Sherry shifted slightly in her revolving chair and took a fleeting glance around this strange place in which she found herself. On these four stages in the years to come, she would see a dazzling array of lights and sounds, a mind-popping potpourri of scenes that would whirl about the audience in an array of colors and textures, lines and rhythms, and silhouettes and sounds. These performances would blend movies and live actors, breaking all the rules of drama and bending her senses. Hamlet would appear as three characters, all of whom would trot about tilted stages that rose from the back, allowing audiences to look down upon the drama as they spun in their chairs to follow the course of the play. Action never stopped. No curtains dropped to cut the movement. No barriers existed across space or time, only action, constantly pouring around the room.

But for now, she focused on the words of a single man, perched upon the edge of one of those four stages and speaking in a way that both bothered and comforted her. Baker warned the students that good ideas or results don't come quickly, or only to a few select people. If you want to learn something, you have to keep working at it. You must explore, probe, question, relate, brush aside failure, and keep going, ultimately rejecting the easy first answers and approaches. You must keep looking for something better. Don't worry, he said, that your first efforts will be pretty "skinny." Better things will come with work. "When I was a boy," he told them, "I was a catcher on the neighborhood baseball team. Before I graduated from high school, I must have thrown down to second base hundreds of times until I could hit a spot" with precision. "But I had to do it over and over again until it was in my muscles." Think about how many times it must take to produce a piece of work with "real maturity" and value.

After class that first day, Paul Baker asked Sherry Kafka and a few other students to go for coffee. They walked next door to one of those old-fashioned drugstores with a U-shaped lunch counter where a sprinkling of students sipped soda concoctions while perched upon round red stools. Baker pulled out a form that Sherry had filled out about herself. "I see you want to be a writer," he noted.

"No sir," she shot back. "I *am* a writer." Baker laughed, but not in a mocking way, only to recognize and appreciate her confidence. "I wasn't trying to be a smart aleck student or anything," she said later, "I was just trying to be accurate. It wasn't that I chose to be a writer; that's just what I had become."

But how did Sherry and other students who took that course later become such creative people? What can you learn from their experiences about your creative self? For Sherry and for hundreds of others who took that magic course, the most powerful ideas emerged from a new vocabulary that Baker gave them, the validation of their own uniqueness, and the exercises they performed to explore those ideas. I share some of the details of those exercises and concepts to help you see how unusual the road to creative development can be, and to introduce you to a simple yet powerful way of thinking about creativity. What the students in Baker's course learned summarize some of the major ideas we'll encounter throughout the book.

Every creative act, Baker insisted, works with five elements: space, time (or rhythm), motion (direction or line), sound (or silence), and silhouette (or color). "Those five elements have always been a part of my thinking on any project I do," Sherry noted. "They became a universal language for the creative process." We'll see the same elements in the creative work of all others we explore, whether they were in the arts, business, engineering, science, or in law.

To help people explore those elements and to understand themselves in relationship to them, the Integration of Abilities course invited students to participate in a series of exercises over a fifteen-week semester, and in each case to write about their inner reactions to them. In the first, they simply walked across a stage twice, once to express tragedy and once to express comedy, using the moments of that experience to think about how they thought about and used space. "There is no right or wrong way to do it," Baker instructed, "and you will fail only if you do not use the exercise to learn something about yourself."

In the second, Baker gave students a word and asked them to write whatever came to mind: he asked them to let the thoughts in their conscious mind flow like a stream and to record those thoughts with no concern about form or the rules of writing. He also showed them a simple line drawing and asked them to start drawing. "Do both everyday," he insisted, "and date your pages so you can go back to them and study your own pattern of thinking."

For the third exercise, Baker asked the students to analyze someone they had known for a long time. Students were to explore the background and origins of their subjects, how they lived and their rhythm in life, and, finally, their values and basic philosophies. Did their subjects come from a city or farm, from a big town or small one? What makes them tick? What do they do for fun? How do they work, walk, sit, and talk? What colors do they wear? Take everything you learn about that person, Baker instructed, and reduce it to a rhythm you can clap with your hands. You already have the ability to understand rhythm, he reminded the class. "You've been doing it all your life since you were lying in a crib, and you understood who was picking you up by the rhythm of that person."

But don't just jump to the rhythm, he warned the class. Anyone can clap their hands in a certain way. That's easy. Instead, use the study to explore your own way of thinking. How do you react to people, and how are all of the elements you discover integrated in the life of an individual? Most of all, how did you create something original? To work through this task, you must stop being concerned about results. Immerse yourself in the process and through that exercise build a new life.

In the fourth exercise, students picked an inanimate object from nature and began writing descriptive adjectives about it—about its color, texture, lines, mass, and maybe rhythm. They looked at it from different angles and in different moods, and wrote as many words as they could imagine. From there, they began to give it a rhythm, and from that rhythm they created a character, a person who began to act. They wrote dialogue for their character and created a scene with words, a space that reflected the nature of the character. "About fifteen or twenty times during the distilling process," Baker told them, "you are going to get a quick result. Every time you do so write it out and go back and make yourself start over." He reminded them again to cease being concerned with results and to engage in the process. "When you are building a new kind of life for yourself, this process of discovery is the key to growth." Don't rush to a fast answer or a quick result, he concluded.

In the fifth and culminating exercise, the students found an object with several different kinds of lines in it, and they drew on paper those lines they liked. A tree limb, a jagged rock, a flower, anything with complex lines. Then they began to walk out the lines, and to feel the rhythm they encountered and the colors and sounds they might assign to different lines. They began to find out which lines pleased them and which they might discard. They might enlarge some lines as their muscles responded to them and toss aside other, less attractive ones. Baker asked the students to listen to their muscles, to let their physical responses to line and rhythm dominate their reactions, pushing aside entirely any intellectual judgments. This final exercise extended over several weeks, during which the students would produce various works of art that extended out of those lines that they kept and expanded upon. Some would write music. Others would paint, and some would produce a sculpture. But the products didn't matter. "It is an exercise in which you are going to listen to your own muscles," Baker told them.

In all of these exercises, Sherry and her classmates found rewards not in the results they produced but in the opportunity that each exercise afforded them to explore their own thinking and how they responded to space, time, color, sound, and silhouette. No one cared what their exercises looked like, only that they used them to have this inner conversation with themselves. Out of these crazy activities, they slowly realized the unique qualities they could bring to any of these dimensions. They began to value the creative process as the central core of their own education, and to see that while it could find expression in the arts, it could also appear in a chemical formula, a new way of looking at history, a fresh way of providing medical services, a new surgical method, a cure for cancer, a well-planned park, a creative meal, or even in what you do with your money.

Each exercise helped students see that the genius to create started both within themselves and in their appreciation of the great works of the mind from others. "I realized," one of those people reported years later, "that an important part of being creative was recognizing good ideas and beautiful creations when I encountered them and finding ways to make them my own." But it also meant—and this was crucial—rejecting the obvious first answers that tradition has given us and pushing for something fresh.

In Paul Baker's exercises, students cultivated a sense of awe and excitement, qualities we found repeatedly in the people we interviewed. They were simply enthralled with the world, with learning, with the possibilities of reaching new levels of excellence, of finding new ways to understand or do. Their enthusiasm extended to not just one specialized area of study or profession but an array of subjects, often mixing the arts and science, Latin and medicine, history and comedy, or journalism and justice, to name a few. With almost childlike fascination, our highly creative best students tackled the unknown, rejecting the commonplace and pursuing their own works of the mind. They found the motivation to do so within themselves and took control of their own learning. Later in the book, we'll explore the power of what psychologists call intrinsic motivation, the stuff that comes from deep within you. Such a power—and here's the catch—can wither and die if you let extrinsic motivators—grades, rewards, prizes—overwhelm you and make you feel manipulated.

These best students also learned that nothing is easy. Growth requires hard work. The world is a complex place. We all become creatures of habit in the ways we think and act. To learn is to strip away those deeply ingrained habits of the mind. To do so requires that we push ourselves, that we keep building and rebuilding, questioning, struggling, and seeking.

In fact, this is one of the major differences we found between highly successful students and mediocre ones: average students think they can tell right away if they are going to be good at something. If they don't get it immediately, they throw up their hands and say, "I can't do it." Their more accomplished classmates have a completely different attitude—and it is largely a matter of attitude rather than ability. They stick with assignments much longer and are always reluctant to give it up. "I haven't learned it yet," they might say, while others would cry, "I'm not good at" history, music, math, writing, or whatever. Traditional schooling rewards quick answers—the person with the hand up first. But an innovative work of the mind, something that lasts and changes the world, demands slow and steady progress. It requires time and devotion. You can't tell what you can do until you struggle with something over and over again.

The high achievers we studied learned that to get themselves to work, they must believe that they can do it—even visualize themselves doing it—and they must understand themselves. "How do you work best?" they asked themselves. How can you motivate yourself?

All had learned the power of intrinsic motivation over working for rewards like grades and honors. "Grades never mattered," they told us. Everything stemmed from an internal desire to learn, to create, and to grow. "Based on my life experience," Neil deGrasse Tyson noted, "ambition and innovation trump grades every time."

Sherry and her classmates began to see that they were responsible for their own education. Don't do it for the teacher, they learned, do it for yourself. Do it because it serves your need to grow. "I came out of that class," she reported years later, "understanding that I wasn't going to school for my teachers. They didn't live my life. I was the only one responsible for who I was going to be."

## Growing the Creative Life

We can begin to see the unfolding of this creative life in people who never went through Baker's course, yet ultimately experienced something similar. Liz Lerman became one of the most celebrated and innovative choreographers in American theater, blending politics and science, soul-searching and personal meaning-making, the experiential with the fanciful. In thousands of dance performances around the world, the Dance Exchange shattered the lines that divide art and science, public and performers, learning and entertainment. Until recently she had never heard of Paul Baker, but she has independently developed similar exercises to spark the imaginations and creativity of business leaders, politicians, educators, and others. In the context of her exercises, as Nobel Prize–winning economist Paul Samuelson put it, "Good questions outrank easy answers."

Liz came from a certain house and a certain soil, from a certain family at a certain time. She grew up in Milwaukee, where her father instilled in her a quest for justice, and where she learned to dance and find fascination with political history and its never-ending struggles between privilege and equality. As a child, she built a rich fantasy world with dolls and later with characters from historical novels. "I read all these books," she said, "biographies and historical novels, and at night before I went to sleep, I'd create these amazing stories, using people from those books."

In that world along the shores of Lake Michigan, where in the winter snow piled up like frosting on a cupcake and children frolicked in an urban water spout on a hot August afternoon, Liz struggled to find meaning and purpose in life, to mold her own values, and to find a place and a way of thinking that would give her life meaning. The lines of her life were often straight, like the grid of streets that crisscrossed Milwaukee, but sometimes they cut at odd angles, like Muskego Avenue, or curved gently along the shores of Milwaukee Bay. Her rhythms came from the seasons, from the parade of ward politics that engaged her father, from the sounds of the city, from dance classes, and from the ancient patterns of religious commitments.

Liz went to school on a dance scholarship at Bennington College in Vermont, where the lines ran up and over hills, not like the flat pancake of land and water that hosted her youth. Milwaukee and the lake had been like a stage upon which the players of her real and fantasy life danced to the music of politics and religion, where Liz had struggled with how she could both dance and "do all the things my father wanted me to do in the world, to fight social wrongs, to create justice," where she had wrestled for "several years" with the "whole question of God." In Bennington, the lines and patterns changed, and so did the space and silhouette, the sounds and rhythms.

"I had a checkered college career," she remembered. "I transferred to Brandeis after two years, got married, and then divorced before dropping out for a year." Liz went back to school at the University of Maryland, where she graduated after another year, and then got a master's degree from George Washington University. Along the way, she had a few memorable learning experiences. At Bennington, a history professor had given her a question and some historical resources, and asked her to draw her own conclusions and write a paper about it. "That was the whole course," she recalled. "My professor met with me twice a week to see if I had any questions. That's where I learned to choreograph, to find my own voice." Later at Maryland, she took a course in improvisation that helped free her to make mistakes and learn from them. Most of all, she loved to explore. "I could spend hours back in the stacks of the library just pulling books off the shelf, letting myself go."

In the years after college, Liz found her own creativity in the experiences of her life and in her ability to explore them. She recognized the unique combination of lines, space, motion, time, and silhouette that poured into her existence and that allowed her to address "topics of cultural, social, and historical importance." She staged acclaimed dances about "the defense budget and other military matters," and her company celebrated the centennial of the Statue of Liberty with a giant production on an outdoor stage in Manhattan. Rather than denying and repressing the fantasy world of her youth, she eventually freed it to soar in the heavens.

How did she do so? In the chapters to come, we will explore how our highly successful individuals realized their visions.

In general, the individuals we chose realized their uniqueness, defined their values, and found a purpose and meaning for their studies and lives. We will see how they used that purpose and meaning to build powerful engines of motivation that produced magnificent results. They found within themselves a way to motivate their work. That intrinsic motivation became their driving force. We will come to understand the power of intentions, and how much they determine outcomes in life. They developed a flexible mindset for themselves in which they came to appreciate their unique qualities, their strengths and weaknesses, and their capacity to grow. We will explore how such concepts of growth helped people to keep trying even after mistakes and missteps. We will see how they came to deal with failure and to use it productively.

These highly productive and creative individuals think about their own thinking while they are thinking. That process, called *metacognition,* allows people to engage in a valuable conversation with themselves, exploring their background, questioning and correcting their thinking in process, and pursuing the dynamic power of their own minds. They also appreciate the messy quality of life and its great questions and the difficulty of drawing conclusions. We will explore an approach to critical thinking that allows the best students to confront and think meaningfully about difficult problems and to become adaptive in their expertise, in this way experiencing Baker's highest level of growth.

They are able to comfort themselves and find personal tranquility, even in the face of the most distressing and potentially depressing developments. These individuals also possess an enhanced capacity for empathy. The capacity for self-comfort—more than any notions of self-esteem—allowed them to confront their own weaknesses and look for areas of growth. All these individuals live balanced lives and learn from a rich assortment of fields, rather than from one narrow discipline. We will explore the power of a broad education, and how our subjects used that kind of learning experience to grow their minds and become highly creative, compassionate, curious, and critically thinking individuals, better able to confront adaptively all of life's challenges.

Finally, those we studied confronted rather than avoided the questions that allowed many of them to shine academically. In a final chapter, we will explore how people can both learn deeply and make high grades. But more than that, we will examine how they read, studied, and learned to write in ways that enabled them to grow their own minds, make significant contributions in the world, and find meaning for their lives.

## Opening a New World

Ernest Butler grew up in a series of small towns in east and central Texas, where his parents taught in the local schools. Like many small-town boys in that state, he lived close to the land, helping his parents farm a few acres on the edge of town. He cared for a cow or two and absorbed the rhythms, lines, and textures of a flat country. He learned to get up early to feed animals and perform other chores (an early rising habit he carried into college), and he learned to play the clarinet because he liked Benny Goodman's music.

Sarah Goodrich grew up in San Antonio, Texas, a city with a strong Hispanic heritage and culture. Nearly half of the people in the city spoke Spanish. In that environment, Sarah became intrigued with Spanish culture and language, and wanted to follow her mother as a schoolteacher. She was an only child, and in the summers she would travel with her parents down to Saltillo, high in the Sierra Madre Mountains in northern Mexico.

When Sarah and Ernest graduated from high school, they went off to college and eventually found themselves taking Paul Baker's Integration of Abilities course together. "It opened up a whole new world," they reported later. "We discovered the theater, music, architecture, and creativity." In college Sarah studied education and

Spanish. Ernest focused on chemistry, took more history classes than he had to, and planned to go to medical school. Yet they both found in that course a life-transforming experience, an exploration of the arts and creativity that influenced nearly everything they did thereafter. Like so many other students who moved through Baker's classroom, they began to see how a work of art challenges your thinking, how it stimulates your mind. Most of all, they began to discover themselves and their own creative abilities.

Ernest did go to medical school after college, and he and Sarah got married. He became an otolaryngologist and eventually set up a practice in Austin, Texas, where he would create what became one of the largest single-practice ear, nose, and throat clinics in the country. A few years into his practice, he bought a failing company that made soundproof rooms where people's hearing could be tested and turned it into one of the largest businesses of its kind in the world. The company branched out into practice rooms for musicians and radio broadcast booths. Sarah taught Spanish in high school, lived a few summers in Spain, and along with Ernest became active in the local arts community. They both enjoyed exploring works of art that challenged their thinking. Together, Ernest and Sarah helped transform the world of music, dance, theater, opera, and museums in central Texas. They gave their time and their money, showering millions of dollars on art museums, scholarship funds, recital halls, awards for outstanding teaching in the sciences, and other enterprises. In one magnificent philanthropic gesture alone, they gave the University of Texas at Austin $55 million dollars to endow the School of Music. They gave away much of their fortune to support the beauty, integration, and challenge that comes from works of art.

Yet the lessons they learned about themselves in college, and the creativity they developed in a course that "opened up a whole new world" found its greatest expression not in the number of dollars they poured into the community, but in the people they became, in the values and attitudes they developed, in the humility with which they approached their wealth and good fortune, and in the creative way they used it to bring the power and beauty of the arts to other people. Since their days sitting in those revolving chairs in the Studio One Theater, Ernest and Sarah had learned to integrate the arts into every aspect of their being and to feel the harmony between various art forms and their own lives and community. When I asked Sarah if they had a large collection of art works in their home, she quietly responded, "Oh, no. That would never do. We've lived in the same modest tract house for years, and not enough people could see a large collection here. We'd want to share art with everyone. We'd put it in a museum so it could become a part of the community."

## Genius Identified

One day while Will Allen was cutting lettuce from his garden, the telephone rang. When the tall urban farmer and former professional basketball player answered, a man on the other end asked, "Have you ever heard of the MacArthur Genius Award?" Will confessed that he hadn't. "We've been following you for about three years," the man continued, "and you are one of the winners this year. You will receive half a million dollars over the next five years, and you can do anything you want with it." Several years later, Will admitted that he almost hung up on the caller. He didn't realize that the MacArthur Foundation annually selects a few people who have been doing highly creative work, calls them out of the blue, and offers them $500,000.

Will, like Liz, also came from a certain soil and a certain family. He used his roots in that land to create one of the most ingenious and promising urban experiments in the world. His parents had been sharecroppers in South Carolina but had moved to southern Maryland outside Washington, D.C., where they survived on a small farm. "We didn't have much money," he remembered, "and couldn't buy stuff, but we always had plenty of good, nourishing food that we grew." When he was thirteen, he learned to play basketball by tacking a peach basket to an old oak tree and taking aim. The lanky six-foot six-inch teenager progressed rapidly in the sport, and he soon became one of the top young players in the country, a high school All-American for three years. With offers from more than one hundred schools to play college ball, he chose the University of Miami. He was the first African American to play on the intercollegiate basketball team at the South Florida school.

A neighbor had taught him to read even before he went to school. Years later, he still remembered going with her to see a production of Shakespeare's *Othello,* and still felt moved by the power of that story. Until he entered the sixth grade, he had attended segregated schools in Montgomery County, Maryland. "We got hand-me-down textbooks from the white schools," he remembered. "Some of the pages were missing and many of them were marked up. You couldn't read them very well." When he went to Miami, a "few Klan people objected, but for the most part it went pretty smoothly." He majored in physical education and sociology, but also took more courses in history than required simply because he found it fascinating. "When I played professional ball in Belgium after college," he noted, "that knowledge of European history came in handy."

When he left his parents' farm to enter college, he swore he'd never go back to that kind of work. As a youth, he'd had chores to do every day before he could play any sport—chopping wood, weeding a garden—and he thought that going to college would free him from that life. But it was not until he learned to draw on his farming heritage that he found the creative activity that would win him both the MacArthur Fellowship Award and the Theodore Roosevelt Award, the "highest honor" the National Collegiate Athletic Association (NCAA) confers on anyone. Four presidents have won the "Teddy," as it is called, and so have senators, secretaries of state, astronauts, and a famous heart surgeon. The first recipient was President Dwight D. Eisenhower. Will Allen won it for being an urban farmer.

When he was in Belgium playing professional ball, he had gone with a teammate to a family farm to help plant potatoes and had discovered "a hidden passion for farming." After he returned to the United States and spent some time in business with a Cincinnati company, he started farming outside Milwaukee, where his wife had grown up, and eventually took over the last remaining farm within the boundaries of that midwestern city. On that two-acre plot he created a revolution drawn from his own history and values.

Will founded and became the chief executive officer of Growing Power, a nonprofit corporation intended to address one of the fundamental problems of urban living. In big cities around the world, people don't know how to grow their own food and usually think they can't. They depend on large corporations to provide them with the stuff they eat, often grown under conditions that can't be sustained forever because of the damage it does to the environment. From that system, city dwellers often dine on synthetic products, more chemical concoctions than organic nutrition. In addition, people without jobs in an urban area have no means to support themselves. Will's nonprofit company teaches them how to produce their own food, even in a big city.

At its home base in central Milwaukee, that two-acre plot would eventually contain the first of a series of community food centers. These centers experimented with new ways of growing food and partnered with local people to help them produce their own. "In a space no larger than a small supermarket," the website proclaims, "live some 20,000 plants and vegetables, thousands of fish, and a livestock inventory of chickens, goats, ducks, rabbits, and bees." In both Milwaukee and Chicago, Growing Power trains people to grow their own food, using methods handed down for generations and cutting-edge approaches that adjust to an urban environment. Satellite training stations have emerged in several states across the South and in New England. "These systems," the organization states, "provide high-quality, safe, healthy, affordable food for all residents in the community." Current plans call for the creation of an innovative five-story vertical farm.

The creative genius behind this revolution simply followed the same pattern that the Integration of Abilities course taught its students. Will Allen looked within his own life and drew from that experience. He analyzed urban space and the time it takes to grow and distribute food, and thought about ways to employ the space and time as no one had done before him. He started Growing Power's dramatic experiment after kids from a gigantic low-income housing project asked him for help in producing their own food. He marveled at their dedication and found inspiration both in the value of helping others, which his parents had instilled in him, and from the determination of those neighborhood children. But he also learned to recognize good ideas when he encountered them. In the process of building his urban farm, he explored a wide range of technologies, from aquaponics, which grows fish and plants in a closed system, to an anaerobic digester that produces energy from food waste. Will has developed new methods of composting to recycle much of the waste and create a sustainable system of farming that doesn't depend on chemical fertilizers, and he now teaches those methods to others. This "Farmer-in-Chief" runs a company with a six million dollar—and expanding—annual budget.

The sharecropper's son who started and runs the nonprofit Growing Power appeared in *Time* magazine's list of the 100 most influential people in the world. He was invited to the White House to help First Lady Michelle Obama launch a program to reduce teenage obesity, and he now counsels universities and community leaders on urban farming. He is a highly respected voice on national and international food policies and emerging agricultural technologies. When he received the Teddy, he told a reporter, "I really value this award, because it shows that student-athletes can aspire to be more than just entertainment symbols for people."[4] Clearly, he valued his days playing a team sport, and he told me he used that experience to learn how to build the personal relationships that made Growing Power a major player in an important urban movement. "It was," he concluded, "the single most influential experience I had in college." And yet he also said, "You can do something positive with your life to impact other people's lives in a different way than just having them watch you play a sport." When I asked him about his most important creation, however, he didn't mention his contributions to urban farming or his basketball career. "I helped my wife rear three wonderful children." Creativity comes in many forms.

# 2

## WHAT MAKES AN EXPERT?

When Jeff Hawkins was growing up on the north shore of Long Island, years before he designed a small computing device that changed the world, he and his two brothers and his father invented stuff, mostly wild-looking contraptions that floated. "My house was a little like the old movie *You Can't Take It with You*," he later reported. At dinnertime, the boys and their father wolfed down their meals and went immediately to the gigantic garage that seemed larger than all the rest of the house put together. In that magic space, they tinkered with plastics, metals, and woods, fashioning a crazy boat that looked more like an alien hovercraft than like any of the usual sailing vessels that plied the waters of Long Island Sound on a Sunday afternoon.

When he wasn't building stuff, he would ride his bike to the library to look up information on history, society, or science. He became fascinated with books on mathematical games, and in high school he joined the math team. Jeff also became intrigued with magic, not just to perform some mystifying trick to baffle his friends, but to understand how people could be fooled by something that so obviously contradicted everything he understood about the universe. He built models in his mind of how the world worked, and if anything challenged those models, he wanted to know why. This future giant in the computer industry became interested in music for much the same reason—not so much to perform but to find out why various sounds would appeal to different people. Why would certain music move you? Why would someone listen to certain patterns of sound and not others?

By the time Jeff entered Cornell as an eighteen-year-old freshman, he had made a list of four great questions he wanted to pursue. First, why does anything exist? "Nothing seems more probable than something," he explained long after he had fathered the first successful mobile computing device and helped build Palm and Handspring into billion-dollar corporations. Second, given that a universe does exist, why do we have the particular laws of physics that we do? Why is it that we have an electromagnetic field, or that E = mc²? he mused. Third, why do we have life, and what is its nature? Finally, given that life exists, what's the nature of intelligence? "In my lifetime, I expected at least to answer the last one," he explained.

Jeff received good grades but never placed at the top of the class. "I did what I had to do in a class," he said, "but I didn't freak out about making the best grades." He usually sat in the front row, paid attention, and did the work, but he focused on what fascinated him. Because simple answers never satisfied, he probed for deeper explanations. "In magic that meant asking not just how the trick was done, but also about how anyone could be fooled by it." In history, it meant hunting for causes and consequences; in engineering, for how and why something worked. Yet he also discovered that for many of the subjects he pursued, there was no place to "look it up," no simple answer.

In college, he didn't have any great teachers or life-changing courses, but he enjoyed his freedom and soon discovered two loves: physics, and the girl he would later marry. "Having someone else in my life made a huge difference," he reported.

He also discovered something else about college. Other people set much of the agenda. "The problem in college," he observed, "is that your interests don't always line up with what you've been assigned to do." So he did what he had to, even if it wasn't his first choice. When that was done, he then went after the questions that fascinated him. "If I had an assignment, I did it, but I pursued thoroughly those things that really intrigued me."

And it was in those pursuits that he took a deep approach to learning, asking in every field why and how, and trying to connect everything together. Most important, he continued to build models of the world in his own mind. "You can build models in math," he noted, "but you could also do it in music, in business, and in engineering." Since childhood, Jeff had been building those patterns, those abstractions that allowed him to understand the world. Now, with the increased knowledge gained in college, he could piece together even more sophisticated ones. He began to theorize from what he learned, to develop concepts, to imagine possibilities and probabilities. Jeff toyed with life, arranging the pieces one way and then another until—from the shadowy world of impressions, confusion, and contradictions—new insights began to emerge.

## Styles of Learning

We live in the midst of some monumental changes in everything we thought we knew about who can do well in school and life. Thirty-five years ago, we thought that people like Jeff Hawkins were an oddity, beyond the reach of mortal students and perhaps a creation of personality, superintelligence, or a mysterious quirk that most of us will never understand. Yet a large and growing body of research suggests that not only can most students achieve Jeff's style of learning, but if they don't, their college experience can become meaningless. This seismic shift in thinking didn't occur overnight, and it is still not widely recognized. It began with the ideas of Paul Baker and others who grasped the essence of works of the mind, and it continued with important research and theory on expertise, student intentions, university learning, and human motivation. In our investigations of the "best students" we attempt to tie these threads together, offering a powerful tool for success in college and thereafter.

Research on these matters began with a single experiment at a Swedish university more than thirty years ago. In that and subsequent studies, psychologists have discovered that college students will take—usually without even realizing it—one of three basic approaches to their studies that will determine much of what they get out of school. Furthermore—and here's the good news—every student can develop the best of these styles of learning. Yet most people never use the most effective approach because they've been conditioned to do otherwise. Why? More on that later. For now, let's understand those three styles or intentions.

In that original investigation at Göteborg University, psychologists gave a group of students an article and asked them to read it.[1] The collegiate volunteers scurried through the composition, some more quickly than others. Yet the speed with which they devoured the piece mattered far less than did another factor that began to emerge. As the researchers interviewed each of the students, they heard some of them say that they had simply tried to remember as much of the reading as possible. These "surface learners," as the psychologists called them, looked for facts and words they could memorize, attempting to anticipate any questions someone might ask them. In subsequent studies, we have learned that surface learners usually focus only on passing the exam, not on ever using anything they read.[2]

Meanwhile, other students expressed much different purposes. They wanted to understand the meaning behind the text and to think about its implications and applications, to search for arguments, and to distinguish between supporting evidence and conclusions. These students tried to comprehend what difference an idea, line of reasoning, or fact made, and how it related to something they had already learned. In short, these "deep learners" approached the piece with all of the enthusiasm of a five-year-old on a treasure hunt but with the added skills of analysis, synthesis, evaluation, and theorizing.

In the years following that first study, social scientists have identified a third style of learning that students will take. "Strategic" learners primarily intend simply to make good grades, often for the sake of graduate or professional school. These people will usually shine in the classroom and make their parents proud of their high marks. In many ways, they look like deep learners, but their fundamental concern is different. They focus almost exclusively on how to find out what the professor wants and how to ace the exam. If they learn something along the way that changes the way they think, act, or feel, that's largely an accident. They never set out to do that. They simply want the recognition that comes from graduating with honors.

## The Perils of Surface and Strategic Intentions

Although making the dean's list sounds great, strategic learners seldom become risk-takers because they fear something new or extra might mess up their grade point average. Thus, they rarely go off on an intellectual journey through those unexplored woods of life, riding their curiosity into a wonderland of intellectual adventure and imagination. They approach college with a checklist rather than with any sense of awe and fascination. As a result, these students often learn procedurally rather than conceptually, following the steps to a calculus problem but understanding little of the ideas behind it because they never intend to do so. To be fair, some of these students are innocently strategic because they've been taught to think of learning in this way. All of them have come to their strategic approach because of conditioning, as we will see shortly. As a result, they can't transfer that problem-solving to a different example involving the same concepts. Strategic learners can plug the right number into the correct formula on a chemistry or physics exam, or put the right words in a properly constructed essay, but it all has little influence on how they think, act, and feel.

Later in life, they may become, at best, what some Japanese theorists called "routine experts," learning all the procedures of their work but seldom becoming inventive.[3] When the problems of life don't follow the norm, routine experts seldom adjust. They have difficulty handling new situations and rarely become pathbreakers, the people who invent new ways of thinking and doing. When confronted with different kinds of problems, they sometimes retreat in frustration. Adaptive experts, in contrast, also know all of those conventional routines, but they have something else we will see in all of our best students and among deep learners in general. They possess the ability and the attitude both to recognize and even to relish the opportunity and the necessity for invention. Such experts love to take on the unknown, to tackle those really difficult problems. They enjoy and know how to improvise, invent, and overcome unexpected obstacles. Our society needs adaptive experts, whether it is to address the ravages of climate change, fix a sagging economy, or end wars, yet strategic learners seldom provide that imaginative flexibility.

But the problems with strategic and surface learners don't end there. They can become bored with school and suffer from major bouts of anxiety and even depression. They often don't enjoy taking on new problems. Most important, they don't learn much. Remember those physics students from the previous chapter, the ones who received A's but still didn't understand motion? They were strategic learners. They discovered how to plug the right number into the proper formula to get the correct answer on the examination, but they had little notion of what it meant. Their counterparts in English or history classes could write a five-paragraph essay in their sleep, but most of what they wrote had precious little meaning for them. Their education had at best only small influences on the way they would subsequently think, act, or feel. No wonder they approached college like a series of hurdles to jump rather than the exciting ride of a lifetime.

Perhaps I should clarify here. If you try to remember something as you attempt to understand it and relate it to other topics and questions, that is fundamentally different than simply trying to poke it into your brain to pass an examination. To take a deep approach means to take control of your own education, to decide that you want to understand, to create something new, to search for the meaning that lies behind the text, to realize that words on a page are mere symbols, and that behind those symbols lies a meaning that has a connection with a thousand other aspects of life and with your own personal development. Such intentions are intertwined with motivation, growing out of an internal drive but also feeding it with an important fuel and direction. The people we examined didn't just take control of their own schooling. They created an education for themselves that would make a difference in their own lives and thinking.

I met recently with a college student who had it backward. "You've got a big test coming up," I said. "You seem nervous about it."

"Oh, I am, but I think I'll be OK. All I have to do is memorize about twenty terms. My friend who took the class last year said that's all there is on the test. If I can just get out of that course with a B, I don't think it will hurt my grade point average too much."

Notice the pattern here. When students fear failure, they often can't sleep. They worry, then decide to memorize isolated facts, thinking that will save the day. Maybe they will succeed, pass the test, and survive the course. Maybe not. But it all becomes pretty meaningless. Nothing in this process has any lasting influence. Not surprisingly, surface learners lose their interest. Who could remain fascinated when you are consumed just with survival?

None of this means that surface learners never go deep, that deep learners don't occasionally settle for shallow knowledge, or that strategic learners never understand anything. The research over the last thirty years or so simply indicates that students will develop strong intentions that *usually* guide their study and learning. They develop a style of learning that is predominantly deep, surface, or strategic, and it is this overriding intention that shapes their lives. Many students never learn deeply simply because they never intend anything more than just to survive or shine in the academic world.

## Do Intentions Matter that Much?

Many people apparently still believe that approaches to learning don't matter, and that if you just teach students good methods for reading and studying, they will use those strategies in their school work. You can see that attitude in hundreds of "how to be a good student" books. Such manuals will show you a multitude of study tricks and other such secrets to academic success without saying a word about intentions or motivation. Of course you must develop good reading, writing, and computational abilities, and learning takes lots of hard work, but if you don't have the intention to learn deeply, all of the skills in the world can leave you short of the mark, as the American psychologist Susan Bobbitt Nolen discovered several years ago.

In a series of studies, Nolen asked students, "What makes you proud?"[4] Some said things like, "I feel most successful when I score higher than other students and I show people I'm smart." She called these people "ego-oriented," and they correspond to our strategic learners. Others responded that they felt most successful when they got a new idea, when something they learned made them want to find out more. She called these people "task-oriented." We've called them "deep learners."

When Nolen looked at students' reading habits, she noticed that the ego-oriented often used surface strategies even if they had been taught to use better ones. They generally tried only to memorize what they read, reading it over and over and trying to remember new words. In contrast, the "task-oriented" students, those people who just loved to learn for its own sake, used much deeper approaches even when no one had prompted them to do so. They looked for basic arguments and decided which information was most important. They thought a great deal about how new information either supported or changed something they already believed, and they asked themselves constantly how well they understood the material. In short, they used strategies that were most likely to produce understanding, critical thinking, creativity, and adaptive expertise.

Nolen also uncovered another type of student. She called these people "work-avoidance" types. We've seen them before as surface learners. They told her they felt most successful when they could "get out of some work," when all the "work was easy" or when they "didn't have to work too hard." What kind of strategies did these people use? Pretty much the same ones that the ego-oriented students had employed. In short, both the surface or work-avoidance students and the ego-oriented students—our strategic learners—used strategies for reading and learning that would seldom lead to any understanding, or, we suspect, to any innovative work.

## How We Come to Think the Way We Do

If you recognize yourself in any of these descriptions of surface or strategic learners, don't despair. You are not locked in those styles of learning. If you think you are too smart to fall into the weaker intentions, think again. We are all possible victims of surface or strategic approaches, but we can all escape them. Neither intelligence nor personality determine what kind of style students will develop. Researchers around the world have found that some highly capable people can grow surface or strategic tendencies while even average students can muster deep ones. Among our subjects, some people moved from strategic to deep approaches, indicating that the style isn't branded in one's soul. Both the shy and the bold can emerge as any of these three types of students.

A complex set of factors seems to drive many students toward surface or strategic approaches, and if you hope to escape them and find a deep approach, you must understand those forces. Some of them emerge in school. If you face, for example, a steady diet of multiple-choice examinations that merely ask you to recognize isolated facts, it seems not at all surprising that you will eventually conclude that the goal in life is to memorize isolated facts, rather than search for meaning. Essay exams that expect students merely to spit back what the book or teacher told them encourage shallow, not meaningful, learning. As a former colleague put it, "If an anthropologist from Mars landed on this campus and tried to determine the purpose of a college education, she might rightfully conclude that it is to learn how to take blue book examinations."

An emphasis on coverage rushes students through material, giving them inadequate time to contemplate deeply. Classes that entail large quantities of work can force people to look for superficial shortcuts just to survive the experience. Students often fill their lives with a variety of distractions that also deny them the time to go deep, and with the cost of higher education escalating and the amount of financial aid declining, many must work long hours outside school to pay the bills. The financial pressures to rush through school, get the degree, and get a job are tremendous. Yet schools do not bear all of the responsibility. They are set in a larger society that constantly pushes people toward the superficial and encourages students to value honors and recognition over deep understanding.

## Intrinsic and Extrinsic Motivators

There is, however, something even more fundamental about schooling that tends to foster surface and strategic approaches and that produces the biggest blow to deep learning. Much of that something lies within a thought problem and subsequent experiment that two young psychologists, Edward Deci and his colleague Richard Ryan, concocted years ago.[5] It goes something like this: Think of something that you love to do—to play baseball, read romantic novels, cook lasagna, do math problems, or study history. Suppose someone pays you to pursue that favorite activity, then later stops giving you that reward. What will happen to the level of your original, internal interest in the face of this external motivator and its subsequent withdrawal? Will it go up because you had that outside incentive, stay the same, or go down? In other words, how do rewards and punishments ultimately influence your desires?

Conventional wisdom and the prevailing social science of the day said that if you want somebody to do something, give them a reward for their work, and they will most likely repeat it in the future. Like rats in a maze, according to this popular doctrine, humans will work hardest and perform best if they have an extrinsic motivator waiting for them. But the two professors had their doubts and turned to their psychology laboratory to find the answer.[6] Over scores of investigations, the Rochester social scientists and others have concluded that external motivators can actually reduce interest, especially if someone feels manipulated by them. In the most dramatic of those experiments, students who had been paid to do a task lost all interest while those who did it voluntarily kept working. These findings have enormous significance because if you don't care about studying, you are unlikely to take a deep approach.

You couldn't think of a better model for Deci's and Ryan's thought problem than most formal education. Even when children enter the experience full of mental excitement, wonder, and fascination, school showers them with extrinsic rewards well designed to kill any internal motivation. At an early age, people learn to work for a gold star or a good grade, and, as one of Deci's colleagues put it, they feel a "loss of the locus of control." In other words, they feel manipulated. As their sense of being an independent person slips from them, their interests fade beneath an avalanche of "requirements" and "assignments." They are no longer in charge of their own education. Their childhood curiosity often languishes and dies.

Even the structure of a formal education tends to reinforce this process.[7] People are most likely to take a deep approach to learning when they are trying to answer questions or solve problems that they regard as important, intriguing, or just beautiful, and they can do so without feeling like someone else controls their education. In most classes, however, students usually aren't in charge of the questions, leaving an enormous gap between the realities of schooling and the conditions that promote deep approaches. Although we can all make a good case that teachers should control the questions simply because they know more and can imagine inquiries that their students will never otherwise consider, the structure nevertheless fosters strategic and surface thinking.

Consider my niece. When she was five years old, she and I took an automobile trip from Austin to San Antonio, Texas. In the seventy-eight miles we rode down Interstate 35, that little girl asked me about seventy-eight hundred questions, constantly peppering me with one inquiry after another. For the most part, she wanted to know about astronomy. "Where's the sun at night?" she asked. "Where are the stars during the day?" Her appetite for knowledge, like that of so many five-year-olds, knew no bounds.

Fast forward about fifteen years. My niece had just started her junior year in college, and I was anxious to hear about her upcoming semester. "What are you going to take this term?" I inquired when I saw her at a family reunion.

"A bunch of required stuff," she muttered.

"Oh, like what?"

"I've got to take some science courses," she pushed back with a grimace and sigh.

"What did you decide to take?"

"I signed up for an astronomy class."

"Great," I exclaimed. "I know you are very interested in astronomy."

She looked at me like I was completely crazy. "Where did you get such an idea?" she asked incredulously. Something tragic had happened to her since that car ride so many years before. She had gone to school. In the process, she had lost that childhood curiosity that had so animated the five-year-old days of her life. It's an all-too-familiar story.

Yet every member of the group we studied went to school, and each eventually emerged as a highly inquisitive and productive person. Indeed, their ability to remain or become curious despite formal education became a key ingredient in their flourishing as critically thinking, creative, and adaptive experts. How did they do it? Across the conversations I had with extraordinarily accomplished individuals, it became clear that they had managed to ignore extrinsic motivators like high marks and to find intrinsic reasons for their studies. Many told me they didn't care about grades, except for what those marks said about their thinking. "I'm moved," Neil deGrasse Tyson confessed, "by curiosity, interest, and fascination, not by making the highest scores on a test." Many of the men and women we interviewed had achieved considerable fame and fortune, yet neither of those gods seemed to drive their work either.

Let me clarify. Strategic and surface learners display little interest in understanding anything. They just want to survive or shine, and for them, grades represent nothing more than a passport to something else, a ticket to survival, or to fame and glory. Grade point averages are like points in a card game that can get you somewhere else. You play the game of school to win against your competition, not to learn. Not surprisingly, grades often feel manipulative to these students. They feel little sense of control over their own education. In contrast, deep learners in general might have some interest in grades, but only to the degree that they convey useful assessments of their work and abilities that they could use to improve. With a teacher whom they respect highly, they might anxiously await the grade because of what it represents, but they are most interested in the substantive feedback to their thinking and work. They aren't interested in the grade per se but in what it says about how well they are thinking and acting. "Keeping up their grades" means maintaining high intellectual or artistic standards. Grades offer a simple shorthand for something more substantial, and deep learners focus on that higher-order meaning rather than the symbols themselves or their "point value" in a competitive game. Motivation remains intrinsic.

Even when someone in our study of deep learners paid attention to her grade point average, as Debra Goldson, a physician in New Jersey, confessed doing, she still didn't lose sight of her primary learning objective. Grades never became her motivation. For Debra, her focus remained on understanding what would help her become an excellent physician, and that is what pushed her through school.

How did these people dodge the scourge of extrinsic rewards or escape from it after first surrendering to it? Part of their secret, no doubt, came from examining their lives and coming to appreciate the qualities and perspectives that only they could muster. Self-examination led students to understand those passions that would excite their soul and even to realize the harm that extrinsic motivators could inflict if they remained unaware of their power. They could unleash a fountain of insights into what they could accomplish, the exceptional nature of their life stories, and the potential of their special contributions. They possessed an empowering and motivating perspective on the educational process.

What did they discover about themselves? While each of our best students found his or her own combination of motives, three key factors appeared in the lives of nearly all of them.

Most basic, they rediscovered the curiosity of childhood. They puzzled over the unknown and stood in awe of the world in which they lived. They appreciated the uniqueness of their individual insights. They found the joy of standing before a body of material or an experience and wondering what it means, how it's connected with other matters, what it implies, or how they might apply it to some question or problem. As they discovered their personal passions, our subjects found ways to build on those initial interests, constantly integrating new subjects with old ones and expanding their relevant world. These best students discovered how to explore human society, the arts, and nature, and how to find links among their interests. They tinkered with the unknown, toyed with life, and found great joy in both the work and the fruits of their labors. More of life became interesting and relevant.

Second, they found great pleasure in learning how to be creative, discovering what Paul Baker had called the dynamic power of their minds. "I studied in major part," one person said, "because everything I learned, all the ideas and insights, helped spark imagination and made me more productive." They found considerable motivation in just learning about themselves and how they could grow. Many of our students even became intrigued with the process of discovery and investigated how their own minds functioned and how they could learn to improve their thinking. Each step in that growth—success or failure—gave them marvelous new ideas about how they could become more productive and creative. They did not, however, just set out to become creative for its own sake. That productive life had a purpose that drove their endeavors. They sought to grow and use their creativity in order to address some issue or achieve some goal that had become important to them.

Because they understood the principle that all of us are unique, they also grasped that each of us can benefit from the special contributions of other people. We can learn to integrate the insights, perspectives, and wonderful works of the mind that others have fashioned out of their peculiar histories. "Part of the creative process," Paul Baker had insisted, "is the ability to recognize good ideas when you encounter them." In essence, then, motivation came in part from simply marveling at even the small accomplishments of others, letting each triumph challenge and inspire. "I came to appreciate works of art," Ernest Butler reported, "that questioned and invigorated the way I was thinking."

## Finding a Purpose for Education

As these best students sought to develop the power of their own minds and to let curiosity drive their lives, those quests became potent parts of their motivation in school, transcending grades and honors. But that alone could not sum up what drove many of our subjects. Most of the people I interviewed had clearly thought deeply about the most profound questions of life. They sought a meaning and purpose for their existence. Who am I? Why am I here? What is my role? Out of that quest they had thought about what they valued, the kind of person each of them wanted to be, and the type of world they hoped to help create. We heard stories from people who had fashioned a keen sense of justice and compassion, and had developed the capacity for empathy. Their deeply felt values defined their sense of responsibility to a larger community and helped drive their work. For some, such thoughts rested in religious convictions; for others, they sprang from strictly personal and family values.

Recent research suggests that most students enter college with similar concerns about values. A seven-year study in the United States discovered that eighty percent of entering college students expect their collegiate experience to help them address spiritual questions about their purpose in life, and two-thirds "say that it is either 'very important' or 'essential' that college 'helps you develop your personal values' and 'enhances your self-understanding.'"[8] Much the same pattern prevailed among the highly creative people we studied. Their lives brimmed with concerns for reason and purpose, and, as we shall see repeatedly, they often found their greatest satisfaction in struggles for social justice. They distinguished themselves because they never lost those values, and they let them drive their academic and personal successes.

"I grew up in a family that stressed giving back," Joel Feinman, a public defender from Arizona, reported. "We were quite fortunate and had accumulated considerable wealth, and my parents and grandparents always stressed the responsibility that we had to others. That's what drove me in college and law school."

As he and his brother grew up in Tucson, he heard that message constantly, both in what his parents told him and in what they did. They encouraged him to read but to avoid television, and stressed the value of a good education for better understanding the world and contributing to it. By the time he reached high school, he had become increasingly concerned with political and social issues related to the city's history.[9]

"My father," Joel remembered, "came from a rich New York family, but he taught us to understand the injustices that many Hispanics often face, and to do something about them. We were immigrants from the Hudson Valley, but we had wealth and didn't cross an international border to get here." The disparities he saw between rich and poor seemed unfair and even cruel, and that feeling helped foster a growing concern for social justice that increasingly drove what he learned.

Not every member of our study became as involved in politics as Joel eventually did, but many of them found similar motivations. They developed a keen concern for issues of justice, the kind of world they wanted to create, and the person they wanted to become. They became curious about the world, and those matters helped drive their studies no matter what field they explored. They didn't always win their battles against the extrinsic forces in their lives, but as we shall see repeatedly, they triumphed only when they let go of all the rewards of academic honors and other external payoffs, and let the sheer joy of learning, an interest in personal development as a creative person, and their concern for the broader society drive their performance. We'll see Joel again in Chapter 8 because of the incredible story his passion for justice began to dictate.

## Taking Control of Your Education

In part, success thus comes simply from taking control over your own education, from realizing that you are in charge. Opportunities to learn matter, and without them, no one can succeed, but given the chance, our subjects had to find their motivation for working.

Stephen Colbert told me he took control of his education and began to decide what areas he would explore when he was ten years old, long before he changed the face of comedy with his late-night television show. He had grown up in a large and happy family on James Island, outside Charleston, South Carolina. In his household, learning and curiosity had value. His parents, both devout Catholics, taught their children to ask questions. His father was the first vice president for Academic Affairs at the Medical University of South Carolina.

Because Stephen came last in a family of eleven children, he received the constant attention and admiration of his older brothers and sisters. "They used the term 'adorable' so often that it almost became pejorative," he mused years later. "They were always picking me up, and carrying me around. I felt valued."

On a hot, steamy summer day, he and his father would sometimes go down to Folly Beach Pier, sit on the dock, and fish the waters after asking the locals where best to drop their line. When he was ten, however, those pleasures ended forever. His father and two brothers died in a fiery plane crash outside Charlotte, North Carolina. "After that," he once said, "I saw my job as making my mother laugh." A house once filled with a baker's dozen of voices grew still, except for the joking antics of a little boy bent on comforting his one remaining parent.

Stephen grew up in an American South that often suffered the barbs of national ridicule. On television and in films, a "southern" accent became synonymous with buffoonery and ignorance. In the popular mindset, if you spoke with a South Carolinian drawl, you obviously played with a crippled mind. To compensate, he sought refuge from this mocking and sometimes mean-spirited stereotype and deliberately set out to make himself over, purposefully and carefully copying the rhythms and tones he heard from the respected mouths of national newscasters. It was one of his first ventures into creating the roles that would help define his place in American comedy and political satire.

Stephen always read a lot—not for school, but for what he found fascinating. "I only did what interested me," he remembered. "I just read so much that I would learn incidentally what I needed to pass my courses." He read ancient and medieval history, in which he could focus on the broad sweep of events and think about causes and consequences. He pored over science fiction, played tabletop roleplaying games, and flirted briefly with becoming a marine biologist. That dream died on the operating table. Surgery intended to repair a perforated eardrum left him deaf on the right side, with no hope of a career that would include scuba diving.

When he went off to college he chose a place where he thought he could study philosophy, but his interest in the theater continued to grow, and after two years at Hampden-Sydney College, he transferred to Northwestern University, where he entered their world-renowned theater program. Within a broad liberal arts base, the school offered a three-year course of study in acting that began in the sophomore year. It included work in all the classics from Shakespeare to Shaw, and offered long hours "working on stage crews" to provide hands-on experience. Stephen was determined to finish the program in two years. That meant, as he explained later, that he worked nearly every waking moment and had little time for socializing, but it also meant that he immersed himself in one of the most enjoyable periods of his life. "I have fond memories of Northwestern," he said, "but I made few lasting friends other than my teacher."

At Northwestern, which is located on a sprawling campus hugging the shore of Lake Michigan just north of Chicago, he met and studied with Ann Woodworth, a wonderful teacher whom I wrote about in my book *What the Best College Teachers Do.* "Ann became a friend and valued mentor," he remembered. "She was very supportive of me; she believed in my ability." More important, he said, "she encouraged me to be honest with myself about my emotions and that was a difficult thing for me to do, for anybody to do. But she was pretty relentless about it, and for that I'm grateful."

When still an undergraduate at Northwestern, he began working with an improvisational theater in Chicago. "That really opened me up in ways I hadn't expected." In that theater, he learned to accept— even love and embrace—failure. Every person we studied had a similar message. "You must be OK with bombing. You have to love it. That's a great freeing experience," Stephen concluded.

For Colbert, the liberating nature of failure crystallized in the theater. "Improvisation is a great educator when it comes to failing," he noted. "There's no way you are going to get it right every time." But that ability to find comfort in bombing had its roots in what his mother had told him repeatedly, perhaps beginning on that tragic day when he was ten years old. "'Momentary disappointments can be seen,' as my mother used to say when we had a heartbreaker, 'in the light of eternity. This moment is nothing in the light of eternity,' and that opens you up to the next moment if you don't put too much weight on the moment where you are failing right now."

"If you don't conceive of things that way," he observed while sitting in his office in midtown Manhattan preparing for his nightly television show, "you are stuck only in this moment, and a failure just extends for as long as you conceive of it as important." That doesn't mean, he quickly added, "that you shouldn't learn from it, but the main thing you should learn is don't worry too much." As for life, "You haven't done it before; how could you possibly get it perfectly right?" Perhaps that attitude helped him see grades not as something that controlled him, but as feedback that he could use.

Stephen had fashioned a philosophy that flowed from his education within the theater, the advice his mother had given him, and the literature he encountered, including the Gospels, and it was that philosophy that freed him to take risks, to explore, to probe deeply, to find self-motivation in what he liked to do, and out of all of that to find an outlet for his creative energies. We found the same general approaches in engineers and journalists, physicians and economists, and a variety of people who learned deeply and worked creatively, who found comfort in the great works of the mind that they produced. Yet for the people we interviewed, the particular ingredients of their worldviews varied, as did the wellspring that gave it life, in each case rooted in individual circumstances.

For Stephen, "don't worry" became a kind of mantra. "Jesus said, 'Therefore I tell you, do not worry,'" he quoted. "'Who among you by worrying can add a single hour to his life . . . Or a single cubit to his height.'" Yet his take on that passage from Matthew had filtered through a life filled with learning, with hard work in the theater and the classroom, through his experience and his conviction that he could learn from each episode, each mistake, and each tragedy, even if it meant simply learning to laugh to keep from crying.

In his senior year at Northwestern, he took a course from Lee Roloff, a Jungian psychologist who helped Stephen explore literature from a psychological perspective. "It was a fantastic class, and one that had a deep influence on me," he remembered. Somewhere along the way, he read Robert Bolt's play *A Man for All Seasons,* and the essay that the award-winning dramatist had written for the published version of the work. "I must have read that essay a hundred times," the late-night television star confessed, "and it influenced me profoundly." Through that essay, he explored what it meant to have some central values that defined you as a person, and the ways in which modern society had stripped many humans of any core essence, turning them into nothing more than consumers of material goods. That quest for values drove much of Colbert's deep educational intentions, shaping the person he became and the comedy he developed.

You can see such influence in a hundred satirical skits, in his appearance before a congressional committee on behalf of migrant farm workers, and even in the guests he chooses for his late-night television show. When he sat down one evening with Sean Kelly, a Harvard philosophy professor, to discuss the Ivy League scholar's work on the western classics and the search for meaning in our secular age, the ghosts of that collegiate reading experience reverberated through that conversation.

I heard stories similar to that of Stephen Colbert in interviews with all of the creative people in our study. They sought not just material advancement or fame, but an inner growth, a curiosity about the world that led them to explore the humanities, the arts, and the world of ideas. Frequently this meant they were as much concerned with their own personal development as human beings and the values they held as they were with obtaining knowledge or wealth. All of that became part of their deep approach to learning.

## Avoiding the Devil

Think for a moment about some other possible outcomes to self-reflection. For some, such a focus on the self might lead to an arrogance that produces little and becomes destructively insensitive. It can also foster a kind of self-delusion. Many students who win their way into highly prestigious institutions, for example, often think that they are solely responsible for their academic success, an idea that highly influences their sense of justice. They come to believe that they deserve their good fortune and other people don't. With such haughtiness, they often can't seem to understand the complex forces that shaped their own lives and those of everyone around them. Sometimes that self-importance can backfire if they ever fall short of their expectations of themselves. They may become depressed, overly anxious, or even suicidal; or they may abuse alcohol, drugs, and other people. Confidence can turn into self-doubt, pity, or a selfishness more reminiscent of a two-year-old. Even if life never turns sour, such people can still lack empathy, compassion, and any sense of justice. People who overcome extreme difficulties like poverty and racial discrimination and rise to great heights of wealth and fame sometimes have the most trouble developing any understanding of other people and the difficulties they face.

Yet those who dwell on the difficulties and disadvantages they face in life can become locked in a life of self-pity and failure, constantly blaming any shortcomings on something else and never taking responsibility for their own education. They can develop a condition that the psychologist Martin Seligman first called "learned helplessness," in which people who have faced repeated obstacles that prevent them from succeeding still act as if they can't help themselves even when those obstacles disappear.[10] They might even blame their shortcomings on themselves and sink into a destructive complacency about their alleged inabilities.

As they discovered the power of intrinsic motivation and took control of their own interests, how did the people we interviewed manage to avoid both blind arrogance and a sense of helplessness? The answer to this question is extraordinarily important in understanding their development as creative people. Primarily, they learned to use their past rather than lionize or reject it. Indeed, an important part of that self-examination became a way to recognize how external forces could influence their lives, and then to find ways to turn those factors into something constructive. As a result, they lived in awe of the enormous complexity of life and how all the intricate twists and turns, the social and historical currents, could shape its contours. They acknowledged the need for growth in themselves while appreciating the work of others. That combination fostered a blend of humility and confidence that characterized their accomplishments as creative people.

Dudley Herschbach, the Stanford football player who later won a Nobel Prize in chemistry, perfectly expressed this quiet confidence and humility. "Real science," he once said, "recognizes that you have an advantage over practically any other human enterprise because what you are after—call it truth or whatever—waits patiently for you while you screw up." He spoke about the humbling experience of standing before nature and trying again and again to figure it out. "Nature," he said, "speaks in many tongues and they are all alien. What science is trying to do is decipher one of those dialects." If scientists make any progress, he concluded, they do so "because nature doesn't change and we just keep trying. It's not because we are particularly smart but because we are stubborn." We saw that same kind of humility and determination repeatedly in the lives of our best students.

## A Musical Journey

When she arrived at the Sony Recording Studios on a warm June evening, Tia Fuller found nearly seven hundred people lined up along the street leading into the building. The young saxophonist from Colorado had already spent nearly eight hours that day rehearsing for her first jazz album, *Healing Space*, but she came to this place like everyone else gathered on those streets in Manhattan to audition for a spot in Beyoncé's touring band. If she could win a place in the ensemble with the internationally renowned rhythm and blues singer, she would join a whirlwind life of playing before twenty thousand people, night after night. Her own fledgling career in jazz would undoubtedly benefit from that experience. She could learn. As the weather grew increasingly hotter in the days to follow, she would return three times to play for the famous diva and her party, constantly ducking in and out of rooms filled with other women seeking a place in the all-female band.

Tia began her journey to this place and time in a musical family in Aurora, Colorado. Her parents, both educators and musicians, filled their house and yard with the sounds of John Coltrane, Cannonball Adderley, and Charlie Parker. Both her mom and dad sang and played music. "If we were cleaning the house or having a barbeque," she once recalled, "music was constantly playing." When she turned three, she started piano lessons, but one day when she was thirteen, sitting in one of the swivel chairs in her childhood kitchen, she announced, "I'm going to play the saxophone."

Years later, when she saw a videotape of that childhood declaration, it helped mark the beginning of a journey she had not yet consciously joined. In high school, she did play the saxophone, but her life became a scramble of pom-pom squads, marching bands, social whirls, and, oh yes, her classwork. She did well in school, but had no particular passion beyond making good grades. She lacked what she would later call a "crystallized vision" of what she wanted to do and be.

In her senior year, Tia won admission to Spelman College in Atlanta. She chose the liberal arts school rather than a conservatory because she wanted a broad education, yet her initial focus fell on "doing well in school," with no particular goal or interest. "In my freshman year," she admitted years later, "I studied primarily for the grades I could get. Nothing more; nothing less."

Every freshman student at Spelman takes a yearlong course on the African diaspora, the history of African people as they spread around the world, often forced into migration as captured slaves. The course introduces students to historical study, fosters a deeper self-awareness, and helps them work on their writing as they compose more than one small paper each week and receive extensive feedback on their efforts. Tia became increasingly fascinated with this history, but she struggled with her writing. In the end, she received a D in the course.

She felt devastated and defeated, but that experience became an important turning point in her education. Because the course lasted a full year, she still had another semester to go, and the prospect of more bad grades. When she returned to campus for the spring, she went to see the professor and simply asked for help. "She told me I had no organization in my writing and didn't support my ideas," she recalled.

At that point, something extraordinary began to happen. Tia seized control of her own education, taking responsibility for her writing and her learning. With the help of friends, she worked diligently, constructing arguments, toying with sentences, twisting them one way and then another. She explored her own thinking, constantly asking herself what she was trying to say, and questioning the reasons behind a particular line of thinking. What am I assuming here? What concepts am I using? What if I move this section here? With each trial, she sought feedback from others in her dorm. "I was fortunate," she noted one day while sipping a cup of tea. "I had plenty of friends who cared deeply about their own work, and who were willing to help me."

In the months and years to come, Tia grew increasingly fascinated with the wide variety of courses she took in science, math, social science, humanities, language, and the arts. In a psychology class, she became intrigued with studies of sleep and the subconscious. In a course on western music, she learned how to integrate that study with her love of jazz, and how the exploration of any music enhanced her understanding of all of it. She became enthralled with big questions, important concepts, and the connections she could draw. Her dorm room evolved into a kind of constant seminar, with vigorous and lively discussions of a wide range of topics. Tia's passion and fascination for her courses grew, and when she studied, she brought that enchantment with her. She carried a dictionary, a notebook, and a highlighter everywhere. "When I read," she remembered one day in West Orange, New Jersey, not far from where Thomas Edison had built his laboratory of innovation a century earlier, "I always took notes and thought about how things connect."

Rather than cramming, she studied over a long period, giving herself time to think about the topic and ask questions, to associate as widely as possible. "Often I made flashcards of key words and vocabulary," she reported, "and I would review those items repeatedly," mulling over each word's implications and applications. "I would review something over an extended period until it became a part of me." She compared and contrasted, and consciously thought about how something new might challenge some older idea or understanding. She usually studied with friends, and they would discuss ideas over and over, often stopping to quiz each other and bounce ideas back and forth until they were at ease with the vocabulary of a new area. She and her friends wrote outlines of possible essay questions even when they expected a multiple-choice test. For Tia, she wasn't just preparing for an examination, she was exploring ideas and information. She often studied in different locations. "I could often recall something," she observed, "because I could remember that I had reviewed it in a certain place."

Her greatest passion developed around her music, as that childhood ambition about playing the saxophone continued to mature. Before her freshman year started, she visited the campus at Spelman and met Joe Jennings, a jazz musician and educator who became her mentor and "second father." Under his careful guidance—he offered "lots of nonjudgmental feedback"—Tia began to flower as a musician, becoming consumed with her desire to play well.

In jazz, the music becomes more powerful when it begins to "seep into your subconscious," she observed, and you build structures that become a permanent part of your reflexes. Tia began to practice six and seven hours a day, and she began to plan. "I set goals for myself, ten years, five years, one year, six months, one month, two weeks, one week, and the next day." Every night before she went to sleep, she would write in her journal for ten minutes about the plans she had made, mapping the next day with precision. "I usually got up at 7 am and went to the Shoot and Run to work out. Then shower, get dressed, and off to class." Between classes she would practice and study. "I tried to live a balanced life," she noted some years later. "I had time to practice, go to class, to the library, and relax with friends, but I planned that out each night before I went to bed." She also planned time for meals, usually ate three times a day, avoided red meat, and always included something green. "Exercise, practicing, studying, meeting with friends, all became a way of life for me."

If she had a large project, she would first "envision herself" finishing it. "I would keep focused on the light at the end of the tunnel," she explained, "and what that accomplishment would mean. That would help me develop a crystallized vision." Once she had developed that vision, she would use all the resources at her disposal to achieve it. In college, she began networking, making connections that would help her learn and grow. She joined professional organizations like the International Association of Jazz Educators and collected business cards. On Friday nights after six, she went out to the local jazz clubs, always taking her horn in case of any opportunity to engage in an impromptu session. During the week, late at night, she sometimes slipped away to a jam session somewhere.

In her second year she joined a social organization that emphasized humanity, nurturing, forgiveness, wisdom, and spirituality. "Everyone thought of it as a sorority," she remembered, "but it was really more than that." Anchored in religion, "but not necessarily in Christianity," the group practiced "weekly rituals," including one in which women spoke to no one except to discuss coursework with their professors or another student. Tia found considerable comfort in such practices, and in her own daily reading of biblical scriptures.

Yet her success in college, the deep learning that she achieved, came primarily from her passion, her ability to approach life with curiosity, and her intrinsic motivation. She began with a vision, took control of her own education, found who she wanted to become, and cultivated the habits that would sustain her. "They had to become part of a lifestyle," she concluded.

When she graduated magna cum laude from Spelman College, Tia didn't plan additional schooling, but the University of Colorado gave her a "free ride" to pursue a master's degree in jazz education. After finishing that degree, she moved to New York City.

On the Friday before Father's Day, Tia had been recording her first album all day long when she got a call from Beyoncé's staff, asking her to return for one more audition. On Sunday, she learned she had gotten the job. In the months and years to come, Tia treated the experience of playing with Beyoncé as she did everything else in her life: it simply expanded her education. "I've tried to take that experience" of watching her work, she once told a reporter, and learn "how to function as a bandleader."

Sometimes that curiosity so essential to intrinsic motivation, deep learning, and adaptive expertise appears early in life and never goes away. For others it comes and goes, and sometimes comes again. Can you rekindle it? I saw my niece recently. "What are you doing with yourself?" I asked.

"I teach astronomy," she reported with a smile.

# 3

## Managing Yourself

"How can you think about your own thinking while you are thinking?" I asked a college student recently who was working in my favorite Peruvian fusion restaurant. She looked at me, puzzled. "That's too much thinking," she finally said, as she laid a plate of roast chicken, plantains, and rice on my table. Yet answering that question is essential to achieving success in college and finding a creative life. It actually makes life and thinking less cluttered and clearer, not more so.

If you understand how you think and work, you have more control over who you will become. Abilities can improve as you understand how your mind works. Paul Baker had it right. Creative and critically thinking people open a conversation with themselves that allows them to understand, control, and improve their own minds and work. Repeatedly, we heard that story in the lives of the highly innovative and productive people we interviewed.

But you have advantages over students from the past. Over the last twenty years, researchers have developed a host of new ways to view ourselves, and in this chapter, we will use some of those fresh categories to help you understand yourself as never before. When Baker talked about opening a conversation with yourself, he meant for you to understand how you work, what motivates you, how ideas emerge in your mind, and how you react to line, color, space, time, and sound. That kind of exploration will serve you well. In this chapter, we go beyond those categories to explore your mind and how it works.

## How Our Brains Construct Reality

In the movie *The Truman Show,* actor Jim Carrey plays a man who has lived his entire life as the central character of a highly popular reality television show. Because he knows nothing else, Truman Burbank doesn't realize that all of the people around him are actors or that the island where he lives is really an elaborate television studio with hidden cameras that capture his every move and broadcast them around the world. In an important sense, you can be a prisoner of your own thoughts—a captive inside your mind—because you have never known anything else. Yet the key to escape this mental jail lies in those very thoughts. Here's how it works.

When you were born, you knew nothing about the world. You had no religion, belonged to no political party, had no favorite sports teams or movie stars, nor had any idea how to drive a car. You had no notion of squares, chairs, lilacs growing beneath a chestnut tree, or anything else. You didn't even know a language. But you could probably hear, see, feel, taste, and smell, and as a million waves of light and sound bombarded your ears and eyes, as you felt fabrics and a parent's touch, as you smelled the odors of the world, and as you tasted your mother's milk, your brain tried to make sense of all that sensory input. You didn't have a dictionary in your diaper that could decode that barrage of signals, so that scant one-pound mass in your head did something rather remarkable. It noticed patterns. Like a little detective piecing clues together, your brain built models of how the world works. At first, those models remained quite simple (if I cry, I get fed), but over time they became more complex, and gradually you began to attach sounds to items and actions.

Even more remarkable, your brain, right from the beginning of this crazy process, used the models that it created to understand new sensory input, and you have been doing that for your entire life. As a result, you can enter a room where you have never been and understand it. Light hits the retina of your eye, or the touch of an object stimulates the nerves in your hand as you feel your way around a dark space. Your brain instantly retrieves a model it has already created from another time and place and you understand "chair." Without that model already in place, the light tickling your retina wouldn't make any sense. In short, you have developed this almost magic power to interpret a completely new situation in terms of mental structures that you forged long ago in another place.

Yet that ability and habit of using previous mental models to comprehend something new can also become your prison, locking you into a single way of looking at the world—especially if you don't think about what is happening. Those physics students I mentioned in the first chapter, the ones who made A's but still didn't have a clue how motion really works, provide a good example of this sort of prison. They had fashioned ideas based on their everyday experience. In their way of thinking, nothing moved without work, and when the effort stopped, so did the movement. Yet physicists have long understood that if any object starts moving, it will keep on going forever unless some force (like friction) stops it. Effort becomes necessary only to start or stop it, not to keep it moving. That subtle change in understanding makes a huge difference if you want to put a satellite in orbit or someone on the moon, or even predict what direction a ball will take if you swing it in a big circle on the end of a string and then suddenly release it. But the students' brains wouldn't let them explore that different way of understanding, and as a result most of them could not predict how motion really works, even when their professors demonstrated the movements to them.

A similar process restricts learning in every field. Students in history develop the perfectly reasonable notion that every historical society operates the same way they think theirs does. Learners will try to stuff fifth-century Greece or early-twentieth-century America into a box they have created about their own world. Thus, they may assume that people have always had the same prejudices, desires, and values, or even the same social customs. They can't understand the motives of people from an earlier time, and they conclude that concepts like race have always been a part of human thinking. Ancient China, for example, didn't have a modern concept of race, but some students think that prejudices they see in that civilization against non-Chinese customs smack of racism (rather than cultural prejudice). Many students think that Christians have always celebrated Christmas in much the same manner as they generally do today, which leaves no room for Puritans, who avoided any special recognition of the holiday. Concepts of war have changed enormously over time, but students who think in contemporary terms will have great difficulty in deciphering the causes of past conflicts.

We all construct reality and then use the paradigms we have fashioned to understand new sensory input. Otherwise, we couldn't move from place to place very easily. We often can't question our own models, let alone build completely new ones, because we have such strong (and usually successful) habits of fitting new ideas into old boxes. Then we find ourselves locked inside with all the windows darkened.

To escape from our boxes, we have to understand how the brain works, how it constructs reality. Only then can we imagine jumping outside our confinements and looking at the world from different angles. But that insight is unlikely to occur unless we find ourselves in a situation where our existing models do not work for us. We call those moments of new insight "expectation failures." The brain expects a certain outcome (because of a model it has built), yet something else happens. As a result, we have to stop and rebuild our understanding. Perhaps we will read a book that contains an earth-shattering revelation, one that calls into question how we understand something. Maybe a teacher raises a question designed to provoke thought. "Life is full of surprises," Neil deGrasse Tyson suggests, "if we only notice them." But we excel at avoiding those challenges to our thinking. To have an influence, the expectation failure often has to be shocking and bold. And, of course, we have to care when our models don't work.

Some people, like those physics students, will cling to their paradigms even under repeated challenges. After the class ended, and the professors realized that their students didn't understand motion, they brought some of them back for a demonstration. They put a ball on the end of a string and asked their students what would happen if someone whirled the ball around in a big circle and then let go of the string. Based on their faulty concepts of motion, the students predicted impossible outcomes. The professors then performed the experiment, and the students observed the errors in their predictions. Even though their expectations had failed to be realized, rather than admitting their errors and reconstructing their ideas about motion, some students argued with their professors, engaging in all sorts of mental gymnastics instead of confronting their mistakes and rethinking their paradigm.[1]

They simply didn't care enough, or perhaps they had too many emotional commitments to old mental models. I have had students in my U.S. history class who entered the course with almost religious convictions about what they thought happened in the past. When they encountered evidence that suggested other histories, they couldn't bring themselves to consider it. In contrast, the people in our study cared deeply about their own education, found the world fascinating and endlessly exciting, and became enthralled with discovery as part of their personal quest to grow their own minds. Finding a new way of thinking didn't bother them. Indeed, they became intrigued with different concepts that would let them see some familiar object or situation in a whole new way. "When I fail," a University of Virginia student told me, "I can learn something."

What kind of students will see and accept new ways of looking at the world? Suppose you gave a group of young people three items: a candle, a box of matches, and some tacks, then asked them to make up a way to attach the candle to a cardboard wall so that it burned upright using only the items they were given. This classic problem has a simple answer. Yet for some reason, the solution doesn't always come to mind easily. (I'll tell you the answer a little later.) It requires the ability to think outside the norms, and it is a good test of who will benefit from an expectation failure. Do the problem-solvers have the highest grade point average or a major in a certain field? What do they have in common?

Researchers at the Kellogg Graduate School of Management at Northwestern University found that most of those who solved the problem quickly had lived in a foreign country and had adapted to the culture of that society.[2] Merely traveling abroad without living there didn't seem to help. Adjusting to a new place with a different culture made people more open to new models and more creative problem solvers. They often had to operate in a different language, get used to when and what people ate, find out what kind of electrical plugs they used (if there was any electricity at all), and adjust to different ways of greeting a stranger. In short, by living abroad they had faced a barrage of expectation failures as they simply tried to navigate through the common practices of everyday life.

Does that mean you have to move to a different country before you go to college? No. It suggests that you need to experience lots of expectation failures and scores of opportunities to speculate even before you know anything. Good teachers will help create those challenges, and you should seek them out and take their classes. You can also challenge yourself and your friends, and they can challenge you. We often heard stories from our subjects about seeking different kinds of friends, ones who would provoke them to think differently. Katherine Phillips, a researcher at Northwestern, discovered that just working with someone from a different social group can make you a better problem solver, even if you feel uncomfortable in doing so.[3] Indeed, social discomfort may be a hidden boon, placing you in an environment that challenges your thinking if you embrace it rather than running away.

In the people we interviewed, we found the same patterns. Our subjects often worked in a variety of cultures and had rich experiences outside the patterns of their normal lives. They also enjoyed the challenge of the unknown, the chance to mix it up with someone different. They often plunged into new situations with almost childlike enthusiasm. They even relished the opportunity and necessity for invention, challenging their existing models of reality with jarring sensations.

If we understand that our brains construct reality, we can help guide that process, and if we realize that it uses those constructions to interpret the world, we can begin to question, to grapple with our own thoughts and even escape the prisons that our existing paradigms build around us. When we place ourselves in an environment in which many of our mental models do not work, we have greater capacity to build new models, to expand our understanding and our capacity to create. We can use the power of those expectation failures, deliberately exposing ourselves to people who may make us uneasy but nevertheless prompt greater creativity. To think about our own thinking begins with an appreciation of the power of our own paradigms, and a corresponding understanding of what it takes to escape them.

As for the solution to the candle problem: Dump out the matches, tack the box to the cardboard wall, stand up the candle in it, and light it with one of the matches.

## We Have More than One Brain

To think about our own thinking also requires that we recognize the complexity of that gray matter we have sitting in our skulls. Studies in neurology and psychology have given us new ways to understand ourselves. These categories and concepts are tools, furthering our conversations with ourselves and enabling us to be effective and creative. Let's utilize some of the key findings of that scientific research by thinking about three brains rather than just one. We'll call one of those brains your Spock brain, another your alligator brain, and one your pleasure brain.

Your Spock brain builds those mental models, stores them (remembers stuff), and uses them to interpret new sensory input. It reasons and makes decisions, and so it is big and complex, incorporating various areas of that mass of cells you have in your head.

Your alligator brain is a tiny piece of tissue that looks like an almond in the middle of your bigger Spock brain.[4] Jeanette Norden, a neuroscientist at Vanderbilt Medical School, explains its function this way. "Let's imagine that you lived a very long time ago, and you are walking down a path, and suddenly your peripheral vision catches some movement. So you turn and look and say, 'Very large kitty with very large teeth.' If you had to use your normal processing brain [your Spock brain] to interpret what this thing was: 'Oh, a saber-toothed tiger,' you would already be his lunch. So the brain needs a second system that is much faster, that can stimulate you to fight or flee. You're already running before your normal pathways figure out what this thing is."

That second system, what I'm calling your alligator brain, triggers that "fight or flee" response. It serves you well in scary situations. Yet, as Norden explains, "your brain can't distinguish between physically threatening developments and things that are perceived as psychologically threatening." When you feel imperiled, your alligator brain sets off a cascade of events that quickly causes the adrenal gland to release cortisol into your body. If you get heavy doses of this chemical mixture repeatedly, that injection can block your Spock brain from forming memories. That's why under high stress, people sometimes can't even remember their names.

For a student that has significant repercussions. If you're really anxious about a test, for example, your alligator brain might keep you from thinking well. People who suffer from test anxiety simply let their alligator brains run wild. The cure, of course, is to relax, but that's probably easier to do if you understand what's happening to you, and almost impossible to do if you don't. Some students told me that they practice relaxation exercises regularly. Others said that understanding stress simply allowed them to stop and begin a relaxation routine whenever they felt pressured. "On an examination," one person said, "if I began to panic, I would take a few minutes to regroup. It was time well spent." For still others, understanding themselves plus developing a broader perspective made all the difference. Remember Stephen Colbert's advice from his mother: "Momentary disappointments can be seen in the light of eternity." Although the moment may seem frightful, worrying about it only makes it worse.

That brings us back to the Spock brain, that series of systems in our noggins that allows us to remember, reason, make decisions, and so forth. It's enormously complex, and we don't want to get bogged down in neuroscience. Yet we need to recognize that this part of our brain functions in complex ways. Ellen Langer, a psychologist at Harvard University, has suggested one way to comprehend that complexity. In her language, your Spock brain can operate as either "mindless" or "mindful." In the first case, our brains run on automatic. You've been down this street or solved this kind of problem hundreds of times. You just follow certain directions stored away without any deliberate thought.[5]

A mindful brain pays attention, but that doesn't mean just staring at something. If I am mindful of some idea, word, event, or object, I'm consciously aware of it, and I think about how I am reacting, about my curiosity, and about how I'm attending to the subject. I turn the matter one way in my mind and then another, looking for new ways of understanding both the object of my attention and the way I'm interacting with it. I'm constantly creating new categories surrounding the event or object, and I'm aware that someone else might create other categories that could challenge mine. I imagine seeing, using, understanding, comparing, and contrasting in whole new ways, and always I wonder what I don't know that might upset my applecart of thinking. What am I missing? How would I understand or use this in different circumstances? What if I thought of this as something else? How would someone else look at this? In short, I'm thinking deeply about it.

We can see that mindfulness in those exercises that Sherry Kafka and her classmates did. In each one, they looked at an ordinary object or event—a walk across the stage, a twig, a rock, a blade of grass—from a new perspective. They thought about an object's rhythm, lines, movement, silhouette, and sound. They thought about a space and how one travels across that space in whole new ways. They played with the novelty of taking an object, exploring its lines, expanding that into a rhythm, and eventually creating a character and a dialogue that flowed from that inspection. Most important, they paid attention to how their minds worked, how they understood something, and how they might understand that entity differently. They learned to be mindful.

If you realize what it means to be mindful or mindless, you can regulate your own thinking. Your Spock brain can operate in either of these two modes. Perhaps the most mindful way of thinking is to be mindful that you are being mindful, and to recognize the difference between mindfulness and mindlessness. Langer sees three characteristics in those who take this approach. Mindful people engage in the "continuous creation of new categories." They possess an "openness to new information," and they have "an implicit awareness of more than one perspective." That means, of course, that they notice novelty and distinctions. They constantly pay attention to different contexts and perspectives, and they live in the moment. "Each," Langer writes, "leads to the other and back to itself." Mindless thinking lies entrapped in old categories, doesn't pay attention to "new signals," and acts as if there is only one perspective possible. "Being mindless," she writes, "is like being on automatic pilot."

You can become more mindful if you simply change an absolute statement into something conditional. Let's say that a teacher tells you that a certain object *is* a thing-a-ma-bob. Would it make much difference in your own thinking if you quietly translated that into "it *could be* a thing-a-ma-bob"? Early in her career, Langer once conducted an experiment in which she gave two groups of students an object.[6] One group heard, "This is a dog's chew toy." She told other students, "This could be a dog's chew toy." Later in the experiment, both groups needed an eraser. Only those who had heard "could be" thought to use the rubber "toy" to erase their mistake. It never occurred to students in the other group.

We must realize how language shapes our thinking, and then we can imagine other words and categories for everything we encounter. Langer has found repeatedly that simply changing the words used with students can increase their mindfulness. That means that all of us possess enormous power to change the world and ourselves by shifting the language and categories we employ. "Maybe I'm thinking about this all wrong. Is there a different way of seeing my problem? Are there different words I might use?" The brain becomes more creative. Life becomes more exciting and fun.

Langer told one group of high school physics students that a short video they were asked to watch "presents *only one of several* outlooks on physics, which may or may not be helpful to you." Use "any additional methods you want to assist you in solving the problems," she instructed. The psychologist and her colleagues then told another group to just watch the video and apply it to some problems. The first group developed a much deeper understanding of the concepts and used more imaginative ways to solve the problems. Although some people in the second group complained about the material, no one in the first group did. Furthermore, they enjoyed what they were doing. In numerous experiments, Langer and her students have found that mindful learning produces pleasure while mindless approaches breed boredom.

Even changing the words in a textbook can make a difference. Students who read phrases like "which could be" and "may be" could imagine far more solutions to problems than students who read the same passages without those words, and they enjoyed their reading more. In general, if students looked for novelty in anything they read, imagined alternative endings to a story, thought about how someone in another time or place might read or hear the same passage, they remembered more, had more fun, and developed more creative skills. Imagine, Langer muses, how boring it would be to memorize parts of the body, but you could have fun playing a game trying to put a friend together or taking him or her apart. You could do the same with history. A professor at Stanford asked students to keep a diary about developments in German history as if they were a particular character. Imagine, she instructed one student, "you were born to a Berlin prostitute in 1900." How would you view the coming of war in 1914, or the rise of the Nazi Party and Adolf Hitler in the 1920s? Anyone can play these games, look for novelty, take new perspectives, create new categories, constantly slice life in different ways.

## In a Rut

While Ellen Langer cuts thinking into mindful and mindless, Keith Stanovich, a neuroscientist, sees automatic and reflective thought. Ever wonder, for example, why some smart people can do some dumb things?[7] Stanovich says it is because your Spock brain is not always so Spocklike. Our brains tend to be lazy, he argues, always looking for the easiest way out. Thus, we will often use automatic thinking, following some well-worn path, rather than thinking afresh and reflectively. We will build little rules for solving problems, then without further consideration, we will automatically switch on those directions when confronting some new difficulty. Research has found a whole series of conventions that automatic thinking uses. Because it takes deliberate effort from your Spock brain to get out of those ruts, it's helpful to know what they are.

### Myside Bias

People tend to think from their own perspective, something scientists call "myside" bias, or sometimes confirmation bias. If I gave you statements by politicians who contradicted themselves, for example, research suggests you'd easily spot those hypocrites—as long as they come from a party you don't support. When they come from your side of the political fence, however, you probably wouldn't see the inconsistency at all. That's what Drew Westen discovered when he gave people statements from American politicians—some Republicans, some Democrats.[8] Ask a group of college students to generate arguments both for and against controversial public policies (like legalizing the sale of body parts), and they will generally produce as many good arguments on one side as they do on another. Get them to do the same for topics that touch closer to home (like raising tuition to pay for the total costs of higher education), and they can't think of many reasons to oppose something they already believe.

Myside prejudice even influences our ability to judge our own prejudices. In study after study, researchers have found that we all tend to believe that we are more objective than others, especially if those people hold opposing views. (When you read about myside prejudice, did you, in fact, think that it didn't apply to you?) In reality, we all tend to generate evidence, test hypotheses, and evaluate policy to confirm what we already believe because it's easier to do that than it is to look for information that might prove us wrong. Yet checking for facts that might contradict our thoughts is one of the fundamental approaches of rational thought.

Keith Stanovich and Richard West provided dramatic evidence of myside prejudice.[9] They gave several hundred Americans a fictional story about a German automobile that was a menace to other people. According to the fictional story, this particular model killed eight times more people in other vehicles than did the typical car. Stanovich and West then asked them if the United States should ban that auto from American highways. Nearly eighty percent said yes. Yet when a comparable group read a true story about an American car that really did kill eight times more people in other vehicles, only half of them thought it would be fair for the German government to ban that automobile from their roadways.

*Vividness Bias*

We are all also subject to the vividness bias. A single vivid example can distract us from overwhelming statistics in favor of the opposite, or if the data comes to us in vivid language, we'll pay more attention to it than we will to dull facts. Again, we simply avoid the difficult task of thinking through our evidence. Ellen Langer might call this a lack of mindfulness. Keith Stanovich says we are acting as mental misers, conserving our brain's energies by using a simple rule—if it is vivid, pay attention to it—rather than using our brains to think carefully.

After the attacks on the World Trade Center on September 11, 2001, for example, airline travel in the United States decreased because more people were afraid to fly. Instead, many of us drove long distances, a foolish act because automobile travel remains considerably more dangerous than commercial air travel. "Researchers have estimated," Keith tells us, "that over 300 people died in the final months of 2001" because they drove rather than getting on an airplane. Yet the "cognitive miser" in all us often fails to do the math until we see it in vivid language.

Which is worse, a disease that wipes out 1,288 people in a village of ten thousand, or one that kills 24 people out of every one hundred? When researchers posed that question to students at the University of Washington, most of them said it was the former, even though 1,288 out of ten thousand is actually a lower rate of death. But the bigger number is more vivid. One experiment in Pennsylvania found that university students were far more willing to give money to the Save the Children Fund if they saw a picture of a little girl and heard a story about her terrible plight than if they read that 3 million Zambians and 11 million Ethiopians faced hunger. An identifiable victim is more vivid than a cold statistic. If I told you that eating red meat would increase your chances of getting the human form of bovine spongiform encephalopathy, would that scare you more or less than telling you it could cause mad cow disease?

Sometimes our personalities can influence what appears to be most vivid. Tell optimistic people that they rank 300 out of 1,000, and they will feel better about themselves than if they hear they rank 30 out of 100. Pessimistic people will have the opposite reaction. Yet both versions represent exactly the same ranking.

Higher numbers appear more vivid to some people than do higher percentages. A few years ago, researchers found that students liked a 9 in 100 chance of winning a jackpot more than they did a 1 in 10 chance, even though the latter represents a greater probability of taking home the money.

### Framing Prejudice

Finally, a frame around a problem or question can influence how you will answer it. Would you, for example, endorse lowering taxes for people making more than a quarter of a million dollars each year? You might favor the idea because you generally support lower taxes. But if I asked you if the tax rate should be higher for people with incomes below 250,000 a year, you might object. Yet these two questions *could* represent exactly the same policy. In the same manner, I could offer a tax reduction for homeowners and you might applaud. Yet I could call it "the rent payers' penalty," as Keith Stanovich points out, and you might find it terribly unfair. If I offered a policy to cut taxes across the board without raising the national debt, would you endorse my plan? Would you still endorse it if I called it a program to decrease government services, like scholarships to students?

Let's say that you signed up for a psychological experiment at your college, and the researcher said she was giving you a fifty-dollar "bonus." Your friend signs up for the same study, but he hears that he will get a fifty-dollar "rebate on tuition." Which one of you will most likely spend the money immediately? You would. Hearing that you get a "bonus" suggests that you are now better off (and can afford to spend more money). A rebate simply suggests that you are returning to some previous state (before you paid your tuition). You don't have any extra money. You're just back where you started, and that frame most likely will shape how you react.

If framing has such a powerful influence, it means that other people can shape your thinking. But if you learn to think about your own thinking, you can train your mind to look for those natural patterns of myside bias, vividness bias, and framing prejudice. A good college education can help you do that. It can also help you develop new ways of thinking that would not normally emerge. In scientific thinking you learn, among other habits, to *look for evidence* that will invalidate the proposition, rather than just for information that will support your suspicions. In statistical studies, you will learn to *think in terms of probabilities.* In history and anthropology, you should learn to *develop a historical perspective,* to understand change over time. You should learn to escape the mental models that your own time and place impose upon you and to understand another culture in another era with different paradigms. Each of the disciplines you study in college offers a way to think, and to think about your own thinking. Highly creative people will explore life from a variety of disciplines and begin to see the interconnections that exist among them. They will learn to integrate, to think mindfully. A mathematician will look at a dance and see the geometry lying behind that creation while the creative dancer might think like a good mathematician to expand the art of moving bodies.

Across higher education in recent years, those who teach in all departments are thinking about what it means to think within that discipline and how that kind of thinking—scientific, historical, sociological, managerial, creative, and so on—might integrate with other forms of thinking to create fresh ways of understanding, appreciating, creating, theorizing, and solving. Professors are exploring new ways to help students think about their own thinking. You should engage in that conversation with them. Seek out those institutions, departments, and professors involved in this enterprise. Demand it of those who are not.

## The Pleasure Brain

Perhaps the greatest discovery of recent neuroscience has been the growing recognition that we also have a pleasure brain. "We're just made to enjoy the world," Jeanette Norden notes. The pleasure brain isn't really a place in your skull but a whole series of connections that find great joy in life. The people we interviewed reflected that pleasure, that awe about the unknown, that enthusiasm for their own work, and a kind of intoxication with life. They became excited about discovering great works of the mind and about the ways those works challenged their own thinking and creative efforts. While others might recoil and even grow jealous in the face of someone else's achievements, our subjects saw opportunities for growth, and they found the sheer joy of taking up the challenges that other people's work presented. Part of their secret in tapping that pleasure potential came in enjoying the ride rather than looking only for a destination. They stopped focusing on results and became immersed in the process of creation. Part of it came in actually enjoying their work rather than seeing it as a necessary evil. Perhaps the greatest power, however, and the one that tied all of the parts together, came from the simple recognition that pleasure with work and life was not only possible but highly likely. Once you know that you have this inner capacity to enjoy, you can look for the switches to turn it on, and you will discover that they reside within you. "What you bring to this class is yourself and your desire to participate, and what you do in here depends finally upon that," Paul Baker said.

A variety of studies have found a connection between having fun and learning. Ellen Langer noticed in repeated experiments that people not only learned more when they became mindful but that they also enjoyed more. She has also found that framing can shape how people react to any activity. In one famous experiment, she told one group that they were going to "work" on something while she described the same task to a second group as a "game." You know what happened. The "work" group found their minds wandering, and often became bored while the "game" students had fun with the same activity. Mark Carnes has found much the same pattern in the history classes he teaches at Barnard College. He has invented "elaborate games" for students to play, all "set in the past," in which they take on roles and run the class themselves. The games have transformed students' interest and involvement, sparking greater appreciation for multiple points of view and deeper understanding.[10] I found much the same result using case studies in Cold War history classes in which students took on roles and played simulations.

If framing is so powerful, it means that when we mindfully pay attention to the frames that other people create for us, we can escape the tyranny of those boxes and cobble together ways of looking at the world that let us enjoy what we do. We can find those switches deep within our brains that allow us to brew pleasure. I think that's what our subjects did constantly.

So much of school can frame everything in a way that makes it boring and tedious. Grades create extrinsic motivators that reduce intrinsic interests. Students often work for the teacher rather than for themselves. They do "assignments" and meet "requirements" rather than pursue goals. Our subjects rose above that milieu, thought about their own thinking, and reconstructed the world. Tia Fuller practiced scales hours at a time because she took control of what she wanted to be and found joy in the process. It wasn't something she "had" to do for someone else but rather what she chose to do. The British comedian Stephen Fry said it just recently: school can't "ruin Shakespeare" for you unless you are "mentally lazy"—if you don't think about your own thinking and don't realize you control those pleasure switches. Claiming that school ruined Shakespeare would be like saying, Fry noted, "I could never enjoy the Grand Canyon or the Lake District" because we studied it in geography class. "Shakespeare is like a landscape. It's there. It can't be ruined for you."[11]

Great teachers made a huge difference in the lives of many of our subjects. They flourished under the best of them and sometimes languished under the worst, but they thrived because they found those pleasure buttons within themselves, took control of their own thinking, reframed the world, and pursued it with vigor.

One recent series of studies even found that laughter can make a big difference in learning. Mark Beeman and his colleagues at Northwestern University asked students to watch short videos of a comedy routine by Robin Williams before they attempted to solve word puzzles. Those students did significantly better with the problems than did students who saw other films that had either "neutral or anxiety-inducing" content. The psychologists have found that a positive mood makes all the difference in the world, and that laughter—and perhaps the enjoyment that comes with it—prepares the brain to solve complex problems, especially to develop that sudden insight that cuts through a jungle of mental confusion.[12] As I interviewed highly accomplished people, I was struck by the ease with which they laughed, the lilt in their voices, and the pleasure they took in thinking about the world.

## Understanding How Society Influences Our Thinking

Social psychology offers us one more important way to understand ourselves. If you are a member of a group about which there is a pervasive negative social stereotype in the society in which you live, the mere existence of that stereotype can influence your performance *even if you personally reject the stereotype*. I put that last part in italics to emphasize that it is the key finding of this research. Back in the 1930s Kenneth Clark had demonstrated that when you accept the stereotype "about your kind," whatever "your kind" happens to be, the negative image of your group will obviously influence your performance. When a popular image says that people like you can't do math very well, for example, and you accept that stereotype as true, then guess what? You won't be able to do math very well.

But the more recent findings, pioneered by Claude Steele and Joshua Aronson, go beyond Clark's research.[13] In a series of experiments, they and other social psychologists have found that you don't even have to accept the popular negative image of "your kind" for it to influence you. If you know there is a popular belief that says that people like you can't do math and you want to do well in the subject, it will simply bother you on some level that other people may think of you in terms of this stereotype. As you become more annoyed, your alligator brain kicks in, causes part of your adrenal gland to squirt cortisol into your body, and then your Spock brain can't even operate on automatic, let alone mindfully. Your body sweats more, your heart beats faster, and your test scores go down.

In the United States and many other countries, for example, a negative stereotype persists about the ability of women to do higher mathematics, the ability of African Americans to do almost any academic work well, and sometimes about the ability of southerners like me to string three coherent sentences together. If you are female, the mere existence of the stereotype can cause you to do worse in math, unless you realize that your own mind is working against you. The same process can occur with male athletes who know about the stereotype of the "dumb jock" and want to prove otherwise. And it can happen to African, Hispanic, and Native Americans in almost any area of study. In a society with racial categories, the ugliest and broadest stereotypes emerge.

Because societies have so many negative and positive stereotypes, most of us have been victims of stereotype threat at some point in our lives. Claude Steele found that you can even create a threat where none has existed before. I know of no popular belief that says that European American males are naturally bad at math. Yet when Steele told a group of such students that Asian Americans usually do better on a math test, those young men suddenly found themselves on the underside of a negative comparison, the victims of an instant stereotype brewed up in the social psychology laboratory like a pot of fresh coffee. Their alligator brains went off like fireworks, spewing cortisol through their bodies. They tanked.[14]

This problem becomes especially acute for anyone from groups that have suffered the barbs of widespread negative stereotypes. "If you're so smart, why aren't you rich?" becomes a stereotype that poor people are dumb, and research finds that such images can depress the performance of students from families with lower incomes. Racial slurs of any kind reflect and perpetuate deep and ugly stereotypes, and harm African, Hispanic, and Native Americans and anyone else who has felt their sting. Remarks about religions and holy wars can do the same. Sometimes a person's speech can cast them in a negative light. Stephen Colbert's quest to change his accent takes on a whole new meaning. Sometimes the wounds from these jabs lie deep within the inner caves of memory, brooding over the patterns that have become so pervasive within society, sulking subconsciously, yet always ready to spring out of the dark at unexpected moments.

When the social psychologist Margaret Shih took up this problem a few years ago, she asked a new question. We have plenty of negative pigeonholes in our culture, she mused, but we also have some that are quite positive. We've already mentioned the negative stereotype about women in mathematics, but in the United States we also tend to think that Asians and Asian Americans possess some secret natural ability in math. So what happens to Asian American women? Margaret found that if you can get these women to think of themselves primarily as Asians, they will do much better on math tests than when they focus on being women.

She created three comparable groups, all Asian American women in mathematically oriented disciplines in which they had done quite well. In other words, she had reliable evidence that if she gave each woman in each group the advanced portion of the Graduate Record Exam (GRE) in mathematics, their group scores would all come out pretty much the same. They didn't, however, because of something Shih did before they took the test, something intended to trigger either negative or positive social stereotypes. She asked each woman to fill out a questionnaire. It looked pretty innocent: name, address, telephone number—nine or ten items. The first group answered a single question intended to remind them of their gender. The second didn't have that item, but had one to remind them of their ethnicity. The third had neither of those two inquiries on their pretest questionnaire. You now might guess how each group did. The young Asian American women who had been reminded of their ethnicity did significantly better than the others. Those who were re-minded of their gender did slightly worse than the group with no reminder.[15]

If I asked you to tell me something about yourself, you might mention your interests or try to describe yourself, but you would also probably say something like, "I'm a southerner" or "I'm French." You might tell me your ethnicity, gender, age, or occupation. In other words, you would identify yourself as a member of a group, and that group would become a part of who you are in your own mind. We all build identities for ourselves that stem from the various roles we play. But if a group with which we identify has become the target of some ugly stereotype, we can feel devalued, fearful that other people will think of us in terms of that popular image. Our very identities begin to feel shaky and sometimes even worthless. On a subconscious level those wounds can fester, and in high-pressure situations like examinations, they can explode in a fountain of anxiety, fear, and even panic.

Yet when you know what's coming, you can keep the train from running over you. If you learn to celebrate and appreciate who you are and the special qualities and experiences you bring, you can maintain that dignity of self that allows you to ride the locomotive rather than being swept beneath it. In part, that's what Paul Baker emphasized when he told Sherry and her classmates to strike up that conversation with themselves. It's what he meant when he told the class, "Each of you has your own philosophy, your own view-point, your own physical tensions and background. You come from a certain soil, a certain family with or without religious background. You were born in a certain house to a certain family at a certain time. Nobody else in the world has done so." You can create in ways that no one else can. The exercises that Sherry did helped her to cel-ebrate and appreciate herself.

# Does Knowing Yourself Really Make a Difference?

At the University of Colorado, a group of students—some male, some female—did something rather unusual in an introductory physics class. During the first week of the semester, when they went to their recitation section the teaching assistant gave them a list of subjects they might value most—relationships with friends and family, or gaining and using knowledge, for example. They were asked to select what they prized most on the list and to respond to a series of prompts about those items. They wrote for about fifteen minutes. Three weeks later, they completed the same exercise as part of their online homework, again writing for fifteen minutes about what they regarded as most important in life. None of what they composed had anything to do with physics, but it did give them a chance to state and celebrate what they held most dear in life, and the personal identities they had created around those values.

Within the physics department at Colorado, like most such departments around the country, women have usually scored worse than men, even when they brought the same scientific background to the class. As a result of such patterns across the country, women received only 28 percent of the physics doctorates awarded in the United States in 2006, and much the same pattern prevailed in math, computer science, and engineering. In introductory science courses, a large gap often exists between the performance of male and female students on both class exams and on standardized measures of conceptual understanding. If such gaps stem primarily from stereotype threat and their attacks on identity—which I think they do—the writing exercise about one's personal values could possibly erase or greatly reduce the gaps.

Sure enough, that's exactly what happened at the University of Colorado. One group of students was asked to write about what was valuable to them while another group spent the same amount of time writing about matters prized by other people. Not surprisingly, women who wrote about what was most precious to them did significantly better in the class. Their scores and grades rose on average a whole letter grade. At the end of the semester, all of the students took a nongraded exam on how well they understood basic concepts. Although men's understanding remained the same, no matter which group they were in (writing about their own values or about someone else's), the women who had celebrated personal values outperformed everyone, including the men in the same group. With writing, they affirmed what was dear to themselves, celebrating their own integrity and worth. In the hostile environment of stereotype threats within the sciences, they had mustered the internal resources necessary to cope.

All of the students were asked if they agreed with the following statement: "According to my own personal beliefs, I expect men to generally do better in physics than women." The women who most strongly agreed with that statement benefited the most from the value affirmation writing, while the men who agreed with the statement generally did worse than the men who didn't, regardless of which writing group they had been in. Prejudice somehow also hurts the performance of the bigoted.[16]

## A Life of Self-Examination, Caring, and Curiosity

On New Year's Eve, Mary Ann Hopkins had spent the better part of the day in Times Square talking with reporters, posing for pictures, and generally making herself available to the press. A little before midnight, she took an elevator to the top of the *New York Times* building, which is located at the south end of the famous square, walked out onto the roof, pressed a button, and triggered the descent of the famous crystal ball that marks the coming of each new year. Her journey to this happy occasion began when she was ten years old.

Mary Ann and her younger sister grew up in the suburbs of Boston, where they attended a private school. "What strikes me most about growing up," she reported while sitting in a Manhattan restaurant, "was this atmosphere of curiosity about the world, of trying to learn about new cultures, of going to science museums in Boston and learning about frogs, or to an art museum to view the work of Shakers or Native Americans." Her house was chock-full of books and art, and when the family took a vacation, they didn't go to the beach to relax in the surf but to explore, to look for sand dollars, and to learn about the tides or sea urchins. While her classmates went off "to the Cape for the summer" or skiing in some exotic spot, Mary Ann and her sister spent their vacations around art or science. "I grew up thinking," she said, "that relaxing is when you are traipsing round robin's barn"—taking the long way around—"looking for something new. I had a very rich childhood."

A restless child who loved to run, Mary Ann became easily absorbed in what she was doing and often arrived late at the dinner table because she didn't listen. "She's too wild. She won't amount to much," a friend told her mother, "and she'll never get into a good college." She and her sister built make-believe villages in their yard and concocted histories and stories for these mini-structures. They dressed up in play clothes that would fit the tenor of their current project and acted out the stories they invented. Indoors, she built rooms out of pillows and imagined that she might be an architect someday who would design "ridiculous million-room homes."

She became fascinated with how things work, and once she and her father took a television apart and put it back together, and on another occasion did the same with the old family car. "My father was a surgeon and had no particular interest in mechanics or just tinkering, but we both wanted to know how it worked." She was also fascinated with the "beauty and logic of math" and loved to do her homework. When a problem stumped her, she turned to her father, who would make her explain it first. "In explaining it to him, I always figured it out for myself," she reported. Using the *World Craft Encyclopedia,* she taught herself to knit, crochet, and sew. She did ceramics and pottery, and other "mechanical, creative things." And she read. When she was eleven years old, she discovered the mystery writer Agatha Christie, and over the next year read all eighty-one of her stories. "I became fascinated with the logic and puzzle of the works and putting it all together by the end," she explained. In high school she pored over Aldous Huxley, Ray Bradbury, John Steinbeck, and J. D. Salinger. She read Archibald MacLeish and a variety of other writers who used rich allusions to biblical tales, and she wanted to know more about those stories. "My family isn't very religious," she reported, "so I joined a Bible study class thinking it was about the literature. The first thing they asked me was 'what does Jesus mean to you.'"

In high school she took advanced courses in math and science, but because she always struggled with words and writing, the school assigned her to remedial English. In a creative writing class, her teacher once gave her a D, and she felt devastated. Yet she continued to read, and in college made reading for pleasure into a ritual, something she did at least every night before going to sleep. "I still do that," she reported, "sometimes to put myself to sleep. One paragraph of Hermann Hesse and I'm out like a light because he's so boring." For Mary Ann, the nightly ritual became a way "to clear my head before I went to sleep, getting me out of all the things I had to do for class, and bringing me into another world. Almost like dreaming."

Mary Ann and her sister grew up in a world where teenage girls often roamed around Europe in the summer or sunbathed on the Riviera, almost as a rite of passage when they reached a certain age. Her parents wanted their daughters to see and understand the world. They wanted them to learn about science and nature, to understand both the beauty of the planet and its ugly underbelly of poverty and misery, and most of all, to develop a sense of responsibility and an ethic of giving back. Travel became a way to achieve all of that and more.

When Mary Ann turned eleven, her parents took the girls to Egypt. She remembered it as "culturally jarring because of the thousands of poor children begging in the streets." (When she returned to Egypt a few years ago, all those scenes had vanished.) In the years to come, she continued to travel with her family: to Greece, Egypt, Peru, and Mexico, among others. Then when she was barely sixteen, she went on an Earthwatch expedition to Costa Rica to live with scientists and help them collect insects, plants, snakes, and other specimens for their research. For the first time in her life, she lived on her own in a foreign culture. "I didn't even know how to braid my long hair at the time," she remembered. "It took six hours on a paved road from the capital, and four hours on an unpaved road to get to our station in the middle of the jungle." She spent a month living there, enjoyed herself thoroughly, but acquired "a lifelong hatred and fear of ants. I had tarantulas in my shower, and I got used to those, but these gigantic ants really bothered me."

The next summer she lived in York, England, joining an archeological dig in that ancient walled city. The summer following her freshman year in college, she had an experience that would strongly influence her future career choice. Her mother arranged for the girls to go to a remote village in India to help manage an orphanage. "For three months, we were a long way from anything, in this small town that nobody ever heard of." The two girls lived all that summer with special needs kids, children who suffered from malnutrition, illness, or some mental handicap. Mary Ann had never been squeamish about the sight of blood, so the orphanage assigned her to take children to the hospital for treatment.

One day, she and her sister took a thirteen-year-old girl with typhoid to the hospital. Along the way, the child died of septic shock. "There was no blood in her when they cut into a vein," Mary Ann told a reporter years later, "and she looked very white." After the girl died, Mary Ann and her sister carried the body back to the orphanage on their laps as they rode in a bicycle rickshaw. "When you have a child die like that . . ." she told that reporter, "that was traumatic. I haven't thought about that for a while. I tend to block traumatic things from my head, or I would probably never go back."

But she did go back, not once but twice. Following her sophomore year in college, she and her sister returned to the orphanage in India, and the next year, they went to Somalia for much the same kind of work. Those summers made a deep impression that would not go away.

Much of Mary Ann's decision about college came from her family. Aunts, uncles, parents, and grandparents had gone to Harvard, and, besides, it was a "local school." She went there thinking she would major in math but took a turn down the Latin and classics corridor instead. "Latin is a lot like Math," she remembered. "In its poetry there is an intrinsic beauty and logic to its rhythm and construction. It reminds me of the rap of Eminem and Tupak. There is

94

that same internal rhyming scheme." She loved Latin too for its beauty. "It's one thing in high school to translate in machine-like fashion; it's another thing when someone has shown you the beauty of the words and how they go together so wonderfully."

In high school, she had joined the speech team and did dramatic readings, and she helped "the physics teacher's wife" make costumes for school plays. "I knew how to sew, so that was relatively easy." In her freshman year at Harvard, she took a theater design seminar, and for the rest of her college years, she and a friend "who later died of AIDS" worked in the theater, designing sets or lights on at least one show a year if not two. "Once you start being in the theater tech world, you're highly desired," she remembered. "I was always hanging lights, or designing lights or sets, or making costumes. One semester, I took an extra class, and did three shows. It was just ridiculous."

In her last year at Harvard, she became fascinated with Asclepius, the god of healing, and how ancient Greeks perceived the cult of Asclepius and healing. So she wrote her senior thesis on the subject and then went to the University of Cambridge, intending to study with Geoffrey Ernest Richard Lloyd, a historian of ancient medicine and science. She never got to work with Lloyd, but she wrote a master's thesis on religious and rational medicine in ancient Greece. For centuries the Greeks had attributed sickness and healing to the gods, but in the fifth and fourth century BC, they developed more rational explanations, a shift in thinking that fascinated Mary Ann. "Why did this shift away from attributing everything to the gods take place when it did?" she asked herself.

As she finished her master's degree and made plans to pursue a doctorate, she felt that her work was increasingly pointless and detached, and one thought kept haunting her: "I want to go back and live in India." As she explained years later, "I realized that if I continued to study ancient medicine, I was operating on the fringes, becoming more and more obscure and irrelevant to the world at large."

"My parents were highly ethical people," she continued, "and they had sent my sister and me to India to make a difference in the world, and I wanted to go back." India needed "educational infrastructure," she told herself, "to train doctors and other experts," and Mary Ann wanted to help design that structure. Now she knew she needed to go to medical school, and then study public health. She returned to Harvard and took organic chemistry. She had abandoned any science courses as an undergraduate after receiving a B− in physics, but with renewed dedication and purpose, she aced the organic chemistry class, getting the second highest grade in the class. After completing other premed requirements, she entered Harvard Medical School, and in her fourth year fell in love with surgery. All of those years of sewing, knitting, and crocheting had trained nimble fingers.

After four years of medical school, physicians must complete four years of residency, and often find another two years of a fellowship in which they work with mentors to learn specialized skills. It's a long and arduous road. In the midst of that whole process, Mary Ann realized that she'd lost sight of her original goal to go back to India, and was increasingly caught up in thinking about setting up her practice somewhere. That's when she volunteered for Doctors Without Borders for the first time. In the years to come, she would volunteer again and again, going sometimes for several weeks every year to remote parts of the world where modern medicine didn't exist otherwise. She lived and worked in war zones at times, operating on people with fresh wounds from conflict, and other times delivered babies.

When Doctors Without Borders won the Nobel Peace Prize, the Times Square Business Improvement District chose the organization for the ceremonial dropping of the New Year's crystal ball. The prize-winning organization then named Mary Ann to represent them, bringing her to the top of that building on Times Square. On that occasion, she didn't have much time to think about her own thinking, yet a lifetime of reflective habits could not entirely escape the moment. When she spoke with reporters, she displayed the same reflective disposition that I found in her several years later.

Like the other people I interviewed, she took her paradigms from their boxes, turned them inside out, belly up, and upside down. She consciously recognized the concepts she had constructed—about the world, herself, her actions, and her personal history—and mindfully reexamined them. She realized that the world and our ideas about it come from constructions, and that all of them can be examined and questioned. She could both use and redesign the particulars of her own life because she thought mindfully about them.

In college Mary Ann had explored the arts, designing scenery, lights, and costumes. When she joined the faculty of New York University's medical school, she brought the same creative spirit and devotion, harnessing rich media and advanced computer technology to help revolutionize surgery education. In the process, she redefined the common paradigms about teaching and learning, and even about what it means to be a professor, mindfully rejecting old notions that didn't make sense to her. Back in school somewhere, a faculty advisor had urged her to concentrate on research and avoid teaching. "Research is academic," he'd smugly pronounced, but teaching isn't. "Thank god, I ignored him," Mary Ann exclaimed. She created a computer program in which surgery students could explore and experience a procedure electronically before seeing it live, or before trying it themselves.

In her fieldwork in the far-flung corners of the world, she recognized that "you have to overcome language barriers, and cultural barriers, and deal with a variety of physical problems. It requires almost all of your energy and creative ability just to show sympathy and care when you have such a huge language and cultural barrier. You are down to your core of who you are."

"It's selfishly exhilarating," she admitted about that work. "When my sister and I went to India, we felt like we were doing something." Mary Ann had discovered an ancient secret like some sand dollar on the beach, and although it had slipped away from time to time, buried in the inner creases of her life, she embraced it now with all her being. "In our society, it is truly hard to be selfless," she reflected. "I have so much here, but when I'm in the field, life becomes simpler and pure. It's not selfless because you are obviously feeling good doing it." Then she added, "Whether it is here or operating on a girl in the Congo and you don't know her language and she's been shot in the leg, I need that personal contact." Mary Ann Hopkins had thought deeply about her own thinking, her emotional needs, and her approach to life. The great insights she had developed about herself helped to shape who she became and what she did.

# 4

## LEARNING HOW TO EMBRACE FAILURE

When I was in school, I failed French twice. I also accumulated a few bad grades in Latin before barely mustering enough credits to satisfy the minimum foreign language requirement. Most of the advice I received focused on propping up my faltering confidence. "You just have to believe you can do it," coaxed a good friend. Others in my entourage of well-wishers took a more fatalistic view. "Some people have a knack for language, and others don't," offered a skinny kid from Seymour, Texas. Still others urged me simply to try a little harder. Meanwhile, I cycled through a range of emotional and intellectual reactions. At first, I blamed the French debacle on the teacher. He assigned us seats, and mine was located in the back of the room, from where I could barely make out the Phi Beta Kappa key that dangled from his waist. Later, I took Seymour's judgment to heart and decided I just couldn't learn French.

Ultimately, I survived both the advice and the bad grades, yet my battle with this challenge might have been my undoing. I could have easily slipped into not caring about any learning, or transformed my difficulties with language into a broad generalization about my capacity to master anything.

Everyone fails at some point. It might be a rejection from a friend, difficulty in learning a new language, or solving an algebra problem. It might be an act of omission, a failure to take necessary action, or a wrong turn deliberately pursued. All of the people we interviewed could tell us stories of some shortcoming. For Neil deGrasse Tyson, director of the Hayden Planetarium, his greatest loss came when the University of Texas booted him from their doctoral program in astronomy. Scientists have experiments that go awry. People lose their jobs, as one of our subjects did soon after we interviewed him. "I failed my freshman year," two people told us at the beginning of our conversations. Forging a creative life didn't depend on avoiding all shortcomings. Rather, it seemed to hinge on how people reacted to them. Ultimately, Neil and all of our other subjects bounced back from those reversals. He eventually finished his doctorate at Columbia University and became an astrophysicist and a leading popularizer of science. Others overcame course failures and other reversals. They learned to weather the inevitable storms of life.

How did they do it? In the last twenty-five years, social scientists have produced some important insights into how successful people overcome their unsuccessful moments. Not surprisingly, our findings among the lives of these remarkable students mirrored the core of that research. The picture that has emerged is both quite simple and far more complex than my well-intentioned friends ever imagined.

One idea has emerged most fully from both that research and the interviews we did. People who become highly creative and productive learn to acknowledge their failures, even to embrace them, and to explore and learn from them. That sounds relatively easy, yet for many people it proves enormously difficult. They won't admit their errors and often pretend they didn't do anything wrong, going to great extremes to justify their actions. They sometimes melt in the face of any mistakes, or refuse to recognize the value they may gain from confronting them. Recently, I conducted a workshop for faculty at a liberal arts college in Pennsylvania, and one English professor in particular objected strenuously even to the use of the word "failure." To her, failures were "too negative," distracting people from the positive thoughts they needed to maintain. She simply could not engage in a process we saw so consistently among our best students. But how and why did our subjects learn the value of admitting failure while so many others didn't? And why did that admission prove to be so significant?

## Fixed and Flexible Views of Life

When Joe was in the first grade, he enjoyed school and did well. He learned to read, count until he ran out of breath, add and subtract. Occasionally, people would tell him he was smart. By the time he reached the sixth grade, however, life began to change. School became more difficult, and when he started the seventh grade, he was going through puberty. His parents told him he needed to do better in school, to try harder. "You can make higher grades," rang in his ears like a bad song. "You used to be so smart. What happened to you?" Gradually, Joe decided that he wasn't all that bright and that he would never be a really good student. "I'm just an average guy," he would tell people, finding comfort in being ordinary. Sometimes he felt quite helpless, and in each class, he fought just to survive.

His friend Karolyn always did well in school, and everyone told her she was smart, something she came to believe deeply about herself. Her father always emphasized that she could do anything she wanted to do, and her teachers said she was one of the brightest students they had ever encountered. When she entered high school, she had a chance to take an advanced course in calculus at a local university, and she signed up without hesitation.

But the course proved to be enormously difficult. The class met in a large lecture hall with more than two hundred students enrolled, and the professor, an older woman with white hair, performed calculus on a series of boards that slid up and down like windows. This professor could have been a trained monkey doing a circus act. She certainly wasn't teaching anybody anything. From her seat in the back of the room, Karolyn could barely make out the numbers, symbols, and diagrams that the woman with white hair scribbled on those windows before shoving them upward to reveal another surface upon which she could splash more chalk shaped into a new set of numbers, symbols, and diagrams. Karolyn took careful notes, fairly confident that she could do calculus if she got down exactly how the professor solved the problems.

On the first examination, she received a forty-three. It contained a whole series of problems, the likes of which she thought she'd never seen before. They actually reflected the same principles the woman in white hair had been using to solve her problems, but because the whole class had focused on following procedures rather than understanding concepts, Karolyn didn't understand the ideas that would allow her to unravel the exam questions. She felt devastated and betrayed. When her parents asked her about the failing grade, she told them the teacher was horrible and she didn't want to go back, and while she eventually returned to class, her grades didn't improve much. She watched in humiliation as other students collected their exam papers after the second test, flashing grades in the seventies and eighties. Although none of them learned much from the instructor either, they had at least encountered most of the material in advanced courses they had taken in high school. Karolyn didn't have that luxury. A few students even made it into the nineties. Karolyn got a forty-eight. In the end, she failed the course.

In the months following that experience, something happened to her. She told her friends, "I'm just not very good at math," and in the inner recesses of her mind, in those dark places where feelings and thoughts mingle like dance couples, she began to explore a new self. Maybe that self wasn't as smart as she had thought. Maybe it couldn't do everything. Maybe she had to protect it. And protect she did. Like a mother guarding a child, she made sure she did not take on anything that might show her to be less intelligent. When she went to college, she avoided science and math courses. She asked her friends about the easiest teachers and then made sure she got into those classes. Once, when she was a junior, she had a chance to study with a visiting professor who had done some pioneering work in her major, but she heard his class was tough, so she took something else instead.

When David was in the seventh grade, his teacher suggested that he take some books home with him for the summer and study. "When you come back in the fall," she told him, "we'll give you some tests on the books, and if you pass those exams—which I'm sure you will—you can get into a special program for talented and gifted students."

That summer, David thought often about the books his teacher gave him, but for the most part he simply looked at them stacked up in the corner of his room. Too many distractions. Too many friends to see. So by the end of the summer, he had yet to crack a single book. Two weeks before school started again, he began to worry about a wasted summer, but the worry soon became overwhelming—too much to think about, too disturbing to consider.

Quickly, he learned to put it out of his mind. He told himself that he probably couldn't have passed the test anyway because "he wasn't all that smart." Getting into the honors program was for really smart kids, he told himself, and I'm not one of those.

To Joe, Karolyn, and David, and to millions of others, intelligence is something you cannot change. In their minds, you are born with lots of brains, very few, or somewhere in between, and something called intelligence determines how well you do in school and life. Joe's refrain about being an average guy was simply a way of saying, "I know what I've got. I'll be OK, but I'm not one of those brainy types." Karolyn held on to her image of being a smart girl, but she was afraid to take a chance, unwilling to risk anything that might question that image. And David concluded that no amount of studying would increase his native intelligence.

When Carol Dweck was a young woman, fresh out of graduate school, she began doing research on such fixed notions of intelligence, and why some highly capable people avoid challenging work. This was an important question because life inevitably involves risks. Think of any long-term goal you might imagine, and it will involve taking chances. There will be roadblocks, tough moments, and, yes, even failures. If some people are afraid to risk making a mistake, if they wilt in the face of coming up short, then they may not even try.

Carol had noticed in her research that she could find two people with almost identical abilities, yet one of them refused to attempt anything challenging while the other pursued the most difficult goals. One would wither and give up in the face of any kind of setback while the other would keep going. One would feel helpless when something proved difficult; the other would try even under the most grueling challenges. Carol could find no difference in their mental or physical abilities, yet she spotted enormous differences in their power to deal with lack of success. She also noticed—and this is highly significant—that some people who really wanted to do well often shot themselves in the foot, acting in ways that would almost guarantee that they wouldn't succeed. Why?[1]

To find out, Carol and one of her graduate students, Carol Diener, created two groups of children, all about ten years old, and gave them a series of puzzles to solve. The first eight problems required some careful thought, but none of them was too demanding for kids of that age. The next four, however, were far too hard for anyone that age to solve in the time they had. On the first eight, all of the youngsters in both groups solved the exercises, and there were no differences in the performance of the two groups. They asked the children to talk about the work as they did it, and clearly all of the kids had fun with it. Once they took on the four impossible problems, however, everything changed.

None of the children could solve the new exercises, but their reactions differed enormously. The students in one group—let's call it Group A—began saying, "I can't solve these problems. I'm just not very good. I'm not smart enough. I can't remember that well. I can't ever solve these exercises. I might as well give up. I'm bored. This is stupid." They also began talking about matters that had nothing to do with the problems, bragging about how much wealth they had, or the big houses and cars their families owned, telling the researchers how good they were at doing something else. In some cases, they even tried to change the rules of the puzzles. And they did all of that even though just minutes earlier, when these youngsters were working on the exercises within their reach, they had responded with enthusiasm, pleasure, and confidence. They had simply wilted in the face of failure.

The children in the other group, however, did none of that (we'll call them Group B). Instead, they kept telling themselves that they could solve the difficult problems with more effort. They changed their strategies and talked about how they could find the answer, constantly searching for a better way to reach their goal. "I did it before," they spontaneously told the researchers, "I can do it again." One child proclaimed, "I'm sure I have it now," even though she didn't. Failure didn't bother them. Instead, they even seemed to welcome a tough problem. "I love a challenge," one little boy announced, rubbing his hands together and pulling up his chair after getting a wrong solution—as if to say, "bring it on!" One of his classmates in the same group looked up at the researcher after failing to get one of the last four problems and said, with a ring of pleasure in his voice, "You know, I was hoping this would be informative."

Something in addition to delight divided the two groups. As children in Group A encountered failure, they began using very poor strategies. Moments earlier, on the exercises within their reach, they had employed perfectly good approaches, the kind of thinking you might expect from a capable problem-solver of their age. Now, they couldn't seem to do anything right. Dweck and Diener later reported that nearly two-thirds of the students in the first group started thinking like preschoolers, using approaches that would never work, no matter how many times they tried. With the first sign of failure, they didn't want to play anymore. They couldn't think straight or do what they had previously done so well, and they wanted to give up, quite sure that they could not do the problems. In the meantime, the students in Group B were as happy as larks, ready to keep trying, and quite sure they could crack the code, even though none did. None of those students began using poor strategies.

Neither group solved the new problems, but that's not the point. Carol had deliberately handed them failure to see how they would react. In many real-life situations, the kids in Group B might eventually solve the tough problems because they kept trying and continued to use good strategies. Students in the other group would never conquer a tough problem because the first sign of failure sent them into a tailspin in which their abilities actually diminished, and they eventually threw in the towel.

What could account for the difference? Certainly not ability. Students in both groups cracked the first eight exercises—the ones appropriate to their age—with equal skill. In fact, the kids in the first group were probably a little better at using good strategies on those initial examples. So why did they flounder so badly once they started failing? Was it interest? No. When the children talked aloud as they struggled with those first eight problems, both groups had clearly remained interested and engaged. But as soon as the hard problems came along and the experimenter had to say "wrong," only the kids in the first group changed their tune.

Why? The answer is fairly simple, yet enormously powerful. The children in Group A, the ones who reacted so poorly to failure, had a fixed view of intelligence while those in Group B believed that you could expand your smarts with effort. To the first kids, you were born at a certain level and nothing could change that. Because they wanted to believe that they were among the brilliant ones, they didn't want anything to challenge that notion. Failure on some stupid puzzle could raise questions in their own mind and in the minds of others—teachers, friends, parents—about their intelligence. When they began to hear the word "wrong," they wanted out. Immediately. They didn't want any words that might suggest that they were not as intelligent as they hoped. They wanted to see some evidence that they were really smart. As the mistakes piled up, they became more nervous and began thinking like someone half their age.

Meanwhile, the kids in the other group thought that effort mattered most. In their minds, intelligence wasn't some central quality fixed for life. Instead, in their view, it was a collection of different abilities, any one of which could be stretched with the right kind of effort. You could expand your capacity, they believed, if you just kept trying. Nothing was written in stone. Thus, they didn't see failure as a sign that they were dumb. They saw it as something they hadn't learned yet. In fact, the two groups had completely different goals. While the kids in the first group wanted to "look smart," those in the second just wanted to get better at solving the problems because they believed that they could increase their abilities with effort.

Before any of the children tried to solve a single problem, Dweck and Diener had asked them questions about why certain things happened to them in school. In general, the kids in Group A, the ones with the view that intelligence is fixed and who wilted with the tougher problems, blamed most of their failures in the classroom on lack of ability. The second group said their failures reflected a lack of effort. When the experiment was over, the researchers asked the kids why they had difficulty with the last four problems. More than half of the first team said it was because they were not smart enough. No one in the second group gave that excuse.[2]

Carol Dweck and other psychologists have given these two types of students names that fit them well. She calls people in the first group "helpless" because they develop the idea that they just can't do something because they "aren't that smart," or not that good at math, music, art, foreign language, or whatever gave them difficulty. Or, if they continue to believe that they are generally smart and that intelligence is something that is fixed at birth, they still often become helpless because they are afraid to try anything new for fear that failure will question their conception of themselves as "one of the bright ones."

Carol says kids in the second group have a "mastery" or "growth" mindset because they believe that they can master something and grow in their abilities if they try. If they don't succeed, they look for new strategies rather than deciding they "just can't do it." Are the mastery students just smarter than the helpless? No. Carol has found considerable evidence that children in the two groups have roughly the same natural abilities, no matter how you measure those, and that sometimes the helpless demonstrate greater native powers with these kinds of problems. The difference lies in whether they have what she called a "growth mindset." Mastery students think abilities can expand. The helpless think they're fixed.

In experiments large and small, Carol and her colleagues have demonstrated the power of a growth mindset. In one prominent study of eleven- and twelve-year-old math students in New York City, they found that kids who believed that intelligence could expand generally improved their math scores during their two years in junior high school while those who thought that it was fixed forever stayed the same. That investigation also demonstrated the relationship between the factors we have pursued in various parts of this book. Students who believed that abilities could grow had a more positive view of effort and were more interested in learning rather than just performing well on an examination. As a result, they took the time and made the effort to understand, which produced higher grades.[3]

Where do helpless students get the notion that intelligence is fixed and you can't do anything about it? They live in a culture that constantly bombards them with that idea, telling them about IQ tests that will measure how bright they are. In her wonderful book *Mindset*, Carol Dweck remembers a sixth-grade teacher who ranked everyone by the scores they received on an IQ test, sitting the students in order around the room and letting only the "smart kids" have certain privileges, such as carrying the flag. Some college professors, especially in certain fields, believe that only "geniuses" can succeed in their discipline and that it doesn't really matter how well they teach. "The smart kids will get it, and the dumb ones won't," a math professor at New York University once told me. That attitude seeps into every action and interaction, and students pick up the message. Every day you can find magazines or Internet sites that claim they can measure your intelligence and invite you to "take the test" as if they were going to tell you how much you weigh.

Even well-meaning parents and teachers can foster that fixed view. We've long assumed that positive feedback always has desirable results. But some recent research has painted a more complex picture. Melissa Kamins discovered that children who receive primarily person-praise ("how smart you are") rather than good words about their efforts will usually develop fixed views of intelligence. When children are young and family members constantly tell them how brilliant they are (or how dumb), they get the message: Life depends on your level of intelligence, not on how you work at something. You've got it or you don't. Nothing can change that reality, they think. In short, fixed views of intelligence or growth mindsets stem from conditioning, not from some inborn character trait.[4] They too can change.

But wait a minute, you say. I'm not helpless. I think I'm smart, and I know it. If that's your attitude, then you deserve a big round of applause for your belief in yourself. That self-confidence will serve you well. There's nothing wrong with it. But if you believe that you were just born smart, that all your friends can be ranked by their intelligence in the same way you might line them up by how tall they are, and that no amount of effort will change this ranking, then you have a fixed view of intelligence. If you think that while you can learn new things, you cannot change your basic intelligence, you have a fixed mindset. If, on the other hand, you think that no matter how capable you may be, you can get better—and so can anyone else—if you believe that if you don't try you probably will lose abilities, you have a growth mindset, and it is that growth mindset that allows many people to find rewards in failure, "to embrace the bomb," as Stephen Colbert put it.

All of the creative people we interviewed for this book—the deep learners who have crafted such creative lives—exhibited a growth mindset about themselves and their friends, and their stories illustrate well the findings of thirty years of empirical research. "I hardly ever use the word intelligence," Neil deGrasse Tyson noted. "I think of people as either wanting to learn, ambivalent about learning, or rejecting learning." Sherry Kafka put it this way: "I believe everybody is creative, or at least has the potential to be." Because our subjects had that basic concept of human nature, they were willing to take risks and try something new, but they didn't worry about making mistakes or looking stupid. They did not see themselves as participating in a competitive game to be the "smartest kid in the class." Rather, they focused on developing their own talents. Yes, they wanted to play to their strengths, and they realized that they had capabilities. But as we have seen already, they didn't give up easily.

## From Disenchantment to Success

On summer afternoons in the sweltering heat along the east coast of Florida, Tom Springer and his two older brothers stretched out on the floor of their cinder-block house listening to their mother read. An electric fan stirred the moist air, whirling in the background as the boys traveled on words and sounds into another place and time. She read *The Wonderful Wizard of Oz* and other L. Frank Baum books about life on the Great Prairie, or Mark Twain's works, set along the Mississippi River in the age of steamboats. On Saturdays they would go together to the local library and bring home a fresh stack of books for her to read. His mother never "read down" to them. She always selected literature that stretched the boys, challenging them to understand new words and ideas, to explore in their minds new places and cultures.

Tom's mother followed the children's interests with care. If she noticed a particular fascination, she picked material on their latest focus, feeding it with carefully selected books to challenge their thinking. When they shifted to something new, so would she. For awhile the boys fell in love with World War II books and wanted to read about battles and politics. As a result, Tom developed a grasp of geography and political developments that went far beyond his years.

In the early grades, Tom went to a school in Melbourne, Florida. His classroom felt the influence of the local space industry in nearby Cape Canaveral. Many of his friends had parents who worked as NASA engineers and scientists, and they made sure their children's school had the best teachers. It was an exciting place to be. A race to the moon unfolded next door, and Tom and his friends explored science, astronomy, and "all that kind of stuff." From their playground, they saw rockets launched into space, unleashing an endless array of speculations about the heavens. They found school stimulating and wonderful.

His parents didn't have much money. "My dad was a barber," he explained. "We were basically a working class family." Nevertheless, they scraped together enough to purchase a small amateur telescope, and Tom and his brothers used it to explore the sky at night. Sometimes they would go to the ocean with their father, and while he waded into the surf with a long cane fishing pole in hand, the boys would wait on shore, digging up little crabs for bait, picking up starfish, and occasionally fishing for shrimp. The boys had a seashell collection, and they accumulated a series of children's books on nature and the sea. "It was just a really rich, sensual experience," Tom recalled.

When he was in the fourth grade, that world vanished in a flash. His family moved from Florida to southern Michigan, and life and his new school didn't have the same vitality for him. "It was a cultural shock," he remembered. School was slower, both less and more demanding, and filled with petty rules and requirements that gave him less sense of control over his own education. The school also had lower intellectual standards. He became bored, never doing his homework or picking up a book outside of class. His grades plummeted. By the time he finished high school they had sunk below a C− average. "I had become," he observed, "a disaffected student" with no ambition. "Much of the education I received thereafter came outside of school," he recalled. "I continued to read about stuff that would fascinate me."

When he graduated from high school, he got a job with an asphalt paving crew, but that was seasonal, so he worked in a couple of factories in the winter. One day, his boss fired him because he had been writing smart aleck remarks on his time card and had asked a friend to punch the clock for him. He then got work as an air-conditioning mechanic with a chain-smoking guy named Porky, but he lost that job too. Failures accumulated on every front. He joined the National Guard, and when he got out decided to enroll in an air-conditioning curriculum at a local community college. His life began to change, even though he continued to fail with anything mechanical.

"I just couldn't get those pipes to fit together," he remembered, "but I had to take a freshman writing class, and that changed my life." In that class, Tom found something that spoke to his childhood in Florida and all the books he had read over the years. He did well and gradually improved his writing, displaying an ability that no one might have suspected a few years before. Eventually, Tom transferred to Western Michigan University, where he appeared on the dean's list, and then on to Michigan State, where he earned a master's degree in environmental journalism. Tom became a successful writer and filmmaker. His work began appearing on National Public Radio, and he published an award-winning book with the University of Michigan Press. He went to work for the W.K. Kellogg Foundation, where he became a senior editor and then a project manager, joining the Learning Innovation Team and working on projects that "seek to reconnect children with nature as a way to spur their mental, physical and spiritual growth."

How did Tom Springer fight his way from failure to success? How does anyone overcome a setback? Reading educated him, but Ernest Hemingway, Twain, Baum, and all the other writers transformed his life because he never allowed some fixed notions of intelligence to freeze him into a sense of helplessness. He had an expansive and flexible view of his own abilities and never saw any of his failures as a reflection on who he was or what he could do as a human be-ing. In general, he didn't think about whether he "had the intelli-gence" to do something, but only that he often didn't do it, and sometimes didn't want to. Furthermore, as Tom struggled through air-conditioning jobs and classes, he fashioned a deep respect for a wide variety of abilities that went beyond "book smarts," as he put it. "The people who can build a barn or a brick fireplace have an abil-ity that deserves recognition," he told me. "I ultimately had more trouble fitting pipes together than I did constructing sentences." That reverence for what other people could do and for the challenges he faced helped him to find out what made him tick. As he learned to respect works of the "hand, head, and heart," as the architect Frank Lloyd Wright had put it, he learned to draw from the unique experiences and body chemistries that defined his soul and to con-centrate on effort rather than on some notion of fixed abilities.

"If something bad happened to me," he said, "I'd try to think about how I could get more power so it wouldn't happen again. It was a kind of 'I'll show you' attitude," he concluded. Tom rec-ognized that he flourished with self-directed learning, staying up nights and reading a book he found fascinating. He would sneak a copy of Sinclair Lewis's *Babbitt* into his lunch pail and then think about the characters he encountered and how they compared to his boss, Porky, and other people around him. In some important ways, Tom never stopped learning, and in one important sense, all those bad grades did not reflect his failure. It reflected instead the inabil-ity of the schools he attended to recognize and honor that learning. Ultimately, he found a way to draw on who he was and the life that he had led, to respect himself as he also learned to appreciate others and what they could do. He drew from his past, the interactions with nature he had enjoyed with his father and brother, and all those wonderful hours he had spent listening to his mother read. "The sounds of good writers reverberated through my mind," he recalled.

At one crucial moment, he learned to convert his learning from curiosity and reading into academic success and with that marriage of achievements to produce a new family of successful work, all growing in its own ways. Teachers—his writing teacher, in particular—provided him with the opportunity and showed interest in his writing and respect for what he could do. His teachers challenged him to find his own voice, to refine its tenor, and to improve on what he produced. He apparently never lost complete respect for himself, even in those dark days of disaffection with school and everything about it, but the missing piece was someone who could appreciate his work and show him ways to expand on it. He found such teachers at Kalamazoo Valley Community College. He discovered a challenging yet inviting world there.

## Blame and Credit

One more important factor often guides people to success, and probably influenced Tom. A growing body of research finds that the way people attribute their successes and failures will have a considerable influence on those achievements and shortcomings. Think of it this way. When something goes wrong, who or what gets the blame? When everything comes up roses, who or what gets the credit?

You could, for example, attribute your successes or setbacks to something that is within you or to some outside force. You could decide that it is only a temporary condition or something permanent, and you could believe that you have considerable influence over it or none at all. In all, there are eight possible combinations, running from "it's something permanent about me over which I have no control" all the way to "it's them but I can change that." Furthermore, any one of these combinations can be used to explain either success or failure. How you decide to put those combinations together will shape how well you deal with any setback.[5]

If, for example, you usually blame your failures on something that permanently infests your soul ("I flunked calculus because I'm just not good at math"), you'll probably think you have no control over that situation. You'll give up and stop trying. And, guess what? You'll also never pass calculus. In contrast, if you say something like, "I don't think I studied the best way; I can do better if I get help from the tutoring center," then you still believe it's you, not someone else, but your math ability can improve with the right kind of effort. With that way of accounting for your setbacks, you most likely will keep trying and will succeed.

How you explain your success will also matter. Which of these two possibilities will most likely motivate you and bring good results?

> I just got lucky on that last exam. All of her questions were right down my alley. But I'm still just not good at math.
> I studied with my friends, and we talked through every type of problem until we understood the concept. That's why we all did well on that exam.

In the first, you attribute your success to something external (luck), temporary, and over which you have no control. In the second, you credit something you did (effort), still temporary, but over which you have considerable influence. No one can find much incentive in the first—why try if it is all luck?—but everyone can find it in the second.

In general, people who are highly successful in handling failure take responsibilities for those shortcomings and triumphs, yet see either situation as highly changeable. Success can evaporate, and failure can be overcome. Years ago, Albert Bandura, a psychologist at Stanford, observed people trying to learn how to handle snakes. He noticed that in order to use the techniques properly the snake-handling students needed to learn the right procedures, but they also had to believe that they could use them appropriately. He called that potent combination of belief and ability "self-efficacy."[6] You must know how to do something, but you must also believe that you can. People who overcome failure possess strong measures of self-efficacy.

How do the best students cultivate the perspectives that allow them to hold a flexible view of intelligence, attribute their successes and failures properly, and maintain a sense of self-efficacy? One central practice comes from what Paul Baker urged upon his students: have a conversation with yourself. Know how you work. Understand what moves you. A flexible view of intelligence and ability, Baker suggested, stands at the base of how successful people handle failures. It allows them to attribute successes and failures productively, work hard and properly at developing some new ability, and believe that they can use their new-found powers.

Baker's ideas escape the debate about whether intelligence remains fixed for life or can be expanded, and most of our subjects managed to take the same route. The distinction I'm making here becomes clear in the metaphors we use to discuss intelligence. The old, rigid view of intellectual prowess was of a ladder with some people fixed at the top from birth and others arrayed on the various rungs. The flexible view that Carol Dweck came to prize still thought in terms of that ladder but believed that people could climb up it. Baker's ideas represent a different metaphor—a tree with an almost countless number of branches—and it is that metaphor we most frequently heard in the conversations with our subjects. Every fork and limb represents someone unique, and the goal becomes not a mad race up the ladder of abilities but the nourishing of those special perspectives within each individual. In this tree every part feeds off every other part. This branch isn't better than that one, only different, and each one has the potential to grow in its own special way. That doesn't mean that there are no standards. But it does mean that people seek to meet those criteria rather than compete with others, and it can mean that different people will flourish in different ways.

In the old perspective, people can develop something psychologists call "contingent self-worth," which is simply the notion that your value as a person depends on where you rank, on what rung you have achieved on the ladder. Melissa Kamins found such ideas among young children who received a steady diet of personal praise and criticism, and as a result built a fixed view of intelligence—even when that feedback was all positive. If you believe that your value as a human being depends on how well you perform, and you also think that fate has predetermined your ability to do something, you are headed for trouble. Those ideas will influence how you react to failure.[7]

If you have a sense of contingent self-worth, if your attitude toward yourself depends on whether you "succeed" or "fail" in a certain domain in comparison with other people, you may stop trying. Subconsciously you decide that the best way to avoid losing is to stay out of the game. If you play, you may give up easily, and retreat into the kind of behavior we saw earlier in Joe, David, and Karolyn. You could even sabotage your efforts, blowing a chance to "win," because you are quite convinced that you will ultimately lose. You may want to withdraw, to give yourself an excuse ("I didn't really try") before tasting the bitter fruits of defeat. As we shall see repeatedly, our best students flourished when they abandoned such comparative thinking; when they looked inside themselves, understood what appealed to them, and focused on what they wanted to *do*, not on how they wanted to rank or look.

I asked each of the people I interviewed, "Are you highly competitive?" To a person, they all answered, "Yes, but with myself, not with other people." That answer speaks volumes about a highly significant factor in their success. For them, as it was for Susan Bobbitt Nolen's task-oriented students, life was all about achieving a personal best rather than merely winning a competition with someone else. A deep intention defined the nature of their learning, sprang from an intrinsic interest while feeding that internal motivation, and reflected their growth mindsets.

Baker offered his students a new vocabulary for thinking about such matters, words rooted in those five senses with which they would experience all of life (line, sound, space, silhouette, and color), and while some of our subjects who never experienced his teaching also trafficked in such language and concepts, the larger point is that the use of those categories rested in a perspective that we saw repeatedly among people who learned deeply and lived productive lives. They believed in growth, and looked both within themselves and at the works of the mind that others had created to find nourishment for that development. They embraced "failures" as wonderful opportunities to learn something rather than as judgments about their souls.

## Lifelong Learning

In the September after he graduated from Cornell, Jeff Hawkins picked up a copy of *Scientific American,* something the budding scientist and engineer had been doing for years. In that issue each fall, the magazine featured articles on a single subject, and that year, all of the content focused on the brain. Jeff had taken an interest in the human mind ever since he had composed those four big questions before going off to college, but one article in particular caught his eye and changed his life.

In it, Francis Crick, the man who helped discover DNA, wrote that although we've learned a lot about the mechanics of that organ that sits in the top of our heads, we still don't have a general theory of how it works. The claim hit Jeff like a bolt of lightning. "After reading that article," he reported, "I became totally devoted to the idea that we're going to figure out in my lifetime how brains function, and I'm going to work on the problem." He had found his life's work: "I'm going to do brains."

While he continued to focus on that three-pound mass of cells in the head and to wonder how it worked, Jeff took a job as an engineer with Intel, first at an office in Oregon, and then in Boston, where he would be closer to his girlfriend. Initially, the young engineer saw a connection between his job and his passion for understanding the brain. If he could understand how the human mind worked, he could build one, and Intel might let him spend his time doing just that. Surely a company that had "invented the silicon memory chip and the microprocessor" would let him use part of his day thinking about "how we could design brain-like memory chips." So he wrote a letter, addressed to the chair of the company. Here was a kid, fresh out of college, writing the chairman of the company, asking if he could get paid to "do brains." That takes passion . . . and nerve. What could anyone expect? Maybe one huge cold shoulder, or a reprimand: "don't spend your time writing me letters about how you should spend your time."

Instead, Gordon Moore may have laughed to himself, but he also sent young Jeffrey to see Intel's chief scientist, Ted Hoff. Jeff flew off to California and met with Hoff. As it turned out, the head scientist had studied human thinking himself, and after listening to this young upstart from Boston, he poured cold water on the whole idea. We don't know enough about biological thinking organs to build artificial ones any time soon, he said. "Hoff was correct," Jeff wrote years later. "Still, at the time, I was pretty disappointed."

Yet that failure didn't stop him. Jeff decided to go back to school and applied to the Massachusetts Institute of Technology, located just across the Charles River from his Boston office. MIT had a big program in artificial intelligence, and Jeff thought he would win admission easily. He didn't. He wrote on his application that he wanted to understand how brains work, but the professors who read that document had other priorities. They wanted to write programs to get computers to do the same things people could do—see, talk, move, calculate, and so forth—but from their perspective, that didn't require an understanding of how the "human computer" functioned. They rejected his application.

I mention this story in part to illustrate the passion that drove Jeff's life, both in college and after, and that ultimately fed his deep approach to learning. He was convinced that brains and computers were fundamentally different, and he wanted to understand how intelligence operates, how we think, create, remember, predict, and all those other wonderful things humans can do.[8]

Jeff Hawkins's intellectual journey illustrates something else about our "best students." They don't give up easily. After rejections from both MIT and Intel, Jeff and his girlfriend, now his wife, moved to California, where he took a job at GRiD Systems, a company in Silicon Valley that had invented the first laptop computer. One day while he was working there, something special happened. It might have been an accident, but I think it occurred partly because Jeff took such a deep interest in learning. He had helped design the first tablet computer, and he let some of his colleagues play with it. As he watched them use this strange device with a touch screen and no keyboard, he marveled at how much they enjoyed carrying it around and using it. The company wasn't thinking of selling this device to consumers, only to businesses. But Jeff observed something, maybe out of his habit of looking behind the obvious, that would send him in a whole new direction. "I noticed how much they enjoyed holding this gadget, and touching the screen, and somebody said, 'I wish I could put my personal contact information in here.'"

That simple observation, plus Jeff's lifetime habit of thinking deeply, sparked a notion that would change forever how we handle and think of information, and land Jeff eventually in the National Academy of Engineers. He simply mused to himself, "I think the future of computing is in mobile devices, things that people can carry around. Why couldn't you put a small computer in people's pocket[s]?" It would be cheaper, easier to use, and more reliable than a big computer. Most of the world's population couldn't afford a computer, but Jeff thought if he could make one small enough "to fit in your pocket," more people would have the money to buy the device.

At the time, this dream of putting small computers in people's pockets looked as wild as those weird boats he and his family had built in their garage back on Long Island, or the even crazier idea of understanding how brains work. "The technology wasn't there to build a small computer and neither was the software." GRiD Systems didn't want to put up the money to develop one because they didn't think anyone would buy it. Another immediate failure.

So Jeff went back to school, still intrigued with the possibilities of building that small computer. He became increasingly convinced that the future lay in gizmos you could carry around with you. But he went to school to follow an old passion, his fascination with the way people think and how it all works. At first he started taking correspondence courses. As Jeff wrote much later, "no one ever got rejected by a correspondence school." He boned up on physiology and other subjects related to biology, and then applied to study human intelligence within a biophysics program at the University of California at Berkeley. As Jeff told the story, "I studied hard, took the required entrance exams, prepared a resume, solicited letters of recommendation, and voila, I was accepted as a full-time graduate student." He was not quite thirty years old.

He took a leave of absence from GRiD Systems, and a few years later, he returned to the computer industry to invent the first successful mobile computer, the Palm Pilot. He had found a way to let people simply write into the computer with a stylus. Millions of people around the world began buying his new device and carrying these little computers in their pockets. Three years later, he and some of his colleagues created a new company, named Handspring, where he designed a small computer that you could use as a telephone, the world's first smart phone, the Treo.

His success in business now gave him the financial resources to follow his passion and "do brains." First, he created the nonprofit Redwood Neuroscience Institute in Menlo Park, California, where he and other scientists studied how the human neocortex processes information. Three years later, he gave the institute to the University of California at Berkeley and created another new company, named Numenta. In this small business, tiny in comparison to the giants that he had helped create at Palm and Handspring, he could explore how the mind works and perhaps build a machine that would think like humans do.

Jeff developed an uncanny optimism about life, and in that perspective, he found further backbone for his deep approach to learning and his willingness to keep trying, even in the face of considerable discouragement. "I understood very early in life that there is a lot of chance in what happens to you, so I never worried about it," he said. Instead, he simply pursued his own curiosity. "If something bad happened, I tried not to become obsessed with it, but to try to find a solution if I could." To believe in solutions is to believe that the world is flexible, that you can change it with effort. That's a growth mindset.

## Changing a Mindset

Can anyone learn to think of intelligence as expandable, and thereby realize the rewards of that growth mindset? Charlie Geaers and his buddies demonstrated that you can.[9] The shy young boy from New York City had never done well on any of the standardized math tests that he took in school. In the sixth grade, he'd scored worse than sixty-five percent of the students who took the same exam across the country. Because his family didn't have much money, he received a free lunch every day. When he came back to school after the New Year's holiday during the seventh grade, a group of psychologists from Columbia and Stanford universities offered him and some of his friends a chance to participate in a weekly workshop for eight weeks to learn about the brain and receive some advice on how to study. Charlie got the required permission from his parents and signed up for the program. Nearly one hundred other students registered as well. Most of them had struggled with math.

The psychologists formed the volunteers into classes of twelve to fourteen students each, and then secretly divided those classes into two large groups. But neither Charlie, his parents, or his teachers knew about the two large groups. Both groups of classes learned about the brain and how it works. They all received instruction on how to use their time most effectively and tips on how to organize, study, understand, and remember new material. Every student also explored how stereotypes can influence thinking about other people and discussed ways they might escape those threats.

Students in both groups had the same experiences—except for two vital sessions. On those special days, Charlie and his friends read aloud an article that Lisa Blackwell, one of the psychologists, had written especially for seventh graders: "You Can Grow Your Intelligence." As they read, the students heard themselves say that when they learn, the brain physically changes. The article explained some recent scientific research which found that the nerve cells in the brain responsible for carrying messages make stronger connections after learning something new. The brain actually grows, the article told them, just like a muscle after daily exercise, sprouting new connections between the cells. The active, learning brain will weigh more than one that doesn't practice. Think about a baby learning to talk, the article concluded. A newborn can't say a word, but by practicing sounds, that infant can eventually acquire a new language. When scientists look inside a child's brain using Magnetic Resonance Imaging (MRI), they can actually see the changes that go on as the kid learns to talk.

When Charlie and his classmates finished reading, the two college students who led the session asked them to think about something they had learned to do by practicing, and got them to explain how their brains might have changed as they learned. The exercise bore a remarkable resemblance to one that Ernest Butler, Sarah Goodrich, Sherry Kafka, and their classmates had experienced in Paul Baker's Integration of Abilities class. They had thought about some creative act they had accomplished and then explored what conditions had led them to undertake that work.

Meanwhile, students in the other group spent those same two days reading an article about how memory works. They learned new strategies for recalling material, and even had an opportunity to practice those memory tricks. In essence, then, they received both study and memory tips.

How did the students do? Most of the students went into the sessions generally believing that intelligence was fixed for life, but Charlie's group emerged from the experience with much stronger notions that intelligence could improve with effort. That shouldn't be surprising, since they read an article about how that happens and the other students didn't. More important, Charlie's group also generally showed greater motivation to do well in math class in the weeks and months following the experience.[10] They sometimes stayed up late to get work done or asked for greater help during lunch periods, something they'd never done before. Most important, for students like Charlie who went into the experience believing that intelligence couldn't change and came out thinking that it might, academic performances in math classes suddenly reversed and started climbing rather than going down.

Lisa Blackwell, who headed the study in Charlie's school, noted that your theory about whether intelligence can change may not make much difference when times are easy and you don't face many challenges, but when you hit a bump in the road and failures accumulate, those who believe that they can improve their basic abilities are far more likely to weather the storm. That's precisely the pattern that we found among highly creative and productive people.

## Weathering Unusual Storms

Debra Goldson lived in Jamaica until she was eight years old, enjoying the upper-class existence of her family's position. But her parents separated that year, and she and her mother moved to Queens in New York City, where life changed significantly. "We moved in with my grandmother and cousins. At one point, we had ten people living in a tiny apartment," she recalled. "It was a big switch moving from grass and trees to concrete and apartment buildings." She loved to read, and the big city gave her plenty of opportunities. "I would go to the library and get 10 books at a time and be done with them before it was time to go back." Murder mysteries fascinated the young girl, and she devoured all of Agatha Christie's novels.

New York City has specialized high schools. "You have to decide when you are about fourteen what you want to do in life and then go to the high school that will prepare you for that career. I was twelve when I decided to become a physician." Debra liked people and taking care of them. "My mom had a heart condition, and no one could tell her what was wrong, so I wanted to become a cardiologist to help her." She had discovered the purpose that would guide her schooling. "I thought if I learned medicine that I could figure out what was wrong and fix my mom."

In the years to come, whenever Debra got sick and had to visit a doctor, her mother would always take the occasion to promote her daughter's career. "By the way," she would say, "my daughter wants to be a doctor; can you give her some advice on what she should be doing." But such requests often fell on deaf and prejudiced ears. "I would get this look," Debra remembered years later, "that said, 'Oh, that's not going to happen.'" That "look," as she called it, said to her, "You're a poor black girl from Queens who doesn't have a prayer of getting into medical school." It was not the last time someone would pass such judgments on her.

Discouraging looks aside, Debra enrolled in the Bronx High School of Science when she was thirteen. "It was a 2½ hour commute," she explained. "I had to leave at 6:00 in the morning and ride the subway." Her grades suffered. For the first time in her life, she faced challenging courses and had to struggle. Literature and math became her soulmates, and in one of those courses she discovered Robert Frost's poem "The Road Not Taken," and it made a deep impression on her. "Like the traveler in that verse, I've always taken the 'one less traveled,'" she explained.

Debra always looked for ways to push herself. "I could have gone to easier schools," she noted, "but that wouldn't have been good for me." By the time she graduated from Bronx Science, her grades had soared, and although she didn't get into the college of her choice, Vassar, she did well enough and packed her bags for Boston University. During the admissions interview for Vassar, they had asked her what she would do with a million dollars. "Give it to my mom," she'd declared proudly, but at that moment she knew she'd blown the interview. "He clearly expected some grand statement, but what did you expect from a child with a single mom who had lived in Queens with 10 other people?"

She chose every course at Boston University with one goal in mind: getting into medical school and becoming a physician. She majored in social psychology because she thought it would help her become a better physician. Social psychology and math—where she also took many courses—made enormous sense to her. Her grades skyrocketed. Yet the experience that made the deepest impression on her was a talk she had with a counselor after she had compiled an impressive academic record. The university required all premed students to see a counselor to make sure they were making the right choice. "He tried to explain to me why I wasn't going to get into medical school. He keep telling me how difficult it would be and that I should give up the dream."

Debra didn't listen. Everything she did in school centered on getting into medical school and becoming a physician. She went to Bronx Science for that reason. She studied social psychology and pushed herself through difficult science classes for that reason. She ignored her counselor for that reason. Yet when she received her first offer to medical school, she turned it down.

Even before she finished college, a friend had arranged for her to interview with the dean of a medical school in Pennsylvania. She had already taken the Medical College Admission Test (the MCAT), and had done "really well," scoring in the ninety-ninth percentile on the essay portion. Even though she hadn't yet finished all of her premed courses, the dean accepted her on the spot. "It was a decent enough school, but they had this one annoying requirement." Every black student had to start taking medical school classes in the summer before everyone else started in the fall. "They didn't give me a choice, which might have made a difference in my decision. They just said I had to do it." When Debra described the requirement years later, she called it a "remedial program," and still bristled over the insult.

"I turned them down, much to the disappointment of my boyfriend at the time, and his father, who had arranged for the interview with the dean. But if I had accepted, I would have always wondered if I could have made it on my own." Debra had been told repeatedly that she couldn't make it. To defeat those skeptics, she had to feel in control of her own education. A requirement suggesting that she needed special help didn't sit well.

The next year she won admission to the medical college at Columbia University, one of the top schools in the country. In the first two years of medical school, students take basic science classes in everything from neurology to physiology. They attend classes, hear lectures, and take tests that often require them to remember large bodies of information. But they don't practice medicine. That comes in the last two clinical years and beyond. "I don't think your performance in those classes indicates what kind of doctor you will be," Debra concluded.

Once she was in the clinic, she excelled, winning constant praise for her abilities. She was finally doing what she had wanted to do since she was twelve years old. Doctors must reason through the evidence they have about a patient, consider all the possible explanations for some health problem, and make a judgment about what's wrong and how to treat it. They must then convince a patient to take their medicine or undergo treatment. Dr. Goldson mastered the science and art of doing that "differential diagnosis" that would eliminate unlikely explanations and center on the one account that most probably explained an ailment. "I would often continue to think about a case while I slept, sometimes waking up in the middle of the night with a conclusion." She became a scientific sleuth, weighing the evidence carefully. Her background in psychology influenced how she convinced a patient to follow her prescription. After her medical training, she established a practice in northern New Jersey that became one of the most respected in the state.

Through all of the struggles, the condescending looks, the discouraging advice from a counselor, and the insult of a required program she saw as remedial, Debra maintained a strong conviction that she could do it. "Negative stereotypes never bothered me," she said recently: "that's not my problem." As for intelligence, she came to believe that effort paid the biggest rewards. "I now define being smart in terms of how hard you try."

# 5

## Messy Problems

One hot and lazy summer day last year, I was sitting on my patio working on this book and watching a six-year-old play baseball with his younger brother. While he pounded the ball into his glove, I had a computer in my lap and was plugging away at the keyboard. At one point he crept up next to me, looked over my shoulder at the work on the screen, and asked the most difficult of questions: "Where do we go when we die?"

Not wanting to get into that discussion, I deflected his inquiry. "I don't know," I answered.

"Can you Google it?" he responded.

At the age of six, this child thought in the same way many college students think. In that perspective, every question has an answer. It's just a matter of finding it. You ask an expert. To learn, you remember the response. Problems have procedures, and if you follow the recipe, you will find a solution.

Yet people face problems every day that defy easy answers. Suppose, for example, that you sit on a jury and hear testimony about an unspeakable crime, and you must decide the fate of a young man accused of committing it. You hear from an eyewitness that Dennis Williams, age twenty-one, and three of his buddies abducted a young girl and her fiancé, took the pair to a motel, and raped the young woman repeatedly before killing the couple and leaving their bodies on the streets of Chicago. The seventeen-year-old woman who sits before you making these charges against her friends shifts nervously on the witness stand while the lawyer for the accused occasionally closes his eyes and seems to catnap. When the testimony ends, you vote with other people on the jury to convict Dennis, and the judge says he must die from a lethal injection.

Eighteen years later, you learn that Dennis Williams and his friends didn't do it, and that the real killers confessed. Williams, now in his late thirties, has lived for years in a six-by-ten-foot cell, sleeping nightly on a thin cotton mattress thrown over a metal frame, and always within days and sometimes hours of having a doctor stick a needle in his arm and squirt liquids into his veins that would snuff out his life. How could you and the other jurors have made such a horrible mistake? How were you fooled?

Such tough problems aren't restricted to the jury box. We struggle with the causes of war and poverty, with why economies fail, or with issues of morality and justice. We battle to understand nature in all of its complexity. In our daily lives, we face an often maddening array of decisions about school, jobs, romances, relatives, friends, health, and happiness. Sometimes the choices test our sense of morality, or bump against some deeply held religious notions. Now and again they question something we have believed firmly all of our lives, or raise frightening possibilities too scary to contemplate. Sometimes, they upset our emotional stability and plunge us into despair.

Is there anything in your education that will help you make better decisions as a juror, citizen, friend, parent, child, student, or in any of the other roles you will play in life? Philosophers and psychologists often talk about two kinds of problems, well-structured and ill-structured ones. The former pop up in those algebra problems you did in high school, in the multiple-choice standardized test in history you took, or even in the addition facts you learned in the first grade. They have definitive answers. Ill-structured problems, in contrast, have no clear resolution. You can't just follow a recipe to find a proper response. What caused the Civil War? What causes overpopulation? Should we vaccinate everyone against an epidemic, even if some will suffer severe allergic reactions to the vaccine?

Even the problem categories themselves can become ill-structured. In the Dennis Williams case, a definitive answer did not emerge until eighteen years after the event. So does our current justice system work properly? What about capital punishment? What changes would make it work better, and how would we know?

Life bristles with messy questions. How can you learn to make decisions wisely? How do the best college students cultivate that ability? In business, science, life, politics, and personal relationships, we face sometimes maddening choices that deeply matter. Can a college education help you make them more wisely?

This is the toughest, most complex topic we'll consider. Let's start with some broad generalizations. In the people we studied, and in the literature on how people learn to handle ill-structured problems, we saw the following patterns:

1. They surrounded themselves with interesting and diverse sets of people, and they engaged in conversations with them about some of those messy, ill-structured problems.
2. They didn't let contrary views bother them emotionally; indeed, they welcomed the chance to duke it out with someone who disagreed with them. Such attitudes reflected the humility with which they drew their own conclusions, and the constant appreciation of

how wrong—or right—they could be, and it indicated their strong
desire to understand the truth.

3. They developed and maintained a fascination with the world, and
they intended to understand deeply, often drawing on childhood
experiences and interests.

4. They engaged in original research on some ill-structured problem
or questions, and they did more than just Google it. They explored
a question.

5. They had the support of a mentor, someone who helped them believe they could do it.

You might say that they learned to tackle ill-structured problems
by tackling ill-structured problems and getting feedback on their
efforts. They didn't learn to play the piano by just listening to someone stroke the keys, and they didn't learn to think by listening to
someone else reason aloud. In the process, our subjects often engaged in a conversation with themselves and used the resulting self-
awareness to channel their interests and craft solutions. They could
see their own prejudices, and fought with themselves to mold more
rational perspectives, conclusions based on evidence and sound reasoning, not on social categories. We can see those paths to a more
productive problem-solving ability in the lives of some of the people
we interviewed.

When David Protess lived in Brooklyn as a child, long before he
became one of the leading investigative journalists in the world, two
fears often gripped his family and friends: Would someone start a
nuclear war? Would anyone get polio? His uncle did develop the
crippling disease, but the possibility of a nuclear war loomed just as
large. In school, children learned to duck and cover, dropping below
their desks at a moment's notice and hiding beneath their hands—

as if fingers and wood could protect them from an atomic or hydro-gen blast. Air-raid sirens often tore through a morning play period.

No one bombed Brooklyn, and most people escaped polio, but the fears continued. When David turned seven, the people in his community, including his parents and the grandparents who lived downstairs, talked a lot about Julius and Ethel Rosenberg, the Jew-ish couple from Lower Manhattan who had been accused of giving atomic secrets to the Russians and who were sentenced to die in the electric chair. Memories of the Holocaust in Germany were fresh in the minds of David's Jewish family and neighbors, and talk around the front stoop or in the local grocery store often turned to whether the execution of the Rosenbergs was the first of a new round of kill-ing Jews. No civilian had ever been put to death in the United States for espionage before. Even if they were guilty, why would these two die, and did they commit the crime? David knew that the couple had two young sons, one of them his age, and he thought about how the state planned to make orphans out of these boys. He still remembers waking on a Saturday morning and seeing the headline in the newspaper: "Rosenbergs Fried." That memory would both haunt him and guide his approach to ill-structured problems. "The execution of the Rosenbergs also made me a lifelong opponent of the death penalty," he noted recently, "profoundly influencing my career as an investigative reporter and educator."

In that era of national hysteria, David learned to love baseball and to speculate about his world. The sport helped him escape. Many summer nights he listened to the game on the radio with his grand-father and analyzed every play. Occasionally he stole away to Ebbets Field in Brooklyn to watch the Dodgers play. Speculating led to the first stages of the most elementary reasoning, an education in think-ing that would later flower and grow. Life constantly forced problems and decisions on his young mind. Did this siren mean a real air raid, or another practice? What's the evidence? Is this when they usually test the sirens? Will there be more killing of Jews? Will the state put them to death? Is Uncle Harold's flu the first stages of polio?

David had little interest in school, but he read a lot and talked baseball with his grandfather. For reasons he still doesn't fully comprehend, he wanted to be a veterinarian, maybe in reaction to his father, who sliced animal skin in the fur district of Manhattan.

When he was eighteen, long before ABC News named him "person of the week," before the city of Chicago proclaimed a day in his honor, and before the network made a television movie about his work, he entered a big state university in the Midwest because it had a strong pre-vet program. But the classes were huge, and he saw no connection between the science courses he took and how he would treat animals. His grades, never great in high school, sank even lower. Following a bout with mononucleosis, he transferred to Roosevelt University in downtown Chicago and found an atmosphere where he would thrive.

Professors at Roosevelt actually spoke with him. They raised fascinating questions in class, provoked arguments, invited his response, then challenged him. They treated him with respect, engaging him in civil discourse and inviting him to challenge them in return. The questions that fascinated David the most centered around justice and how to create and maintain it. Discussions that began in class spilled into the hallways, cafeteria, and offices of the building. "The university became one continuous classroom without walls," David recalled.

Outside the university, the world was changing rapidly. A thriving youth culture raised new issues, questioned old social patterns, and engaged in the intellectual struggles that emerged in David's classes. Many of the discussions revolved around the growing struggle over a war in Southeast Asia and the way the society treated people of color. For decades, the United States had segregated African Americans and many Hispanics into separate schools, hospitals, areas of town, drinking fountains, swimming pools, restaurants, hotels, and every other institution of life. In increasing numbers, people began to question those laws and practices of discrimination. They marched in the streets, broke the segregation rules deliberately, sought changes in the law, resisted peacefully until arrested, held public meetings to question and discuss, and sometimes broke into belligerent opposition, or more frequently faced the violent response of those who sought to uphold segregation and racism. As a war in Southeast Asia grew, so did the public opposition to it. Conflicts over the hostility in Vietnam festered inside college campuses across the country—and in board rooms, labor halls, Sunday School classes, parties, and picnics. National news spoke frequently of the Civil Rights and antiwar movements.

For David, his professors, and his classmates, such matters became fodder for the intellectual exchanges that drove their conversations. How could you maintain a democratic society and segregate some people into separate and unequal facilities? What caused society to adopt segregation in the first place, and what tactics would best confront it? How do you make up for years of discrimination? Was the war in Southeast Asia fought on behalf of a democratic future for the people of Vietnam, or waged to protect U.S. imperial interests and to prop up an unpopular and often dictatorial government in South Vietnam? Would the American government and people support "self-determination" for the peoples of the world if some of those people chose a future that ran counter to the wishes of the United States?

David's schoolwork spoke to childhood memories of working in political campaigns with his mother, handing out leaflets on street corners for candidates they thought would bring peace and justice in the world, and battling verbally with doubters. They spoke also to the elementary reasoning that the threat of war, disease, and execution had thrust upon him as a child. That reasoning now rose to a higher level of sophistication. David was forced to examine his assumptions and values, to take into consideration all that he was learning about the world, and to mark carefully the way he inferred his conclusions.

Roosevelt University had a room where students would go to play chess, and David often went there, fascinated with imagining the next move and where the game was going, speculating about what his opponent would do, and trying to stay one step ahead in his reasoning. He found parallels in the debates and discussion emerging in class. He had to think constantly about his own reasoning, to respond to the counterarguments thrust back at him, to imagine various possibilities. But in the classroom or a professor's office he wasn't just playing a game to trump his opponent. He sought to understand the issues better and to build a model that would help him examine the problem and raise new questions. How do we know this? What's the evidence? What does it mean? Faculty members became mentors rather than just lecturers. They challenged his thinking with questions about his assumptions, evidence, and reasoning, and David often stopped by their offices to continue the exchange.

As he learned to reason, a thousand new kinds of questions sprang into his mind. Why do I believe what I do? What don't I know? What am I taking on faith? Can I tolerate ambiguity and uncertainty? Sometimes David would deliberately try out a "wild line of reasoning" just to hear the responses, to examine his own thoughts, to form new models, and then to question those structures. What am I assuming here? Can I dig into my own mind and find those assumptions that I've never spoken to myself, bring them into the sunshine, turn them belly up, and poke at their soft undersides? And if they explode in my face, can I go on reasoning, probing, looking for alternative perspectives? Can I accept the death of one idea or the uncertainty of another? Can I live with the messiness of life while continuing to untangle its mysteries? Do I recognize what I know from observation and what I've concluded from some previous reasoning? What are the implications and the applications of what I'm saying? David came to recognize the enormous power that previously formed concepts might have on current reasoning and the necessity of identifying those preconceptions.

When David was growing up in Brooklyn, he inhabited a world in which IQ's were weighed and measured like potatoes. Schools and test scores pronounced some people smart and others dumb. All the conventional wisdom of the day told him that intelligence formed at birth, and nothing could change it. Much of what he encountered at Roosevelt challenged those notions. Every corridor brimmed with people like David, who came there after underachieving at other institutions. "Yet, they proved to be sharp, imaginative, full of insights, and capable of brilliant reasoning," he remembered. In the right environment, they blossomed into curious, inquisitive students, toppling old ideas about intelligence.

David would sometimes read for hours on a topic of interest. He particularly loved his political science classes, but biology also became more interesting, perhaps in part because his professor introduced the social controversies surrounding science. His instructor taught a Darwinian, evolutionary understanding of biology while confessing a personal and emotional attachment to traditional religious explanations of the origins of life.

Libraries became important to David, but so did the whole city. "Chicago became our laboratory," he remembered. He joined civil rights and antiwar groups, immersing himself in the stew of politics. He learned to approach issues more systematically, to seek evidence, to speculate, and then to ask what would count as good reasons to reject or support his ideas. All the while, he was developing a strong sense of social responsibility and convictions about justice. His confidence as a student soared along with his grades, but that mattered less than the intellectual life in which he now engaged. Based on the available evidence, he decided he had to do more than think about problems; he had to take action. The consequences of doing nothing seemed increasingly unacceptable.

When he graduated from Roosevelt, he entered a joint graduate program in political science, community organization, and social policy at the University of Chicago, where the conversations continued, "but now on an even higher level." Each day he tested and grew his hard-earned skills of analysis, synthesis, and defense. "I learned best," he recognized, "in small group environments where people have an opportunity to interact," and where he felt comfortable making mistakes. "New inferences led to rational discourse and gave me an opportunity to receive challenges so I could refine my thinking and draw new ones." David came to recognize that words are mere symbols for ideas, and realities lurked behind the language. Each challenge to his thinking helped root out common informal fallacies in reasoning. He could no longer simply appeal to authority as indisputable proof of some claim, or dismiss someone's conclusions and evidence because he didn't like their general views on life or politics. Merely because "everybody" believed something offered no support for its truth. The future journalist and educator had to recognize when an argument flowed from specific examples to general conclusions (inductive), and when it moved in the opposite direction (deductive), and to realize what kinds of questions he should raise with each form of reasoning. He had to evaluate constantly his own reasoning for internal consistency.

By the time he got to the University of Chicago, he knew he would never be a vet. After graduating from that school four years later with a doctorate in public policy, David became an investigative journalist, and eventually joined the faculty of the Medill School of Journalism at Northwestern University. In that position, all of the years of questioning and rational discourse came into play. Out of his own experience with learning, he had cobbled together ideas about how people learn most deeply. In that view, experience teaches best, yet he also recognized, as John Dewey, the American educational philosopher, supposedly once said, that we don't learn from experience; we learn from thinking about experience.

Protess engaged his students in investigative journalism even before they knew how, primarily exploring whether people convicted of capital crimes and sentenced to die at the hands of the state had been wrongfully convicted. His undergraduate students formed a team of reporters who dug out evidence, asked anew what would count as proof, pursued leads that no one else had considered, and in a series of spectacular investigations exonerated men condemned to die, convicted on flimsy evidence. Many of them were poor and black. Dennis Williams and his buddies escaped death primarily because of the reporting by David and his students. For that work, David received the prestigious Puffin Prize for creative citizenship.

More important, his work led directly to a moratorium on executions and eventually to the end of the death penalty in Illinois.

In 2011, after nearly thirty years at Northwestern, he left his faculty post and created the Chicago Innocence Project. As president of that organization, he offered interns a chance "to investigate cases in which prisoners may have been convicted of crimes they did not commit," as the project's website put it. "Our fundamental goal is to expose and remedy wrongdoing by the criminal justice system." Within a year, the program had eight student interns from four universities who investigated wrongful conviction, and they had won their first case. Men who had been freed after spending years in prison for crimes they didn't commit worked with these students. "You learn from experience," David noted recently, "and we've demonstrated that the experiential learning model we developed at Northwestern can work almost anywhere."[1]

## From Privilege to Responsibility

Shawn Armbrust grew up in a privileged environment, and she knew it. "Through an accident of birth," she declared, "I enjoyed advantages that many other people didn't have." In time, she came to regard that reality as neither just nor avoidable. Life had dealt her several winning hands, but she wasn't content merely to play those cards for all they were worth. Instead, numerous developments along the way encouraged within her a sense of civic responsibility. Her parents certainly favored such views and attitudes, and, as a child, she absorbed the social justice teachings encountered in a Catholic education. She read extensively and met the injustices of the world, the uneven opportunities and cruel fates that some people endured, and those encounters heavily influenced her commitments to justice.

The Holocaust had been a seminal event in the thinking of many Americans, exposing the ugly possibilities of racial thinking. Many people in the United States looked at Nazi atrocities and saw reflected in that catastrophe the logical extension of race thinking and practice in their own country. They were horrified by the possibilities. Shawn had a similar reaction decades after the mass killings ended. In the months following her junior year in high school she spent part of her summer in Berlin reading about fascist brutality under Hitler, and that experience deeply impressed her.

That summer marked another important step in her thinking and ambitions. She had stumbled across the old movie *All the President's Men,* about the young investigative reporters Bob Woodward and Carl Bernstein, who had unraveled for the *Washington Post* the Watergate scandal that ended Richard Nixon's presidency. When Shawn traveled to Germany on a study abroad program, she took the book about those two young reporters with her to Europe. She came home convinced she had to become an investigative journalist. She went to college to pursue that dream, enrolling in Northwestern University's Medill School of Journalism.

In her first three years on the Evanston, Illinois, campus, her intellectual development came as much from volunteer work as it did from the classroom. She did take a course on the Cold War that highly influenced her views on foreign policy, but she also babysat kids whose parents were studying to get a high school equivalency degree. That experience shaped her views of politics and poverty.[2] In the summer before her senior year at Northwestern, she took a temporary job at the White House, working in the correspondence office, and that work convinced her to focus on policies and not candidates.

When Shawn started her senior year, a friend suggested that she take the David Protess course on investigative reporting. "I didn't want to take magazine writing," she later explained, "and besides I had wanted to be an investigative journalist since I was seventeen." She didn't put "a tremendous amount of thought behind it. It just seemed kind of fun." But it would change her life and the lives of people she'd never met, and she would help alter the system of crime and punishment in Illinois.

In the days before the class began, Shawn read *Promise of Justice,* the book that David Protess had written with Rob Warden about Dennis Williams and his three friends. She became increasingly intrigued that reporters could have such influence. In early September, David told the students about the case of Anthony Porter, a poor black man from the south side of Chicago convicted of killing a young couple near a swimming pool in Washington Park. A previous class had unearthed evidence questioning Anthony's conviction, but not enough to exonerate him. Porter had fought through appeal after appeal to stay the hand of the executioner. He had been living on death row for more than fifteen years. On more than one occasion, he had come within a whisper of death before winning still another delay from the courts. In his latest escape, the court delayed his capital penalty because prison officials had tested his IQ and scored him at 51. Nothing in Illinois law, however, prevented the state from killing a retarded man, and this latest delay could evaporate at any time. Shawn decided to work on the case in part because of the urgency. "We had to realize that he could be put to death during our class for something he might not have done," she reported.

Yet she knew that merely because there were questions about his conviction didn't prove that he was innocent.

On a blustery Saturday in November, Shawn and a few other students went to Washington Park to reenact the crime. "We were all a little tired and not quite sure why David had asked us to do this," she remembered years later. The state had argued that Anthony Porter shot and killed Marilyn Green, a nineteen-year-old girl, and her eighteen-year-old fiancé, Jerry Hillard, in an attempted robbery while the victims sat in bleachers next to a swimming pool. Everything seemed to fit. The twenty-seven-year-old Porter had staged a robbery in that same park once before, and an eyewitness said he saw him commit the murders of Green and Hillard. Porter had gone to the police to clear his name but had been arrested and, after a short trial, convicted and sentenced to die.

When the Northwestern students tried to duplicate what happened, however, something appeared to be terribly wrong. "I stood where the murder had taken place," Shawn recalled, "and others stood where the eyewitnesses said they had been. The distances were just absurd. My colleagues could see I had red hair, but that was about it," she explained. "You certainly couldn't identify a killer from that distance even in the daylight, and the killings occurred at I AM." But that observation didn't prove Anthony had been wrongfully convicted, and the aspiring journalist knew it. In the American system of justice, people are considered innocent until compelling evidence establishes their guilt in a court of law. The burden of proof rests with the prosecution. But once a jury has convicted someone of a crime, the defense must offer evidence to overturn that judgment. The burden of proof shifts.

One of the two eyewitnesses who fingered Anthony as the killer had died. Shawn and her colleagues wanted to talk with the other one. When one of her classmates finally interviewed that witness, he related a disturbing story. He told the journalism student that his testimony was all a lie, coerced by the police. If true, that confession could explode the whole case. But was this guy making it up?

Did the authorities merely want to wrap up this murder because a poor black man had killed a poor black couple and nobody cared? Given the level of prejudice in American society that was a plausible explanation. But merely because something could happen doesn't prove that it did. The only evidence came from a man who was lying either now or when he testified in court. Could anyone trust his word on anything?

As Shawn dug through the records of the case, she learned that the police had briefly considered an alternative suspect, Alstory Simon, before focusing on Porter. She wanted to talk with Simon's estranged wife, Inez Jackson, but finding her would be no easy task. "Over the Christmas holidays, I knocked on the doors of scores of people with that name," Shawn remembered. In late January, the student reporter finally found the right Inez Jackson. "We took her out to eat and talked about a hundred unrelated things before raising anything about the crime," the former journalism student related. "As she stared right at me," Shawn wrote some years later, "she told us that Simon used to beat her, that he once took a coat-hanger to her, and that she often thought he'd kill her."[3] The small black woman grew progressively more angry as she talked. At the right moment, David suddenly asked, "Inez, we know what happened that night in Washington Park, so why don't you just tell us?"

In short order, Inez divulged everything. She had been sitting next to her ex-husband, Alstory Simon, at the pool that night and wasn't paying much attention to anything when she heard him arguing with Jerry Hillard. She heard six shots and saw Alstory stuff a gun down his pants. He then grabbed Inez by the hand and pulled her out of the park, "telling her to shut up or he'd kill her too."

"We then took her to my parents' house and videotaped her statement and gave it to a CBS news crew," Shawn explained recently. Four days later, the story and the tape of Jackson ran on the evening news. The next morning the private investigator working for the journalism class interviewed Alstory Simon. "It just so happened that CBS ran the film of Inez's confession again that morning," Shawn remembered, "and Alstory happened to have his television on a CBS station when the investigator was there. Within ten minutes, he was on videotape confessing, claiming that he'd done it in self-defense."

Everything had happened so rapidly, and some of it by sheer accident. Two days later, the state of Illinois released Porter from jail, and a month later officially dropped the murder charges. Twenty-one-year-old Shawn Armbrust and her fellow students suddenly found themselves in the middle of a media frenzy, with appearances on *Good Morning America* and stories spread across the American press. That attention didn't, however, center on the justice system and whether it had worked or the role of chance in saving an innocent man from execution. Rather it focused on the novelty of middle-class white university students who had freed a poor black man from death row. For Shawn, the whirlwind of publicity was both exhilarating and profoundly disturbing. "Simon's confession," she recognized, depended on a "bizarre coincidence." CBS ran the Inez Jackson tape in only five markets that morning, and Alstory Simon just happened to tune his television to the right channel in one of those markets. "If it weren't for some genuinely lucky investigative break," she concluded, "Porter would have been executed."[4]

On the day Porter walked free, the governor of Illinois at the time, George Ryan, watched on television as the former death-row inmate ran toward David, Shawn, and her fellow students Syandene Rhodes-Pitts and Tom McCann, lifting each one in the air in triumphant celebration and thanks. The chief executive of the state wondered how a few undergraduate students, their professor, and a private investigator could uncover evidence that no one else had discovered. It raised serious questions about the fairness of the death penalty. "How the hell does that happen?" he asked his wife. "How does an innocent man sit on death row for 15 years and get no relief?" A year later, Ryan declared a moratorium on state executions, and a decade later, Illinois abolished the death penalty.

Shawn emerged from the ordeal deeply changed. "The system didn't work the way it was supposed to. Flimsy evidence cost a man eighteen years of his life," she summarized for me. "Twenty-one-year-olds shouldn't be freeing innocent men from jail," the young woman kept telling the press at the time. "Police officers, trial attorneys, prosecutors, appellate courts didn't do their fundamental job of protecting the rights of the accused" or "convicting the guilty," she later wrote.

After graduation, she worked for two years with the newly formed Center on Wrongful Conviction at Northwestern before going to law school at Georgetown University. She clerked for awhile with a federal judge. "The greatest thing that happened to me," Shawn reminisced, "was that I got fired from my clerking job. I was devastated for about fifteen hours, before I realized how much I hated clerking, and that it would let me do what I really wanted to pursue." Six years after she worked on that team to help Anthony Porter prove his innocence, she became executive director of the Mid-

Atlantic Innocence Project serving the District of Columbia, Maryland, and Virginia.

## Reflective Judgments

How can we best understand changes in the way people think as they learn to solve those messy problems of life? In what ways did their thinking change? When Patricia King and her friend, Karen Kitchener, took a graduate class together at the University of Minnesota, they worked out a model to capture the kind of changes that go on when people learn to make what they called "reflective judgments" about ill-structured problems.[5] The work they produced didn't bottle simple answers, however.

After interviewing hundreds of students, Patricia and Karen saw seven broad ways to make judgments. They call them stages of development, which might imply that we try out all of them, generally in order, as we march up the ladder toward more sophisticated ways of thinking and problem solving. Yet that's not exactly what they mean. Instead, they believe we, like circus acrobats, hang from three or four rungs of this ladder at the same time. One day, in one area, we will think on one level; some other time, we've climbed higher—or slipped a step or two. King and Kitchener describe these rungs as stages so we can understand the different ways we think, but they realize that we can and probably do use several ways of thinking at the same time. "In fact," they write, "most individuals appear to use two and occasionally three (typically adjacent) stages." And, of course, some people never reach the highest levels of thinking.

The creative and highly productive people I interviewed did generally think on the highest levels, but they didn't think that way when they were born. They developed the capacity as they progressed through life. If we deliberately become aware of all of these stages, we can understand our own ways of solving problems, and out of that understanding move toward that rational ideal.

One warning before we examine that ladder: if you find you are hanging out on the bottom rungs, don't despair. Everybody started out there. Just try thinking like a student who seeks new challenges rather than giving up. Remember also what Paul Baker told his students: "When you are building a new kind of life for yourself, this process of discovery is the key to growth." It takes time.

On the bottom rung of King and Kitchener's ladder, we think that knowledge "exists absolutely" and in the flesh. We just have to observe it. A child tells his grandmother, "when you die, give me a call and tell me what it's like." A college student says, with absolute conviction, "I know what I've seen. Don't question me." In this way of thinking, abstractions don't exist. Children think this way because it makes sense to them.

In the second stage, we assume anything is knowable; we just have to ask the right person. Rather than thinking through matters, we assume that all knowledge comes from authority. We don't ask how or where those authorities got their knowledge. Like the city kid who says food comes from the grocery store, we never see the farming operation that lies behind a "fact" or idea. We can hear this stage in the language we might use: "I know that's true; I read it on the internet."

On the third level, we also appeal to authority but recognize this authority's limitations. Some things no one knows, we might say, so we can fill in the gaps with our own beliefs. "When there is evidence that people can give to convince everybody one way or another, then it will be knowledge; until then, it is just a guess," one student told the researchers.

You should notice something these first three stages have in common. King and Kitchener call it "prereflective thinking." At these levels, people believe that knowledge comes from authorities. It's what the teacher—or your grandmother—tells you is true—or what you see "in front of your eyes." You just remember it, and you've learned. No questions asked, and no doubts. What you see is what you get.

When we arrive at the fourth level, we think like the cab driver who drove me to Penn Station last night. "You can never know anything for sure," he offered as he rounded a corner. "It all depends on how you look at it. Sure you got to have evidence, but one guy might look at it one way, and another is going to see it completely different." Patricia and Karen once heard a student say, "I would be more inclined to believe evolution if they had proof. It is just like the pyramids: I do not think we will ever know. Who are you going to ask? No one was there." For the cab driver and student, knowledge is uncertain, but what you believe pretty much depends on who you are. You can justify anything, according to people at this level, by offering evidence and good reasons, and what evidence you pick depends entirely on you. Students at this level will simply look for reasons and evidence to support their most cherished beliefs. Richard Paul, a philosopher who studies critical thinking, calls this kind of reasoning "critical thinking in the weak sense."

Few of us climb to the fifth stage, but if we do, we see everything as someone's interpretation of the evidence. We may say we can know but not judge those interpretations. One philosopher might put it this way, and another might put it that way. "I read all these different interpretations, and I know how you want me to evaluate them," a student once told me, "but can you really say that one is any better than another? It's so confusing." Patricia and Karen heard a student say, "People think differently and so they attack the problem differently. Other theories could be as true as my own, but based on different evidence." Students at this level see themselves awash in a sea of different contexts, but they find great difficulty in reaching any conclusions.

Levels four and five also have something in common. At these "quasi-reflective thinking" stages, as the Michigan psychologists called them, evidence becomes important, but how you use that evidence to draw conclusions depends entirely on you. Students operating on these levels see a jumble of interpretations. They endeavor to understand each one but can't compare them. "Although they use evidence," Patricia and Karen write, "they do not understand how evidence entails a conclusion (especially in light of the acknowledged uncertainty), and thus tend to view judgments as highly idiosyncratic."

Even fewer of us reach levels six and seven, what King and Kitchener call "reflective thinking." When we get there, we understand that some problems and questions are terribly complex and messy. We look for interpretations and ideas that come from evaluation of evidence, with a lot of perspectives in mind. We compare evidence and opinions from different perspectives, and in a variety of contexts. To construct a tentative solution to a complex problem, we look at the weight of the evidence we see, but we also ask, "How useful will it be to draw a conclusion at this point? Do I need to draw a conclusion, or can I just live with uncertainty? Does the tentative solution I draw solve some problem, or does it raise more questions than it answers?" Here's what one student told the researchers: "It is very difficult in this life to be sure. There are degrees of sureness. You come to a point at which you are sure enough for a personal stance on the issue."

We are approaching the top level, so let's stop for a moment and consider this sixth stage in order to distinguish it from the final one. At level six, we may look at a variety of different studies on any problem, weigh the evidence carefully, and draw a tentative conclusion. We compare evidence and opinions from different perspectives and consider their relative weight, determine how useful the solution will be, and decide whether there is a practical reason to draw a conclusion at this time.

Only at the seventh and highest stage, the level at which students like David and Shawn learned to operate, do we consciously recognize that we must construct knowledge and decisions about ill-structured problems through a process King and Kitchener call "reasonable inquiry." We can't just make up stuff or believe what we want; instead we draw the most reasonable or probable conclusion from the current evidence, and when new evidence comes along, better ways of looking at the data emerge, a fresh perspective blossoms, or new tools of inquiry become available, we reevaluate. When we look at evidence, we ask what is most probable. What are the chances we are wrong? How does everything fit together? One of Patricia's and Karen's students offered this summary: "One can judge an argument by how well thought-out the positions are, what kinds of reasoning and evidence are used to support it, and how consistent the way one argues on this topic is as compared with how one argues on other topics."

Earlier I maintained that you have to intend to learn deeply before you can do so, but I also promised that we'd return to the subject and consider what it means to learn deeply. That's a major part of what we've explored here. Those highest stages of rational inquiry reflect a deep understanding of knowledge, and it is that deep understanding that influences how you make judgments about difficult choices in life. How you make those decisions will determine what kind of student and person you will become. If you still think on one of the lower levels, the question "What is knowledge?" may sound pretty silly. Knowledge, you may say, is stuff you know. But, as I hope you see, nothing is that simple.

John Biggs, an Australian researcher and thinker, has suggested some additional ways to define deep learning. At the highest levels, in Biggs's view, students can see how something fits into a larger picture. They can take problems and arguments apart and apply general principles to their solution. They can compare and contrast ideas, explain causes, and integrate ideas together. But they can also take the ideas and arguments of one subject and apply them, where appropriate, to something completely different. They can generate new theories from what they know already, and then imagine ways to test their hypothesis.

A few years ago, a documentary film crew had some fun with Professor Biggs's ideas. For a short documentary, *Teaching Teaching & Understanding Understanding*, which was made with a Danish university, they had students illustrate different approaches to the knowledge of cows. A surface learner might say something like "Cows give us milk, and when slaughtered, they give us oil, meat, fat, and bone." A deep learner, however, wouldn't be satisfied with such a simple list of items. She would probe further and develop, perhaps, theories about why cows come in different breeds. Her explanation might sound like this: "Cattle, or kye, are domesticated ungulates—a member of the subfamily Bovinae. And it seems to me that humans must have been the root cause for the diversification of cattle, because they were selected for different genetic characteristics like draft, milk, meat, size, color, and behavior, to name a few."[6] The University of Queensland in Australia suggested that surface learners might be expected simply to "list four species of mosquito," whereas a deep learner could respond to this question: "Discuss how you might judge the relative importance of similar threats to public health; in your discussion use various species of tropical mosquito as examples."[7]

## From Spiders to Science

In her senior year at Yale University, Cheryl Hayashi got a job feeding spiders. Every day, she opened the door to a room that looked like an industrial walk-in refrigerator and crept inside to serve the eight-legged critters their lunch of fruit flies and crickets. Spiders roamed freely in the hot and humid air of that room as she carefully wrapped these delectable morsels in the silky web the spiders had woven. It was like a "Panamanian rain forest," Cheryl told a reporter soon after she had won a MacArthur "Genius" award for her groundbreaking research.

By her own admission, she never had the same kind of experience in college that Shawn and David enjoyed. She had grown up in Hawaii, and had gone to Yale in part for the wide blend of students she hoped to meet there, and to "get off an island where all the highways go in circles." Indeed, she met students from every state, social class, and many foreign countries, and she talked primarily about that invaluable variety in recalling those years, and how that rich tapestry of ideas and perspectives challenged her thinking. Those associations gave her ample opportunities to exchange ideas with classmates, and she valued those conversations. "One of the advantages of going to a school like Yale," she admitted a few years later, "is that you are surrounded by people who are highly accomplished and they constantly challenge your thinking and their curiosity becomes contagious."

In that environment, she developed a keen appreciation for the "ambiguity of life," the sense that there may not always be final answers. She had first grasped that notion when observing how she and her classmates often reacted differently to works of art, but in time, she came to use such perspectives to understand herself and the field in which she participated. "I realize that I am a product of certain historical contingencies that shape what I've done and how I look at the world," she mused recently. "We are all unique, all products of our own history." She grasped the power of both her personal background and the experiences and viewpoints of others.

Cheryl came to Yale with a broad appetite for learning. "My friends and I would thumb through the course catalogue, dog-earring nearly every page with markers of courses we wanted to take," she remembered. "I didn't think of college as some kind of professional training for a job, but as a chance to explore and learn." She had no desire to go to medical school, "but other than that I had no idea what I wanted to do with my life. I just wanted to pursue my curiosity." For the future MacArthur Fellowship Grant recipient, that learning meant "developing my critical thinking and creative abilities, expanding writing and speaking skills, understanding how to fit knowledge into a broader picture, and knowing where and how to find information." It didn't mean just "memorizing stuff."

Cheryl struggled most with foreign languages and chemistry but kept trying. The budding scientist learned much from all her failures, always trying to understand what went wrong and how she might improve on another try. "Failure becomes extremely important in doing experiments," she observed. "You have a chance to learn something every time it doesn't turn out the way you expected."

As a freshman, she took a "mind-blowing" course, an experience given to few first-year students. Most people never encounter much thinking in a typical introductory college course. Instead, their professors feed them a plate of well-barbequed facts to memorize, never offering many hints about how those morsels had been cooked, how anyone came to believe them, how anyone had tackled ill-structured problems. Introductory courses rarely offer mysteries, reasoning opportunities, or challenges other than the necessity of stuffing it all in your brain before the exam. Students typically develop little understanding of how the discipline raises and answers questions. They seldom examine messy, complex questions or even hear how anyone else does so. Cheryl lucked out. She got to take a class on evolutionary biology usually reserved for more advanced students.

"We explored one central question," she recalled. "Where did life originate, and how and why did it change over time?" Cheryl had always been a hypercurious child—"elephant ears," her parents called her because she tried hard to hear adult conversations. She'd puzzled over the countless variety of animals in the world, whether in the wild of her native Hawaii or in the passel of stuffed critters she collected. "As a little girl," she reminisced, "I had tea parties for cloth bears, tigers, and other animals, and told my parents, I had to have that anteater in the window." Not surprisingly, a course that proposed to explore the origins and history of life fascinated her. "I had asked those same questions when I was a little girl," she recalled. "Why does this tree look like that? Where do we come from?"

For fifteen fascinating weeks, she listened to a series of scientists who examined the evidence from fossil records, DNA research, and other sources and drew their conclusions. "We don't have a time machine; so how do we know what happened?" What's the scientific evidence? From inference to inference, her professors marched toward the most plausible explanation. If we have this fossil record, what should we conclude, and with that conclusion, how do we read this evidence? The final classes were like the climax of those murder mysteries that had fascinated Mary Ann Hopkins, Shawn Armbrust, and Debra Goldson, the part where the wily detective unravels the evidence and points to the guilty party. In every biology class thereafter Cheryl would ask herself what evidence she had, and how she knew it. "I took a historical approach to the study of biology," she concluded, "trying to understand how life evolves and changes."

For all their benefits, however, neither that course nor anything else she encountered at Yale as an undergraduate gave her much experience in grappling with ill-structured problems. She didn't get the chance to plunge into the stew of her discipline, to pursue evidence and weigh it, until she reached her senior year, and even then only on a limited basis. When she worked with those spiders, she did complete a senior thesis on the web spinners, "but that was little more than a glorified term paper," she remembered. "I still didn't know what research was all about."

When she went to the library, Cheryl encountered millions of books and articles on every aspect of biology. "How could I ever do research and find anything new?" she remembered asking. "All these smart people have written about it in the past, and all these smart people are doing work on some question. How could I contribute anything?" She finally decided, "I had to get my butt out of the library and into the field."

That chance came in the summer following her graduation from Yale. She went to Panama to work as an assistant to the spider professor. For the first time, she saw researchers making observations in the field, asking questions, piecing evidence together in strings of inferences, raising more questions, and returning for additional observations. "I began to realize that there is so much about the world we don't know."

Cheryl began to piece together an understanding of original research. "You don't want to reinvent the wheel," she noted, "so you have to know what's already been done. Yet it isn't about what we know already, but how you raise new questions, collect data that will give you a better understanding of the world and how it works." You raise questions, plan, gather data, "then adjust to all the things that will inevitably go wrong." Cheryl realized she was joining a new society of knowledgeable peers, and that support from this community would be essential to the work before her. She had entered a conversation and could speak with other researchers about the evidence that she was collecting. She could compare notes and reframe questions. Communicating with her scholarly peers became an integral part of the way she tackled those fuzzy and complicated questions.

As an undergraduate, Cheryl's focus narrowed from that broad array of courses she dog-eared as a freshman to the specialized focus of her life's work, but it also became more intense, penetrating layers of nature that no one had explored before. "I was asking questions," she observed, "that I could not even imagine as a freshman." In the process, the Hawaiian native came to show the unexpected richness of the spider, how diverse its system had become over millions of years, and the enormous potential springing from cracking the secrets of this eight-legged creature. Yet as she specialized on one arthropod, the emerging scientist also marshaled a wide array of disciplines and perspectives to build the questions and models that began to emerge from her work. "Everything I learned influenced how I looked at spiders," she concluded. She became an engineer, a scientist, an artist, and a historian, and the blend helped her to see the spider and its web-building capacity in ways that no one had ever imagined.

She finished a doctorate at Yale, did postgraduate work in Wyoming, and opened her own lab at the University of California, Riverside, where she began to blend biology, phylogenetics, biomechanics, and material science to probe the history, design, structure, and function of spider silks.

That question she encountered in her first biology class at Yale about the origin and changes in life forms continues to fascinate her, and much of her study centers on the evolution of spiders and their abilities to spin such miraculous webs. In the process she discovered materials with incredible strength. "What could you do with a silk thread one tenth the diameter of human hair yet each ounce is five times tougher than the same weight of steel?" Maybe you could make a bulletproof vest, biodegradable surgical sutures, or super-light but strong athletic uniforms. Her research with spiders promises to revolutionize the world.

"I've had a lot of luck in my life," she concluded. "I'm lucky to have had teachers who gave me their time and the opportunity to work with them. I'm constantly learning from other people. Things could have been very different," she recognized, "if I had encountered lots of people who were quite negative and didn't want to invest any time in me." But it also helped, she admitted, "that I'm so stubborn."

The deep learners we've discussed here learned to make wise judgments by making decisions and getting feedback on their thinking. They conducted original research, asked questions, gathered evidence, and drew conclusions. They engaged in a deep conversation with friends, professors, and themselves, imagining what no one else would consider and testing their own thinking against rigorous standards. Yet the progress they made depended on more than that experience or those conversations. They could have practiced until the cows came home, but if they had not changed the way they understood knowledge, they would have learned nothing. You don't learn from experience; you learn from reflecting on experience.

# 6

## Encouragement

Kristin Neff had a problem. The young psychologist from Texas was going through some rough personal times, and she had every reason to become anxious and depressed.[1] At that point in her life, she could perhaps read with renewed interest and understanding a growing debate within her field. For decades, Americans had seen self-esteem as the key to a successful, happy life. Psychologists had provided study after study to show that loving and admiring yourself offered advantages in the race for happiness and well-being. Self-esteem breeds confidence, scholars and counselors kept saying, and confident people try new things and enjoy greater successes. Conversely, students who don't like themselves and doubt their abilities drop out of school more frequently, suffer from anxiety and depression in greater numbers, and muster generally lower levels of motivation.

American culture celebrated the value of thinking well of yourself. "Self-esteem," exclaimed one of the gurus of the movement, "has profound consequences for every aspect of our existence." Waxing eloquent, Nathaniel Branden concluded that he could not "think of a single psychological problem—from anxiety and depression, to fear of intimacy or of success, to spouse battery or child molestation—that is not traceable to the problem of low self-esteem." We just don't have enough "self-love," proclaimed another promoter of this psychological elixir.[2]

Schools began programs to help students increase this valuable commodity. Guide books on how to succeed in college often included a section—or at least a word or two—on why students should love themselves. In many ways, the worship of self exposed a deep vein in Western cultures, one that had long celebrated individualism and the importance of feeling good about who you are. One group of psychologists argued, "North American society in particular has come to embrace the idea that high self-esteem is not only desirable in its own right, but also the central psychological source from which all manner of positive behaviors and outcomes spring."[3]

A small band of researchers, however, had begun to question the conventional wisdom, and Kristin read their work with great interest. Did this magic concept of one's self always pay rich dividends? Did it change lives? If you sought a strong sense of self-worth, what price would you pay? Would that pursuit damage other aspects of your being, doing more harm than good? Sometimes in life, if you chase some quality, you virtually guarantee that you will never catch it. The hedonistic paradox in philosophy, for example, holds that if you pursue happiness directly (by doing only those things that feel good), you will never achieve it. Like a beach swimmer caught in a riptide, every effort to swim directly ashore washes you out into the cold depths. Does self-esteem fall into this frustrating category?

Is it even possible to increase this magic quality in anyone's life? Much of the research and evaluation of existing programs reported disappointing results. As Kristin pored over the emerging literature around these questions, and as she began to search for alternatives to this increasingly controversial quality, she found insights that not only spoke to her personal needs but reflected the thinking and attitudes we saw among highly creative people. What Kristin began to piece together from the research literature would fundamentally change the way we think about the road to success and happiness, and about what highly productive and creative students do in college to address these issues.

We might think, for example, that if students built a strong sense of self-esteem around doing well in school, they would learn more. Not necessarily. Indeed, a growing body of research finds that people who base their sense of worth primarily or exclusively on what kind of grades they get will likely take a performance approach rather than a learning approach to their studies. You will recall from the discussion in Chapter 2 that performance-based (or strategic) learners focus on getting approval for their work (high marks), whereas those with a learning (or deep) approach want to understand more, to think about implications and applications. And it is the latter approach that drives highly creative and productive people. If students focus on raising their grades just to boost their self-esteem, why should they care much about understanding the material or using it creatively? These strategic learners will often, so the research suggests, single-mindedly pursue those grades, sacrificing all else.[4]

But their problems do not end there. People who build self-worth around good grades may not learn much and may not even get the high marks they so desperately covet. Here's the problem. If what I think of myself depends on making the academic honor roll, then any test, paper, lab experiment, or other assignment that heavily affects my grades will most likely produce great anxiety and tension. My sense of self-worth rides on the outcome of that schoolwork.

Who wouldn't become highly nervous with that kind of pressure? The grade becomes more than a letter on a transcript; it becomes a statement on how I can feel about myself. If I have placed great importance on maintaining high self-esteem, and I have let my marks in school define whether I've achieved that goal, then every failing or even mediocre score becomes a threat to what I think of myself. The more I try, the more nervous I become, fearful that a single failure will reveal that I'm not a worthy person.[5]

No one contends that high self-regard hurts your grades and learning. Far from it. It's the *pursuit* of this quality through high grades rather than through learning that becomes the match that kindles anxiety, especially when the academic stakes are high. In other words, if you base what you think of yourself on how high your grades are rather than, say, on how kind you may be, how much you learn, how hard you try, or what you contribute to society, then you have a fairly reliable sign of trouble ahead. Worry about outcomes often leads students to think about grades rather than about learning, and if they take that *performance approach* to all their school work while believing that their worth as a human being depends on making the high marks, the tensions will likely become so great that they will neither learn nor make superior scores.

There's no harm in respecting yourself, and we certainly know that if you don't, you are unlikely to have much motivation. There's no harm in getting high grades, either, and in the best of circumstances those A's and 100's reflect how much you have learned. But caring too much about your marks can trigger a disastrous series of developments, especially if you think your class rank indicates your true worth.

We saw that process earlier among people who become victims of negative social stereotypes. If you are a member of a group that has been labeled as less talented in some academic area and you base your opinion of your self-worth on your performance in that area, it will bother you that other people think that you will perform poorly. It can disturb you so much that you confirm the stereotype and perform poorly under pressure, even though you may personally reject the popular belief. If you also worry that your lousy results will give others like you a bad reputation, the pressure can become too intense. Indeed, the more you care about doing well —because, for example, doing well defines you and a whole bunch of other people—the worse you are likely to do because of the greater pressure and anxiety.

Yet such reactions occur not only among the victims of negative stereotypes (often in U.S. culture that means people of color or women but can also include the overweight, the poor, the "dumb jock," the less attractive, men, and, at some point, almost anyone). They can even arise among white American males who face fewer popular images that cast them in a bad light. Jennifer Crocker and her colleagues demonstrated as much in a series of experiments they conducted with college students. Tell a group of European-American students a test measures their basic abilities. If they have built how much they like themselves on how well they do in school, such an exam will seem like it is measuring each person's worth as a human being. The stakes become too high and many students will choke. If you tell the same group you are merely trying to find out about their "problem-solving styles and approaches, and not about the number of correct answers," their scores will actually rise.[6]

Repeatedly, social scientists have found that if they give students a difficult examination and tell them that it will measure their intellectual abilities or future success in life, they will generally perform worse than students who see that test as a challenge, a game, or as an opportunity to learn something.[7] If those students tie their sense of self-worth to doing well academically and "being smart," they are likely to feel enormous pressure when they think something evaluates their innate abilities, and they are likely to choke—even if just a little. When they believe that humans can't expand their intelligence, the pressures grow even more as they face those tough exams. Too much rides on the outcome.

Repeatedly in recent years, surveys of college students have found large numbers reporting that they suffer from acute anxiety, depression, or severe eating disorders. One study at a large public university found over half of the students suffering from one of these problems.[8] No one cause produced these illnesses, yet scholars began to suspect that the frenzy over maintaining the ego might play a large role. A maddening conflict began to emerge within the literature. Low self-esteem could clearly increase depression, but so could the crazy dash to love yourself. Not always, of course, but it could trigger an avalanche of cascading emotions. You simply attach great importance to making the grade. You come to think those high marks define your worth as a human being. School becomes more competitive and the dean's list more difficult to reach. You falter. Anxieties grow. Fears of more failures increase. Who can think when you are worried? Those emotions may trigger a parade of poor grades (or at least lower grades than you expect). Anxiety and depression may follow. The more you care, the worse it all becomes.

Kristin knew that the troubles with an overemphasis on loving yourself did not end here. In their push for this valued commodity, people could become so centered on number one that they turn into bigheaded bores, always seeking other people's praise and constantly focusing on themselves. They could act in selfish and arrogant ways, neither of which we noticed in any of the highly successful and creative people we interviewed. They could even become more violent. Studies of violence and self-esteem had uncovered complex patterns and relationships. People with high regard for themselves don't always become more violent than others, but if their self-love slips into extreme narcissism, they frequently do. Bullies often think highly of themselves, but so do the people who stand up to them. That magic quality simply doesn't guarantee positive results.[9]

Just thinking highly of yourself doesn't ensure good things, and can even blind you to something you need to fix, such as ignorance. People can feel so good about themselves that they fail to recognize how much they need to learn. Students with less knowledge often express great confidence in what they don't know. Perhaps behind their exaggerated assertions about how much they believe in themselves lies an uneasy doubt that can't admit any shortfall for fear that it might jeopardize some carefully constructed facade of self-regard.

For those who concentrate only on the feeling rather than the accomplishments that might spawn those good emotions, the results can be particularly agonizing. Caught in a world of ignorance and unable to admit any weakness, they stumble about in the dark, incapable of accepting guidance or criticism. Rather than achieving a sense of competence, connection with the world, and independence, they become slaves to their ego.

They may even sabotage their own chances of success. When failure leads people to question their worth, they feel anxious. To ensure that any failure isn't their personal responsibility, they begin to invent excuses even before a project is finished. At those moments, people sometimes procrastinate, or even undermine their own work so they can blame someone or something other than themselves.

Because they see failure as an attack on their self-worth, they must protect themselves from it by not even trying. "Self-handicapping" like this destroys initiative and creativity, and often springs from the pursuit of self-esteem at all costs.

Other extreme self-lovers may become so focused on themselves that they ignore or mistreat others. Research has found that in the quest to protect egos, some people can become more prejudiced as they look for someone else's supposed misery to make them feel better about themselves. In one recent experiment, for example, white students from Arizona State University received some highly negative feedback on something they wrote, the kind of harsh response that could challenge what they thought of themselves, especially if they built their self-esteem on getting high marks. Another group received no feedback on what they did. Then both groups ranked black candidates for jobs by looking at their credentials. Theoretically, the average rankings should have been the same. Instead, the people who had just received the scorching attacks on their work gave the black candidates lower ratings. Meanwhile, black students did the same to white candidates after they encountered a response to their work that cut to the bone. The researchers put it this way: "Expressing prejudice against members of another group can buffer one's self-esteem against failure or other self-image threats."[10]

The real problem is that it's often unclear what self-esteem means. This supposedly magic quality can come in too many forms to declare it a universal cure for all that ails the human soul. Some of it seems to flow from genuine accomplishments whereas other versions appear to sprout from artificial soil. People with high accomplishments usually have it, but so do others who have a lot less to be proud of. It makes you feel good and can be a great motivator, but if you go after it like an addict seeking a fix, you might be caught in the trap of constantly trying to prove to yourself and others that you have worth.

Indeed, it is the quest for the magic elixir that seems to cause most of the problem. Jennifer Crocker and Lora Park, two University of Michigan psychologists, put it this way: "The pursuit of self-esteem, when it is successful, has emotional and motivational benefits, but it also has both short- and long-term costs, diverting people from fulfilling their fundamental human needs for competence, relatedness, and autonomy, and leading to poor self-regulation and poor mental and physical health."[11]

So what can you do? In a series of research and theoretical articles, Kristin Neff laid out three major approaches. The first is self-kindness, which is simply the practice and intention of being "kind and understanding" toward yourself when you are going through a difficult moment, whether it be a failure or some loss or pain. People who are kind to themselves aren't "harshly self-critical." The second approach, common humanity, is the recognition that whatever pain or failure you may face, others have gone through something similar. It's all part of the human experience. Remember Stephen Colbert's advice: "Momentary disappointments can be seen, as my mother used to say when we had a heartbreaker, 'in the light of eternity.'" Finally, Neff suggests practicing mindfulness, which is the habit of acknowledging "painful thoughts and feelings" but not "over-identifying with them." Kristin called this collection of approaches "self-compassion."

Think of an occasion when you had compassion for someone else, maybe when a friend lost a parent, suffered an injury, failed at something they strongly valued, or made a terrible mistake. When you commiserate with someone else, you understand, accept, and even feel their pain without judging them. Because you care about the person, you don't forget about what happened to them. Instead, you want to relieve their suffering. If they did something wrong, you don't pile on blame but rather help them see that nobody is perfect, and although they have to take responsibility for their actions, they can do better. So it is with being compassionate with yourself. Kristin put it this way: "Self-compassion . . . involves being touched by and open to one's own suffering, not avoiding or disconnecting from it, generating the desire to alleviate one's suffering and to heal oneself with kindness." It also means, she continued, "offering non-judgmental understanding to one's pain, inadequacies, and failures, so that one's experience is seen as part of the larger human experience."[12]

Self-compassion isn't feeling sorry for yourself. If you do, you can become so wrapped up in your own problems that you can't think straight. Rather, self-compassion allows you to step back from the problem and exercise a more objective approach. As you practice self-compassion, your empathy for others grows with the recognition that everybody, including you, suffers, comes up short, and stumbles from time to time. Forgiveness of yourself doesn't allow you to keep on making the same old mistakes. If you constantly beat up that person in the mirror, thinking that will get you on the right track, you may protect yourself from such abuse by avoiding any thoughts of the bad behavior. You quietly forget about that resolution to do better and slip easily into old habits. Only when you confront your actions with compassion and understanding can you change them. To achieve any of this, Kristin came to believe, you must become a mindful person—one who is aware but not too self-involved. "Mindfulness," she concluded, "is a balanced state of awareness." You see your problems clearly and accept "mental and emotional phenomena" as they pop up in life. You neither "run away with nor run away from" your feelings.[13]

Finally, self-compassion in Kristin's terms doesn't mean self-indulgence. It isn't an excuse for taking lots of hot baths. It means taking responsibility for your actions and confronting their consequences mindfully. Self-compassion calls for a sense of responsibility toward yourself and others.

What does all of this get you? In a series of research studies, Kristin and her colleagues have discovered that learning to comfort yourself pays all the rich dividends that high self-esteem offers without any of its downsides. People who discover how to comfort themselves generally suffer less anxiety. They take greater responsibility for their own lives. They are more peaceful, their minds are more open, and they are less likely to make those social comparisons that breed prejudice. College students who score high in self-compassion suffer less anxiety and depression, develop greater satisfaction with themselves and their lives, find more joy in just learning for its own sake, and avoid the trap of worshiping high grades. They know how to pursue a goal with vim and vigor, but they can also walk away without regret when something doesn't pan out. Because they can adopt a new purpose they know how to cope with failure, learning from the experience rather than ignoring it or freaking out.[14]

## Self-Compassion

What Kristin found among contented people, I found among the highly productive and creative. Indeed, you can see all of the aspects of self-compassion in the biographies of people I interviewed. In their language and lives they displayed a remarkable ability to comfort themselves, to understand their connections to a much larger community, and to confront life with honesty. That capacity for what she called self-compassion enabled them to triumph through all the peaks and valleys they encountered. It allowed their creativity to flourish, less encumbered and distracted with the anxieties and depressions that often plague human existence, but it also undergirded and complemented a broader set of perspectives and attitudes, including compassion and empathy for others. I interviewed people who had rooted themselves in communities rather than in themselves, and had found purpose in life within those broader relationships. They had recognized their own interdependence with the world and relished the connections that they could build and maintain.

They set high standards for personal growth, but not in some mad anxiety-ridden quest to best someone else. People I interviewed had found great joy in finding and pursuing a purpose that defined their lives. Because of this self-knowledge, they accepted criticism easily and used it to benefit that personal growth. They could confront their own lives—even the tragedies—and find ways to use those events to bolster, inform, inspire, stimulate, and guide. I was struck by the way several of them discussed the most bittersweet moments with solemnity and mindfulness. Sometimes they washed those feelings, attitudes, and approaches in religious traditions and expressions; other times they did not. "Keep trying," Stephen Colbert advised, "but don't worry." And then he added: "Who among you by worrying can add a single hour to his life . . . Or a single cubit to his height." Rather than pursuing self-esteem, they sought goals that were larger than themselves and focused on others, and while a sense of self-worth came from those commitments, that was never their goal.

## Understanding

"My sister committed suicide when I was in college," Eliza Noh said calmly one afternoon. "She was a student at a college in Houston, and I was a junior at Columbia at the time." Eliza and her older sister had grown up in the prosperous suburbs of southwest Houston. They had a rich cultural heritage. Their father came from Korea, and their mother from Vietnam. Their parents had immigrated to the United States together before the girls were born. Eliza's dad became a physician, and the family did well in Sugarland, Texas, where a small but growing Asian American community took pride in the academic achievements of their children.

"We faced a lot of pressure to make the top grades," Eliza remembered, "and my sister caught most of the force because she was the oldest." Eliza took honors AP classes in high school, devoted herself to making the highest grades, and eventually graduated second in her class. "I remember the fights that went on between my sister and father over her performance in school," Eliza related. "I was usually just trying to control the chaos going on around me, and to do that I learned to avoid emotional involvement."

Her parents wanted the best for their daughters, and that meant making the honor roll, getting into prestigious colleges, eventually going to medical school, then on to fat paychecks in medicine, which would provide economic security. "I became consumed with making the highest grades," she confessed. "As Asian Americans, we were supposed to be the model minority, the ones who succeeded."

And succeed she did—at least with grades. Year after year Eliza racked up high marks, honors, AP credit, and all the trappings of a highly successful high school student marching toward that moment on the graduation podium when she would take her bow as class salutatorian.

Eliza also had a strong curiosity, and her friends and family sometimes called her the "walking question mark" because she constantly peppered people with queries. Yet throughout high school, as she recognized later, she never enjoyed discovering something new just for the pure joy of it. "I think I missed out on a lot because I was so focused on grades rather than on learning," she concluded. Seldom if ever did she read anything that wasn't part of an assignment.

When she graduated from high school she went to New York City to enter Columbia University. She chose Columbia "largely to escape," she reported. In her freshman year, she began to discover a different kind of educational environment, one filled with provocative ideas and less competition. Yet the old habits and approaches persisted, clinging to her soul like a bad cold. She had long before learned how to get good grades, and throughout her freshman year, that's the approach she took. But Columbia was a different kind of place, and the culture there began to whittle away at her strategic learning style. "In high school, everyone concentrated on getting into the best colleges," she recalled, "but at Columbia I encountered a world of ideas and people who cared about learning."

In her sophomore year, she took a course that finally shattered the remaining walls of her well-worn strategic intentions. It was an elective that fulfilled a distribution requirement, but it became her path to deep learning. That course raised questions she found important, intriguing, and sometimes just beautiful. "It really opened my eyes," Eliza reminisced. "For the first time in my life, I realized that learning could be about me and my interests, about who I was." That course asked about power in society: who has it, how is it used, how do different roles you have in life influence the power you have? How does your gender, occupation, race, sexual orientation, or social and economic class influence the power you can exercise? How does your power change as you move from one role to another?

As Eliza explored those questions, they sparked even more inquiries as her mind raced from one idea to another. If some people have more power, everyone isn't equal. So how do you maintain a democratic society? How do people use their power? What happens to people who lack power? She realized that in some contexts she had enormous sway over other people, and in others, she had none.

Eliza spoke up more in class, raising questions and making arguments, and that habit carried into other classes and subjects, transforming her into a student with deep-learning intentions. It changed the way she studied everything. When she read, she engaged the text. She wrote notes in the margin, raising more questions or advancing some counter-position. She didn't just follow someone's prescription for good study habits. It all sprang spontaneously from her growing fascination with the world. "My thoughts about gender hierarchies led me to explore how various ethnic groups had different hierarchies." She noticed that nearly all the subjects and people she studied were male (from Plato to presidents), and nearly all were from European backgrounds. Asians, Asian Americans, and women received virtually no mention. This led her to ask why.

Her whole approach to education began to change. "I always asked a lot of questions," she noted, "but in high school, I was so consumed with grades that I didn't realize how much I enjoyed thinking critically, having an inquiring mind, advancing arguments." Learning became more intellectually satisfying when she was liberated from the urgency of making the dean's list. "In high school I never thought of education as being personal." It was just a game she played for high scores. But in that class on power and in classes to come, "I didn't just listen to lectures, but began to use my own experiences as a jumping off point for asking questions and wanting to pursue certain concepts."

That elective course introduced her to worlds she had never known, to modern-day sweatshops where women and men toiled in conditions she'd thought belonged to the darkest days of the nineteenth century. It provoked an examination of political and social ideas, as she began to see her education as highly personal and concerned with what she would believe and why, the values she would hold, the actions she would take, and the problems she would encounter in holding any of her thoughts.

Eliza actively pursued her education. She sought meaning and thought about the implication, applications, and possibilities for that meaning. The young girl from Sugarland, Texas, asked big questions and looked for answers that integrated multiple disciplines. She read, raised questions about arguments and evidence, then searched for a personal connection. She and her friends lobbied the administration at Columbia to offer courses on Asian American affairs. The university had long emphasized Western European traditions and had put every student through a core curriculum that focused on political, social, intellectual, and artistic developments in the West, from ancient Greek philosophers to modern thinkers and actors. Students read five or six books a week and went to class prepared to discuss their ideas, but none of that touched on any of the traditions and experiences of Asian Americans. Eliza wanted more, and became increasingly driven by what was missing from the traditional education. She and her colleagues successfully lobbied the women's studies department to hire a part-time lecturer to offer classes on Asian American history. She had taken control of her own education and found those powerful intrinsic motivators to fuel her life.

Then came the terrible night of her sister's death. Eliza had spoken with her older sibling by phone and had written her a letter. She was concerned about her growing bouts with depression. "I told her I supported her, and I encouraged her," Eliza later told a reporter.[15] But all the words of encouragement did no good. Her sister joined a growing epidemic of young Asian American women who took their own lives.[16] "I was in denial and shock for a long time," she confessed. After the funeral, she went back to class, almost as if nothing had happened. "I tried to move on, to distance myself emotionally as I had always done when my sister and father fought." But she could not so easily dismiss it.

When she began working on a senior thesis the next year, Eliza decided to explore suicide among Asian American young women, to probe its causes and consequences. Doing the research, however, brought a wave of deeply sad emotions to the front of her mind. "It produced an emotional breakdown, and I could not finish the paper," she told me. Along the way, she had a few teachers, both in high school and college, who took an interest in her as an individual, and one such person appeared at that crucial moment in her life. "She accepted what I had written up to that point. I eventually published that paper and it became the basis for the research I've done in the field, but when I could not finish it for academic credit, I had one caring professor who understood the emotional difficulty I was having, and didn't just write me off."

Listening to her story, two powerful factors became apparent.

First, as she reported to me, she was able to come to terms emotionally with her sister's death only when she stopped seeing it as an individual tragedy and placed it in a larger social and political context. Once she understood it as "part of a larger human experience," as Kristin Neff had described one of the three key ingredients of self-compassion, she could see the powerful role that the idea of a "model minority" had played in her own family's tragic moment. Society had constructed a positive stereotype that Asian Americans were smart and particularly good at math, and that notion became both an extrinsic motivator, with its own possibilities for diminishing intrinsic drives, and an immense pressure that sometimes became unbearable. Like so many other Asian American families, her parents had unwittingly become the instrument of that social force.

She could understand also the larger social elements that had driven her sister to hate her own looks and to seek plastic surgery in order to conform to some popular notions of beauty rooted in European models and appearances. "The standard of beauty she wanted to emulate was white women," Eliza told a reporter. As Eliza came to understand those larger forces, she could exercise that mindfulness of acknowledging her painful thoughts and feelings rather than over-identifying with them or repressing them. "Until I began to study the social basis of suicide among Asian-American women," Eliza concluded, "I was in denial about what had happened."

The joy she had found in learning and thinking critically overcame all of the extrinsic motivations to "make the grade," allowing her to shed those stifling pressures that diminish rather than increase the pleasures of life. She found an intrinsic delight that left her at peace with herself. That inner serenity, in turn, helped give her the strength to treat herself and others with kindness. The understanding she developed about society and people, forged not from any one discipline but from a variety of perspectives, allowed her to comprehend and deal with the tough moments of life.

After that emotional breakdown, Eliza dropped out of Columbia for a semester, but returned to finish her degree with honors. Yet the academic accolades mattered little to her now. She had discovered a deeper meaning for her work, and as she did, she learned to be more empathetic and self-compassionate. "In high school, I didn't deal with failure well because my whole goal was to get good grades. If I didn't, I was really hard on myself," she recognized. "I was so focused on being number one that I didn't realize that I was actually getting my greatest satisfaction from asking questions and thinking critically."

As that began to change at Columbia, her thoughts about failure shifted too. "Before, I was so concerned with being number one. Now, learning for me is no longer about success versus failure. Rather it is a process. It is about continuing to learn and grow, not a constant test to see whether I'm succeeding or failing." With that change in perspective, she went on to study at the University of California at Berkeley, where she received a doctorate in ethnic studies. Thereafter she pioneered work on the epidemic among Asian American women that had taken her sister's life.

## Self-Comfort and Creativity

Duncan Campbell grew up with two alcoholic parents. At the age of three, he had once stumbled out of his house looking for his father and mother before the police found them in a local saloon. "Early in my life," he remembered, "we had a house of our own," but as his parents sank into the arms of their disease and his dad went to prison, the family spiraled downward into ever more dingy housing in low-income and high-crime areas of Portland, Oregon.

In the lonely hours of his childhood, often deserted by inebriated parents, Duncan learned the element of self-comfort, including the capacity to think mindfully about his plight rather than to repress it. "When I was eight or nine," he declared, "I made a conscious decision not to be like my mother and father. Everything I did over the next twenty years came out of that decision." But that choice rested both on his power to confront his life as it existed and on his ability to keep it in balance. He didn't sweep it under some mental rug, repressing it, nor did he spend much time just pondering it.

The future millionaire and philanthropist was a small kid, "one of the smallest on my high school football team," but he had a huge curiosity, and in the lonely hours of his childhood, he used that fascination with the world to comfort himself and to learn. "I became street smart, but unbelievably naive," he confessed. "Because your world is so small, you don't always know what you don't know." When he was ten, he discovered the public library, where he eventually read everything in the sports section. He discovered also the corner drugstore, where he could buy comic and sports books. "No one told me to do that, but that's one of the advantages of being left alone," he remembered. Duncan became enamored with puzzles, and on solitary nights he would sometimes find an old movie playing on television and do jigsaw puzzles on the floor in front of the set, fidgeting with those little pieces like the parts of the problems he would tackle later in life. He also enjoyed crossword puzzles, manipulating letters and words.

Because Duncan was poor, he faced considerable discrimination when he was growing up and felt the sharp and painful emotions of that experience. When children suffer the attacks of prejudice, they often strike back with their own bigotries, finding someone lower than themselves. That brush with the unjust doesn't always breed a concern for a fair society, but it did in Duncan, perhaps because no one had bothered to teach him about the ugly, racist underbelly of his civilization, or perhaps because he found his contentment in self-comfort. He emerged from childhood with an almost insatiable desire to help other children overcome the prejudices they face. "I developed great empathy for anyone who faced discrimination," he once explained, "because, coming from a family with no money, I faced so much of it myself."

Duncan had a purpose in life: to avoid being like his parents. "If you are familiar with some of the literature on adult children of alcoholics," he offered, employing that ability to step back from his problems and see them in a larger context, "you know that most of the positive attributes center on creativity and being resourceful. You learn a lot of skills from the street." He emerged from those hard times with the rudimentary elements of a creative process he would refine only years later when he was a law student at the University of Oregon. "For me," he summarized, "creativity is rearranging existing things in ways that have never been done before." That ability to do so, first sculpted on the streets of his childhood, began with considering his options and exploring the possibilities, then choosing between alternatives and taking action. He learned to draw on his own experience and concentrate on what he could do rather than what he couldn't. "So many people cut the process short," he observed, "often stopping just short of taking action."

Society gave him some of those pieces he needed in the form of public libraries and schools, streets and sidewalks, and a healthy economy in which to operate, but he had to find ways to use those resources. He sold stuff door-to-door to make extra money, everything from seeds to magazines, scraping together enough coins for sports and puzzle books. "I never had an allowance as a child," he explained, "so I had to make my own money."

In school, he worked hard. "I knew I wasn't anybody, and I wanted to make good grades so I could be somebody." He tried to keep up because falling behind would be a disaster. "I didn't associate school with any love of learning or with a desire to understand and be creative," he admitted. "I just wanted to perform well." In German class he aced every quiz because he sought simply to memorize, and he could do that. In major examinations, however, he was expected to have acquired the language, and those quick-fix memory schemes left him with little working ability in German. On the final, he earned a D.

Most of his grades were higher, but few classes really challenged him to think. Piece by piece, his strategic approach began to crumble, sometimes entirely by accident. An English class in high school required him to read a novel, and he looked for the thinnest book he could find. That's when he pulled from the shelf a little volume by John Steinbeck called *Of Mice and Men* and discovered the great American author. "It was the first good book I had ever read," Duncan recalled, "and I began to read everything that Steinbeck wrote."

In college, first at Portland State and then later at the University of Oregon, "I majored in paperbacks," he conceded with a laugh. He continued to buy books at the local drugstore or co-op and to read what fascinated him, but only in a few classes did he find much to challenge or motivate him to think. In a freshman class in composition, he learned to weigh evidence and reason carefully, then draw conclusions and defend them. Although he'd learned some of that on the streets, it was the first time a teacher had asked him to express his thinking in writing.

At college he had the chance to design a course. "You could create a class as an elective, and there was a lawyer who taught a business law class, and I asked him if I could do a range of readings and discussions around a topic," Duncan recalled. "He would suggest readings and then we'd get together for an hour and talk about them. It was the best class I took as an undergraduate." Only in law school did he finally encounter an education that systematically challenged him to think critically, weigh options and evidence, make choices, and write out his reasoning.

Duncan Campbell eventually became a lawyer and a CPA. He worked for an accounting firm "doing mostly tax work," but then created an investment firm in the timber industry ("nobody had done that before") called the Campbell Group and made millions when he sold it to a New York Stock Exchange company. That wealth then allowed him to do what he had always wanted to do: work with children. "I'd gone to law school because I thought it would be about justice," he explained, "but I discovered it was about winning." With considerable financial resources, he created and funded what eventually became the country's most successful effort to help poor children overcome the pressing burden of their poverty. He has established four major initiatives to address the problems that such children face, including Youth Resources, the Children's Course, and the Children's Institute. His premier program, however, has been Friends of the Children, which hires full-time professional mentors to work with children beginning at age five or six and continuing until they graduate from high school. Each mentor shepherds eight children, and spends at least four hours a week with each one. Unlike other mentoring programs that help a wide variety of kids, Friends of the Children targets only the toughest cases: those who come from high-poverty backgrounds and have severe behavioral and emotional problems. Yet the success of the program has been phenomenal. While most children from such backgrounds will drop out of school, get into trouble with the law at some point in their young lives, and start having their own children when they are still in their teens, the overwhelming majority in this program finish school, stay clear of legal trouble, and avoid early parenting. Many go on to college. For his work in creating such programs, Duncan Campbell received the Purpose Award, which the Robert Wood Johnson Foundation gives annually to people "focused on solving seemingly intractable problems."[17]

Duncan emerged from a ragged childhood and a formal education that he never really enjoyed to live a highly productive, compassionate, and creative life. Three personal ingredients helped shape that journey and determine its outcome. First, he had an insatiable curiosity ("I was always a kind of 'curious George,'" he noted) that he fed primarily from the paperback books he bought at the corner drugstore. He read books, enjoyed music, and experienced life. When he graduated from college, he traveled, first from Oregon to Los Angeles, then east to Alabama and Georgia, north to New York, and eventually on to Europe, sometimes taking odd jobs along the way. Second, he learned to comfort himself, easing the pain and healing those troubled moments. Third, he had followed the advice that Paul Baker had given his students: draw from your own life. Realize how unusual you are and use those uncommon pieces to create something no one else could even imagine. "I wouldn't wish my childhood on anyone," he said recently, "but I'm so thankful for it now because it gave me an opportunity to do something I love."

Duncan built his own creative process from the tough streets of Portland's poorest neighborhoods.

Law school and other small segments of his education had helped him refine his critical thinking abilities, but why didn't he enjoy that formal education more? "Perhaps," he said recently, "I couldn't let go completely of that strategic approach." So much of the education system he encountered judged students more than it tried to help them grow. In many schools students are constantly tested, as if education existed to weed people out rather than to foster their talents. Duncan and other people we interviewed prospered because they were ultimately able to find their own path to creative growth. When he was older, Duncan took a course at Harvard that had no credit and no grades, just the opportunity to learn. "I really enjoyed that experience," he beamed. "They didn't treat you like pond scum."

## A Higher Purpose

Singapore sits on sixty-three islands off the southern tip of the Malay Peninsula in Southeast Asia. The city-state has become a prosperous melting pot of Asian and world cultures, and living in that polyglot environment, Meixi Ng had learned English and two dialects of Chinese, including Mandarin. She spoke Thai and would later study Spanish and French. When she was quite young, her family lived in Evanston, Illinois, for three years while her father worked on a doctorate in communication studies at Northwestern University, and when they returned to Singapore, he did family counseling and leadership development.

At the age of ten, Meixi took up gymnastics and trained three and four hours a day for competition. But in high school, she fell and injured her back and had to stop. "That gave me a chance to explore other areas," she recalled with a smile. As she was growing up in the island city, her father had a large circle of friends who called themselves the Eagles, and their children became her constant companions. Born out of Christian beliefs, the oddly named association stressed humility and commitment to a "common vision to support one another."

"I grew up in a huge fellowship of people and we were always together," she recalled. "Everything was about the group." They learned to care about one another, and to seek justice within their community and within the broader world, something the adults stressed constantly. "We had a strong sense of responsibility toward other people," she remembered.

When she turned eleven, her mother sent her and her younger brother to the slums of India to help people who were less fortunate. The next year, they lived in Myanmar to do the same. "I got the long end of the stick," she concluded, "but I saw how unfair the world could be for other people." Both of those excursions made a profound impression on Meixi, but her exposure to injustice didn't end there. In high school, she went with the Eagles to Thailand, enrolled in school there, and became good friends with a Thai girl in her class. "She was my best friend," Meixi Ng declared. "She loved school and wanted to learn, but one day, her parents sold her as a bride because they needed money. She was just sixteen. I tried to raise the money to buy her back, but failed."

That shocking event might have triggered any number of reactions from anger to depression. In Meixi, it sparked a crusading desire to address a whole host of social issues that revolved around education. "It was a very painful experience," she said. "It made injustice and inequality very personal." "What happened to Da was always on my mind," she told a reporter recently. Influenced by her friend's fate, she decided to attend Northwestern and major in education and international studies, with a minor in communication sciences and disorders. In high school, she was "always in the middle of the pack academically," but now, with a greater purpose for her studies, she regularly made the dean's list in college. "I don't consider myself naturally all that smart," she told me, "but I'm dedicated."

More important, she took a deep approach to everything she studied and looked for ways to put her emerging ideas into action. She learned to organize and to act. Even in high school, she directed a large conference to help young people address personal issues and later co-founded the Amber Initiative, an international organization working all across Southeast Asia to advocate "for the restoration and protection of human dignity through a global movement of youth." The group created mentoring programs for "disadvantaged Singaporean youth" and "an art competition for children living in the red light district" of Kolkata, India, among other initiatives.[18] It sought to end human trafficking by expanding educational opportunities around the world.

Once she arrived in Evanston, she co-founded the International Studies Association, and then within that organization created a Northwestern version of the World Cup. That event eventually became the "largest student-run athletic tournament" at the Illinois university, all devoted to using sports to "bridge cultures" and help students realize the rich diversity on campus. Once a week, she tutored schoolchildren and coached swimmers in the Special Olympics.

She sought also to integrate a sense of community and commitment into the curriculum of the university. "What we really want is for civic engagement to become a Northwestern value, something that we all have in common," she told a student reporter. Meixi joined with other students to create the Northwestern Engagement Coalition, a superorganization devoted to coordination events and collaboration of all groups involved in civic engagement. The newly founded alliance immediately initiated a letter-writing campaign to convince the university to select a new president who would push for civic and global engagement across the curriculum and extra-curricular activities.

Amid all these commitments, one goal remained paramount, and it drove her studies. She wanted to improve educational opportunities around the world. In her junior year, she sought and received a Circumnavigators Club Foundation Around-the-World Travel-Study Grant that would allow her to circle the globe, visiting schools in marginalized communities. "I wanted to find out what worked," she reported, "so we can learn more about what needs to be done." Her own education focused on a higher purpose that never confined itself to a classroom or a single course.

## Resilience

When Reyna Grande was two years old, her father left home to look for work in the United States. Like so many Mexican men of his age, he found the oppressive poverty of his home village unbearable and trekked north to seek a better life. "Our village flooded often," Reyna remembered, "and we escaped to the roof of our little hut to avoid the rising waters and the dead animals floating by."

Her father planned to return home once he'd made enough money but never did. Instead, he became part of a growing economy in the United States that depended on paying low wages to Mexican immigrants desperate for any work, and constantly afraid that the government would send them back because they didn't have the right entry documents. Señor Grande was "good with his hands" and "could do plumbing and electricity," so he found a job working as a maintenance man in a convalescence hospital making fifteen thousand dollars a year.

After four years, he sent for his wife, but Reyna and her older sister and brother stayed in Mexico with their grandmother. They didn't have the right immigration papers, and perhaps their parents feared the children would be caught and arrested at the border. "He was gone for eight years," she recalled, "before I saw him again."

When she turned ten, he came for the children, and Reyna and her siblings crossed the border to join their father, but by then her parents had divorced and both had remarried. "It's kind of sad," she reminisced, "our family from Mexico didn't exist any more." She and her older brother and sister lived with their father and step-mother and saw her biological mother only once a month.

Reyna didn't speak English when she entered school, so the teacher put her in a corner where an assistant would translate everything for her. "I felt really bad," she admitted many years later, "because I couldn't participate with the rest of the class." She learned English mostly "by reading a lot" and from English as a Second Language classes, which she took in middle school.

She and her siblings faced enormous pressure from their dad to do well in school. "He constantly threatened to send us back to Mexico if we didn't make good grades," Reyna recalled. "My father was never satisfied, really angry if we had even one tardy." He told his children that "uneducated people don't go too far in this country." Reyna was especially curious about music and art, anything that would allow her to create. In middle school she joined the band

and then tried playing every instrument in the school collection. "I brought home trombones, clarinets, trumpets, and nearly everything else," she related. She took art classes and thought about being an animator for Walt Disney. Every week, she went to the public library and checked out a new book, marching through the young adult section. There were "a lot of books about twins with blue eyes and blond hair," she remembered. "There wasn't much substance to them, and because I didn't have any guidance, I didn't read any serious literature until I got to college."

Her father continued to support his family on the poverty-level wages he received from the convalescence home, but that grew progressively more difficult as they matured. When the two oldest children reached college-age, he took out a loan to send them to school, but both of them dropped out within a year. When Reyna reached that point, he had no more money or patience, and told the young girl that she would have to fend for herself. Even though she won admission to the University of California as an art major, he wouldn't let her go.

After staying out of school in the fall, Reyna entered Pasadena College in January. Life at home, however, became increasingly more difficult. Her father had become a violent alcoholic who beat his children regularly, and Reyna, as the youngest, often bore the brunt of those attacks. "He never touched my stepmother," she said, "until one day he beat her so badly she had to go to the hospital." The police came and arrested him.

Years later when she talked about that traumatic day, Reyna remembered the desperation that gripped her. "I had to talk with someone," she explained. "I was scared and lonely." She went to campus and looked for her English professor, Diana Savas. Savas had studied French literature at Oberlin College before getting a doctorate in applied linguistics from UCLA. Nothing in the curriculum she had pursued prepared her for this moment. Reyna told her what had happened, and Diana responded simply, "Why don't you come live with me?"

That invitation transformed Reyna's life. "She took me out of an unstable situation and gave me a new home," and in that environment, the young student thrived. Diana had already admired Reyna's writing in the English class, and increasingly she had encouraged the girl to become a writer and to go away to school. "Put some distance between yourself and your family," she advised.

Through all of her ordeal, Reyna Grande had an intense capacity for self-comfort. "I had this double personality," she explained. "One Reyna was scared, always depressed, and had low self-esteem, but I developed this other person who was strong and who would tell me that things are going to be OK." Much like the characters she would later fashion for her award-winning novels, her alter-ego became a figment of her imagination, a product of both her drive to create and a growing belief that she could accomplish something. "I kept my eyes on the future so I wouldn't have to think about the present," she said. "I kept telling myself that life isn't always going to be like this, so I have to keep going." Reyna came to believe strongly in her capacity to grow, and that conviction, coupled with her push to avoid failure and an inner hunger to create, drove her work. "My brother and sister dropped out of school, and I wanted to avoid that."

Diana Savas played a huge role in helping Reyna to imagine that she might use the experiences of her life to become a novelist. "I used to think that only white people wrote books," she confessed. But her English teacher began to change that impression. In class, Reyna studied *Rereading America: Cultural Contexts for Critical Think-*

*ing and Writing*, and in that collection and in her writing in response to that work, she discovered a diverse cultural landscape. These voices challenged some of the popular images that girlhood reading in the library and the broader culture had given her. At home, Diana gave her novels by Latina writers, like Sandra Cisneros's *The House on Mango Street*. That author had taken her unique experiences of living in Chicago and in Mexico and turned them into literary treasures. Reyna began to imagine that she could do the same with her own life.

In that English class with Diana, she also learned to write nonfiction, and developed the habits of critical thinking, constantly asking herself, "What's my evidence, what conclusions will I draw, what are the problems I face in reaching this decision, how will I demonstrate and support my reasoning?" Later those habits served her well. "I would think about a paper for days, exploring the argument I wished to make and the evidence I would use, and when I sat down to write it out, it came naturally."

Diana helped her secure loans and win a scholarship to the University of California at Santa Cruz, six hours from her family. "In Los Angeles, I lived in ugly, gang-infested neighborhoods. In Santa Cruz, it helped me spiritually and emotionally to have my own dorm room on this beautiful campus and to come out of my room and to know that no one was going to yell at me or beat me up. I didn't have to be afraid any more." In that environment, Reyna continued to grow, majoring in film studies and creative writing, taking anthropology, getting hooked on dancing, and playing saxophone in the band. Even at Pasadena, curiosity had driven her into myriad fields. She had aced physics and biology, had taken a course on Shakespeare simply because she wanted to know what the fuss was all about, and, as it turned out, had understood the Bard's Elizabethan English far better than most of her classmates. At Santa Cruz, she continued her learning tour, taking botany because she loved gardening and wanted to know about composting, studying Chinese literature to explore another culture, and taking Spanish for native speakers to rediscover her native tongue. Reyna struggled with math and found history classes boring with their emphasis on timelines and memorization of dates, although she continued to devour historical novels and the histories she learned through her literature classes. "I had a ton of interests, but I had to watch myself and not get too overinvolved." Indeed, her appetite became overwhelming, and only in her junior year, at the advice of her Spanish teacher, did Reyna focus on writing.

Reyna wrote for pleasure and to heal the wounds of her troubled past. For her senior project, she began composing a memoir, but the experience became quite painful. She discovered, however, that if she turned it into fiction, the tales that emerged liberated both her imagination and emotions. As she explored the life of a girl left behind in Mexico, the emerging novelist could twist and turn the events she had experienced years before, playing with them in the fictional lives she created in her novel. "It became easier to create this character who was like me, but when the writing got tough, I could always say, that's not me. That's her."

Writing fiction taught Reyna to empathize with the people who populated her stories, an ability that she transferred to her life. "As a writer," she offered, "I have to understand what motivates a character, and I see other people as characters in the story of life. When someone makes mistakes, I always look at what made them act the way they do." Writing even gave her the capacity to understand herself, and with that power to use rather than reject her own life. With such deep calamities coursing through her experiences, she might have easily slipped into acute depression or despair, surrendering quickly to a brooding preoccupation with her own troubles or even hatred for all those forces and people responsible for her tragedies. Such alternative paths might have immobilized her. Instead, she used a combination of empathy, self-comfort, self-examination, a growth mindset, and that habit of trying to understand what motivates other people to discover the dynamic power of her own mind and forge a creative life.

I do not want to suggest, however, that Reyna or any of the people we have met were solely responsible for the successes that eventually came their way, or that her story somehow demonstrates that anyone can overcome the most egregious injustices that befall people; and I certainly do not want to excuse those unnecessary barriers that societies have created, or to belittle the structural forces that shape students' successes and failures. Rather, I seek to understand the attitudes, concepts, and practices that enabled her and some others to handle highly depressing and confining experiences. We must acknowledge that Reyna and others had a bit of luck. She found a caring teacher at the right moment and experienced the opportunities and support of an extensive public higher education system. Even her father—for all the sickness that sparked his later violence—fought to bring his children to a country with better opportunities and constantly pushed them to learn.

Reyna lived at both the right and wrong moment. She was born across a border that had been laid down in war more than a century before her birth. That frontier at first became a barrier to a little girl's wish to join her family. But a year after her father defied the law and brought her to Los Angeles, a Democratic Congress and a Republican president in the United States granted three million people a chance to get legal immigration status, and Reyna and her family got their green cards. From that moment they could stay in the United States without fear of deportation. If she had been born a decade later, her life might have taken a quite different turn.

As I heard Reyna's story, my mind flashed to an incident I witnessed nearly fifteen years ago. When I arrived at my office one morning, police cars surrounded an old pickup truck in the alley next to my building. A brown-skinned man with a handsome chiseled face sat stoically in the driver's seat of the dilapidated vehicle. His clothes and leathery skin suggested he had worked a lot in the burning sun. In the back seat of that pickup, his teenage son (I presumed) sat crying loudly while occasionally pounding the back of the seat with his fist. An older woman, perhaps his mother, had her arm around the boy, trying to calm him. "Do you speak Spanish?" one of the policemen asked me. "He doesn't want to speak any English." I asked what he'd done, and the officer explained. "We caught him going along the alley picking up items that people have thrown away, but we think he's probably an illegal immigrant." What will happen to him? I asked. "He'll get sent back to Mexico after doing some jail time. Maybe the whole family. That's what his kid is so upset about."

Reyna graduated from Santa Cruz, and then earned a master's degree in creative writing from Antioch University. She published *Across a Hundred Mountains,* an autobiographical first novel, three years later. Highly applauded by critics for its "stunning and poignant story of migration, loss, and discovery," the book won numerous honors, including the Latino Books into Movies Award and the Premio Aztlán Literary Prize. Three years later, she published her critically acclaimed second novel, *Dancing with Butterflies,* which drew on her experience with *Folklórico* dance.

# 7

## CURIOSITY AND ENDLESS EDUCATION

On a hot September afternoon, four hundred students crushed into a small auditorium, looking for seats on the long rows that curved around like giant horseshoes. As the room filled with chattering voices, each one grew louder to compete with the clamor around them.

After a few minutes, a tall, thin man wearing white running shoes, brown trousers, and a blue shirt entered and stood at a podium in the front of the room. From their seats, most of the students could look down at the top of his head. He clipped on a lavalier microphone and cleared his throat.

"I know it's hot in here," he said, almost shouting over the chatter. "But we've got work to do." As the students stopped talking, he continued. "This is History 112, and I suppose most of you are here because you think you're required to take this class. Well, you are not," he said as he moved from behind the podium and looked toward the back row.

A soft murmur rippled across the room as students turned from side to side and whispered expressions of disbelief. "But wait," he quickly added, thrusting his hands in the air as if to stop an oncoming locomotive. "This course is by definition a part of getting a liberal education at this institution, but nobody in the world is requiring you to pursue such broad learning. You will not be whipped in the public square if you don't. No one will imprison or fine you. You are in charge of your own education."

As students listened, he continued. "I want you to think about whether you really want to get this kind of education. I want you to understand both its beauty and utility, then you can decide if it is for you." The room grew still now, and a soft breeze floated around the space as the air conditioning finally kicked in.

Within a few minutes, he had unfurled a brief history of liberal education, and told them that "liberal" came from the Latin for "free" *(liber),* and it was the kind of schooling that free (as opposed to slave) children received in the ancient world. In the modern version, students explored a host of disciplines from the sciences to the humanities, taking a deep approach to important issues that those disciplines could help them address.

When the professor finished, he asked the students to do something rather strange. "This evening, when you go home or to your dorm room," he said, "I want you to decide whether you really want to pursue such an education. Run everybody out of the room, sit in the dark for at least thirty minutes, and ask yourself, 'do I really want to get a liberal education?'" If you do, he concluded, "come back on Wednesday, and prepare for the ride of a lifetime." But if you don't, "you also know what to do. You don't really want to attend this college. You should pursue something else." No one dropped the course.

Many students would now reject that appeal. They believe that if you want to do well in an increasingly specialized world, you must concentrate on a single area and become an expert in that field, forsaking all other subjects. Students study to become doctors, plumbers, business executives, lawn specialists, account managers, computer technicians, and other professionals. They often see no reason for the large number of "general education" requirements they face in most traditional colleges and universities, and "liberal arts" sounds to them like something you pursue if you don't have a real major. They speak of courses one must "get out of the way," and their advisors help them "check off" those requirements. In the most extreme version of this thinking, students believe that schools exist merely to get you the right certificate or degree, not to help you develop as a creative, critically intelligent, compassionate, and concerned human being.

If truth be known, many professors and deans also don't understand and appreciate why anyone would need to take all those general education requirements.[1] They have few notions about what the whole tradition of liberal education entails, except for some vague sense that it's "good for the students to be well-rounded."[2] But this is an old metaphor that has little appeal anymore. Who wants to be a ball in a world that seems to require a Swiss army knife, someone with multiple specialized tools to address increasingly complex problems?

I met recently with a group of influential policy-makers in Washington, D.C., and they too had difficulty understanding anything of value about education other than preparation for a job. They dismissed as meaningless anything about higher learning that didn't center on training someone to do a task that would make them money.

Our most creative and productive subjects, however, bucked the trend. They found great value in general and liberal education, yet they didn't become jacks of all trades and masters of none. They didn't just flit about from subject to subject forever, never landing anywhere long enough to make a difference. "You see so many kids coming to Harvard," one professor in that Ivy League school noted recently, "who are involved in too many activities." Our highly creative and productive subjects, in contrast, learned to make some tough choices. But here's the point: their broad educations helped them to make those choices as they learned to see connections between liberal education and the specialty they would pursue. We saw that ability in Reyna Grande and others, and we'll see it again here. If we are to understand and use what our subjects did that enabled them to fashion such highly productive and creative lives, we must appreciate why they valued a broad education before specializing in one or two fields.

## Liberal Arts and Creativity

An important part of the creative process is the ability to recognize good ideas when you encounter them. The implications of that notion are profound. To grow on the ideas and creations of others, we must encounter them, and to do so, we must explore the great works of the mind found in the arts, sciences, mathematics, philosophies, and historical perspectives. We have to get excited about probing a vast array of subjects and disciplines. The world of ideas and scholarship becomes our oyster, and the possibilities become almost unlimited, at least as large as all of human endeavor and achievement throughout history.

I could make an argument that such creativity benefits society, but that wasn't the only reason given for the diverse interests of the highly accomplished people I interviewed. They valued creativity because it helped fulfill a basic human need. It could make their lives richer and more robust. The American philosopher Richard Taylor echoes similar ideas in his classic work *Virtue Ethics*. He argues that humans, because they have a special intelligence, can live the good life only if they become creative. It is, Taylor wrote, "what distinguishes us from all other living things."[3] Taylor believed that original work could occur in any domain. "When we think of creativity," the philosopher wrote, "we are apt to construe it narrowly, as the creation of things, sometimes even limiting it to things belonging to the arts." But that is too thin, he concluded. "Creative intelligence is exhibited by a dancer, by athletes, by a chess player, and indeed in virtually any activity guided by intelligence." It can occur in gardening and farming or in "the rearing of a beautiful family." In his own quest for an innovative and good life, Taylor became both an internationally renowned beekeeper and a philosopher.[4]

The subjects in our study didn't just sit around expounding on the value of creativity. They found something that fascinated them. They became interested in problems they could solve, in work that they could do. They became creative because they became lost in something other than themselves. Our subjects realized that their growth as creative individuals needed food, and that they would find that nourishment both in an increasing appreciation for the creative work of others and in the special perspectives that they could bring to any situation, problem, or project. They had to understand how their brains worked best, how ideas came up in their own minds, how they thought, and where they got those thoughts. Fundamentally, they had to understand themselves as a product of history and society, and that required deep comprehension and extensive study of both the past and their own world. Driven by their desires to fulfill that human capacity and need for originality, our best students explored the rich world of the liberal arts, mining the humanities, arts, and social and natural sciences for the concepts and information that fed their minds.

Curiosity and the fun they experienced in learning more played a huge role in shaping their focus. A liberal arts education afforded them the chance to enjoy a richer life because they could get more out of every moment and every experience. What is life, after all? It is experiencing reality over time, but if you can take any moment and enhance it, know it in historical context, explore its social context, dissect it and all its many voices, and integrate it into your experience, you can derive far more out of any one time and place. You can extend your life. As Andrew Abbott, a sociologist at the University of Chicago, told some students a few years ago, "given the opportunity, you are a fool not to avail yourself of every means to extend your experience in the now. The quality of education is our central means for doing that."[5]

History, for example, is the broadest of disciplines because it encompasses all of human affairs—from the arts to the sciences and everything in between. Imagine that you are trying to see different shades of a color. You can see the difference most clearly if you put them next to each other. So it is with understanding yourself and your own times. Until you have other historical points of reference, you can't really say much about your own society or yourself. You might think that certain attitudes—such as racism—are quite natural until you learn that those feelings and concepts have a history and have not always existed. You might think certain people and religions tend toward violence until you explore the long history of those same groups and compare them with other societies. You might think that the people in your society have some superior gene because of their enhanced ability to build indoor toilets and other technologies until you study the lengthy historical forces that shaped their prosperity, and realize that in earlier times your ancestors had little to brag about.

## Engaging with History and Justice

Long before he became one of the few economists to predict the economic collapse in 2008 and a leading advocate for economic justice, Dean Baker built a summer seminar with his older brother. Like two siblings constructing a tree house, the Baker brothers hammered together their own line of study. Dean had just finished his freshman year at Swarthmore College, outside Philadelphia, and his brother had completed his junior year at Reed College, in Portland. The Baker brothers had grown up on the north side of Chicago, living with their mother and grandparents, and they returned home that summer to the old Lakeview neighborhood full of ideas and questions. The older brother had studied history at Reed and had encountered a school of American historians who questioned many of the popular assumptions about the country's past.

"I didn't do that well my freshman year," Dean recalled, "especially in language. I think it was because I didn't try hard enough." But he had always taken an interest in politics, spurred in part by the struggles he saw around him in Chicago, and when his brother came home with new research and ideas, the boys found a topic that would change Dean's whole approach to learning. "I spent a lot of time with my brother that summer," the economist remembered, "and it changed my motivation in school."

As summer temperatures edged upward, the boys debated and discussed, shared books and perspectives, challenged arguments, and examined evidence. The older brother had been reading books by, among other historians, Gabriel Kolko and William Appleman Williams, scholars who disputed the conventional historical narrative, and he shared those books with Dean. In them, they found ideas that lit a fire, questioned much of the orthodox interpretation, and introduced them to narratives they had never encountered before. The boys pored over the texts, interrogating ideas and evidence, exchanging passages, debating the implications, and pursuing more information.

Chicago temperatures along the shores of Lake Michigan floated between the seventies and nineties that summer, as they do in most years, and on the hottest days the sandy beaches lining the edges of Lake Michigan filled with bathers. On the coolest days, a refreshing and brisk breeze swept across the lake. Not far from where the boys conducted their running conversations, the Chicago Cubs played baseball at Wrigley Field on those magic days of cool weather and in the heat of an afternoon game on the fourth of July. Even on the hottest days, however, the nights usually turned cool enough to sleep without an air conditioner.

One historical development in particular piqued Dean's interest that summer and for years to come. Years later when he sat in a jury pool waiting to join the panel that would decide someone's fate, he remembered those stories. "It was about Mosaddegh," he explained, "the prime minister of Iran," who had been elected to that position in 1951, long before the boys were born.

Mohammad Mosaddegh, the sixtieth and sixty-second parliamentary leader of modern Iran, came from an aristocratic family but carried out economic reforms that benefited workers and peasants. He gave them unemployment benefits and pay when they were sick or injured. Peasants won freedom from forced labor, and Mosaddegh taxed landlords to build public projects to benefit common folks. In Iran at the time, what later became BP (British Petroleum) controlled much of the economy through its ownership of the oil reserves in the country. The prime minister ran afoul of both the U.S. and British governments when he said the wells should belong to the Iranian people, and on August 19, 1953, the American Central Intelligence Agency organized a coup to oust him from power.

Even though it happened before the Baker brothers were born, the violent overthrow of a democratically elected government in another country shocked and disturbed both of the boys as they read the historical account. Every childhood mental model they had constructed about U.S. foreign policy came into question, rocking their most cherished beliefs and raising new curiosities about how the international system really worked. "We'd been told that the overthrow of Mosaddegh was part of the Cold War struggle against tyranny," he remembered, "but that didn't make sense in light of the historical record. Mosaddegh wasn't a Soviet agent, just a progressive reformer seeking justice for his own people, and he wasn't a tyrant. The coup against him protected the financial interest of a large oil company." The Baker boys' seminar explored those issues all summer, driven by curiosity and their own sense of justice. They read what intrigued them. They understood and remembered what seemed important. As July trailed into the warm days of early August, the boys debated and discussed, picking their own path through material that the older brother brought to the table, and the younger now adopted as his own.

The fall after that magic summer with his brother, Dean didn't return to school but took off to travel around Europe. When he came back to campus a year later, he applied for and won admission to the honors program at Swarthmore, which had produced many creative and critical thinkers. In an environment of small seminars meeting weekly, students engaged in dialogue and often led the discussion with their own work. Dean learned to question everything.

He looked for the assumptions behind arguments and the concepts they employed. He thought about their implications and applications, and asked for evidence, questioning the source and nature of that supporting information. He analyzed the reasoning employed by his classmates and in the source material, noting in particular the way language is sometimes used to distort thought and enflame passions.

Even before joining the honors program, he took a multidisciplinary course on behaviorism and explored one central question: What controls human actions? "You had to understand before you could critique," Dean explained, "and the professor didn't tolerate a bunch of stupid criticism." The next year, he took a course in U.S. economic history, in which some of the questions of that sophomore class once more came into play.

In the honors program at Swarthmore, professors became primarily coaches and mentors, helping students to prepare, rather than judges making final assessments of students' work. Dean and his classmates spent two years preparing for two days at the end of their senior year when outside examiners—experts in the field— would come to campus to evaluate their work, engage them in conversations, exchange ideas, challenge their thinking, and decide whether they received honors for their work.

Dean came to understand his own learning style and knew that he worked best when he had more freedom, when he could help design his own education. "That's why I went to Swarthmore," he explained. "I chose it also," he said, "because they had an emphasis on undergraduate education and good teaching." The quality of instruction made a difference to him, but his growing fascination with and concern for the world carried the day. "Most of the teachers I had were quite good," he noted, "but even if they weren't, I could usually find something interesting to read in the course."

Increasingly, Dean became fascinated with how economic forces shape people's lives and how economies work. As he plunged into a wide variety of disciplines, he could tap the wisdom of those fields while thinking constantly about what he believed and why, integrating and questioning. "I was always looking for arguments in something I read," he explained, "and then pinpointing the evidence to see how it was used." His deep empathy with other people bolstered his quest, but so did his ability to chuckle at himself and the absurdities around him. With laughter and seriousness, he learned to solve problems and ask questions that no one else bothered to raise. By bringing his own, broad perspective reasoned from the evidence and from the insights of others, he could sift critically through a rich array of arguments and keep only those that met his highest standards of reasoning and evidence. Years later, after he had acquired a doctorate in economics from the University of Michigan, he used those critical habits to see through the faulty arguments of economists who wanted to roll back social security payments and later to see a looming economic collapse when few others saw it coming. Grades, however, never played a large role in his education. "I just didn't care about them," he explained. "They were decent enough, and that's all that mattered. I was more interested in what fascinated me."

The philosopher Andrew Chrucky could have been describing the kind of education Dean received when he wrote that liberal education helps people find just ways to resolve conflict. "Liberal education should," he wrote, "empower individuals to try to reach agreements . . . on what is economically and politically advantageous to everyone." Such an outcome stems from dialogue, he argued, from struggles with moral problems drawn out of "history, anthropology, sociology, economics, and politics."[6] In that kind of liberal education, students learn to engage in those exchanges as they come to understand the nature of discussion "through a study of rhetoric and logic," and as they discover how to express themselves in writing and speaking. They engage in discussions in which they challenge one another's arguments, pointing out any problems with evidence or reasoning. They reject or accept arguments not out of personal whim but because they have engaged in the highest rational judgments. A liberal education helps them develop the ability to do that reflective thinking.

Our best students generally crafted that kind of education for themselves, engaging in dialogues that brought their own perspectives to bear yet tested them against the values and concepts of others and against the rules of reason and the standards of evidence. They told us about long discussions with friends in the dormitory and library; the sometimes fierce debates that erupted; the personal struggles they had with questions of morality, justice, and other issues; the sometimes all-night mental battles they joined with an author they had read. They pinpointed the differences between agreeing (or disagreeing) with someone's facts, or agreeing (or disagreeing) with their attitudes.

Stephen Colbert, who made his fame and fortune in comedy, struggled with Robert Bolt's essay on values. Jeff Hawkins, the computing pioneer, pondered the work of philosophers, using the thinking of John Searle to distinguish in his own mind between what computers and human thought can do. Journalist David Protess engaged in those running seminars with professors and other students. Duncan Campbell looked for justice, entered law school hoping to find it there, but eventually discovered it in his own project to help disadvantaged youth. Mary Ann Hopkins explored the performing arts, humanities, and the sciences, searching for examples of justice for war-torn and poverty-ridden worlds, but ultimately finding the answers in her own actions. Repeatedly, we heard stories of multidisciplinary expeditions; of conversations late into the night; of lifetimes of reading absolutely everything; of explorations for those insights, ideas, and facts that could feed their brains. We heard in all of that a thirst for knowledge, a quest for originality, and a pervasive concern for justice.

## The Freedom to Choose

Emma Murphy majored in political and social thought, studied Russian literature, and had never taken the standard pre-med courses or the MCAT examination that usually determines who gets into medical school. Yet during her junior year at the University of Virginia, she won admission to Mount Sinai School of Medicine. If she accepts the appointment, she will join a long line of students with humanities and social science backgrounds who have attended medical school.

Mount Sinai School of Medicine began the program to attract students with broad liberal arts educations into a profession that doesn't always encourage that kind of educational depth. How have these students performed in comparison with students who had more traditional preparations that focused almost exclusively on the sciences?

Researchers at the school recently compared the two groups and found that on a wide variety of measures the liberal arts students did just as well or better than students who didn't necessarily pursue that broad undergraduate education.[7] They performed with distinction in the clinic, in clerkships, and in the classroom, and were more likely to do scholarly research and "graduate with Distinction in Research." Furthermore, they more frequently chose primary care specialties. Emma believes that her experiences have made her more compassionate and empathetic, able to understand better the plight of her future patients. "These students," noted Dennis Charney, dean of the medical school, "help to diversify our student body" and create a "vibrant educational community and a more stimulating training experience."

Much of Emma's schooling and family life had nurtured deep approaches to learning and a concern for big issues in life. When she was growing up in suburban Maryland, her parents, both physicians, encouraged her curiosity. "My father would sit down and discuss anything with me," she recalled. Emma came from a home with rich religious roots where values, purpose, and faith filtered into nearly everything she did. "Religion was always a structure in our weekly routine," she related. "In high school, personal faith became a very important aspect of my life." From the first through the twelfth grade, she attended a "wonderful independent private school" that offered small classes and an emphasis on the liberal arts. "My classes were no bigger than ten or twelve people," she recalled, and in those surroundings, she explored major questions and learned to read critically and to write well. Her teachers shared their passion "for what they were doing," and their devotion had a strong influence on the young girl. "I was encouraged," she emphasized, "to ask questions."

But Emma lived in a world that also fostered strategic concerns and buffeted her with powerful extrinsic motivations. Her parents wanted their three daughters to do well in school academically, and her society took pride in the students who won admission to the most prestigious private colleges. Her older sister went to Princeton University, and she saw herself going to an Ivy League school as well. In class, she faced subtle pressures to make the grade. "I had been trained in high school to measure my studies by what the teacher said, as if I was quantitatively mapped on some graph," she confessed. Like many young girls of her social class, she took up ballet, in which she also excelled. But in this activity, as in her schoolwork, she felt pressured to follow a certain path in life. "In that pre-professional environment, I developed anorexia and had to enter a treatment center for a month," she explained. Confined to a hospital, Emma felt isolated and abandoned but never hopeless. The incident had a profound influence on her thinking and values, and later encouraged a deep empathy for anyone facing incarceration. It was perhaps the beginning of a transformation that extended into her work at the University of Virginia.

When Emma went off to college, she stood between two worlds, one ready to intensify those extrinsic pressures and drive her toward a concern for strategic considerations, the other appealing to life's purpose, its values and personal development. The first might have promised a fast trip to academic honors, glory, and a fat paycheck, but the second raised questions about the meaning of life. She came to Virginia almost by accident, with an application for the Jefferson Scholarship program submitted at the last minute. She visited the campus before she entered and found "passionate and creative" students. "It was an easy decision to make," she decided.

Her curriculum allowed the Maryland native "to chart her own course of study" around politics and society, and that freedom sparked deep intentions and broad interests. Early in her studies, she took several classes from Bill Wilson in the religion department that helped shape the direction she would take. "When you were grappling with a text," she explained, "he never took the attitude that he was the expert and if our interpretation didn't match his we were somehow failing." Emma remembered that her professor valued the questions she raised and how she tackled them in her writing and thinking. "Grades became irrelevant to that discussion," she concluded.

In her junior year, Emma took an unusual class that cemented her commitments to a broad and deep liberal education. Students in a Russian literature class conducted regular seminars for residents of a juvenile detention center. "We weren't reading to write papers just to sit on some professor's desk," Emma explained, "but to search for key meanings and personal connections. We had to explore the Russian classics from the perspective of the child who had been marginalized by the justice system." Emma's life had little in common with the boys she met at the detention center. Yet she could pull from her own experience as she struggled to comprehend their plight. "I could remember," she explained, "when I was confined to the hospital and wanting to get back to a healthier place." The experience sparked a larger concern for justice, and for the issues of purpose and the values that the literature raised. She emerged from the class conscious of the common humanity we share, and with a strong sense of control over her own education.

Emma isn't sure if she will take the offer to attend medical school. She wants primarily to pursue a career that brings her into contact with other people and allows her to be creative. Among the people we studied, we saw the same pattern repeatedly of wanting more than a rote challenge or prestige from their careers. They sought an education that didn't leave out contemplation or a sense of wonder, even if they had to blaze their own trail.

## Selecting a Path

On a crisp spring day in northern California, young Dudley Herschbach walked along a creek bed looking at everything around him. He took such walks often, marveling at the trees and rocks, ripples of water that stood in small pools and flowed gently to some other spot, and the little creatures that populated these miniature worlds. He noticed the birds, the incredible array of flying feathered species that sometimes perched on a limb or swooped in for a meal. Many years later, long after he had gone to Stanford University to play football, turned down an invitation to try out for the Rams professional football team, won a Nobel Prize in Chemistry, and done a voiceover for the Simpsons, he remembered those birds and the walks he took. They were like good teachers, raising questions, sparking imagination, and invoking awe with his world. "I had a lot of time to myself just to daydream," he remembered.

Dudley was the oldest of three boys and three girls, children of parents who struggled during tough economic times. His father built houses to make a living and took pride in the details of his work. "My father would tell stories about his craft and how important it was to do a job right," the scientist recalled. "He always said, someday someone will take this house apart and realize how well it has been built. Doing it right requires a little longer."

Stories became a big part of his young life. When he was four and five, his house often filled with aunts and uncles—his father's brothers and their families mostly—who gathered to tell tales of their adventures in the world. His grandfather could spin a yarn about encounters with bears that were bigger than a garage, which would both scare and beguile the young children gathered around him. Soon Dudley learned to read his own stories. "When I was three and four," he reported, "I kept wondering what was in those balloons that pointed at the heads of the cartoon characters in the funny paper." Like an archaeologist deciphering an ancient Mayan code, Dudley painstakingly uncovered the secrets of all those letters in the comic balloons. "I remember once," he said, "going through the newspaper with a red pencil and underlining all the words I knew." His mother helped him with some, but he read others in context and decoded their meaning.

After he learned to read, his family bought him a three-volume set of the history of the world that had been written for children, and Dudley raced through all of them before he started the first grade. "We didn't have an intellectual household," he stated. "Before that encyclopedia we only had copies of the Bible, Ellery Queen mystery novels, and Reader's Digest." When he was nine or ten, those books perished when his house burned to the ground early one morning. After the fire, Dudley became dependent on the library and a librarian who recommended books. "She played a large role in my education," he recognized.

He read history, science, and some literature. His parents often gave him books for Christmas or for his birthday, and he explored *Treasure Island* and traveled with *Robinson Crusoe*. When he was eleven, he picked up an issue of *National Geographic* that focused on planets and constellations and fell in love with the mysteries of nature. He searched for other books on the heavens and made star maps. It was his first major scientific exploration, and while science and math increasingly became his focus, he continued to explore literature, history, and biography. "I realized," he explained, "that you are only one person in one period of time. Reading allows you to expand, to live other lives in other times. You learn to write from what you read." In high school, he discovered the rich tapestry of

Shakespeare's plays and eventually loved the music of mathematics and probability.

Such exploration produced an extraordinary imagination. He learned to hop easily from one perspective to another, to make connections that few had imagined, and to ask questions that no one had framed before. "Because I had a lot of time as a kid to daydream without any adult telling me what to do," Dudley observed, "I learned to think like a hound dog sniffing out its prey. My thinking bounces around a lot rather than following a linear path."

Dudley Herschbach fell in love with life—its mysteries, intrigues, beauties, problems, challenges, and even its tragedies. Like so many of our other subjects, he pursued a broad education, dipping into a variety of disciplines, yet ultimately concentrated deeply on the world of chemical science. He enjoyed the thrill of conquest and the fascination of an unsolved problem, and took that joy into playing right end on the football field, but he also took it into the classroom. Dudley has a strong sense of his uniqueness, born both out of his personal history and from the learning he achieved. In his mind his intelligence and personality are not frozen in place but constantly evolving, permanently changed by everything he learns. "You think of yourself differently," he said, "if you have mastered something. You realize that you are separate, you are different. You have been empowered in a special way."

Like so many of our subjects, Dudley discovered early in life the power of teaching. In high school, he began to tutor his football buddies who struggled with history, math, chemistry, and a variety of subjects. In their conversations, Dudley and his teammates built their understanding, socially constructing the ideas that emerged. It offered the budding scientist a chance to make sense of complex concepts and to explain them to others in ways that made sense to him. He once took a math class in high school from a rotund fellow fresh from the war who lacked deep insight into his subject but expected each student to "explain why you calculated the problem the way you did." In more than one class, teachers insisted that their students take the lead and explain matters to one another. "I think this might be called peer instruction today," Dudley surmised many years later.

Dudley loved sports and keeping physically fit. The games he played—football and basketball—came from a twentieth-century corporate culture and trafficked in time, space, and lines. Unlike the nineteenth-century game of baseball, in which every individual stands alone at the plate exercising an individual opportunity to hit the ball, these competitions emphasized coordination and cooperation, and in that sense bore a resemblance to the world of scientific research, where he would eventually land. When he entered Stanford, the university had offered him both an academic and athletic scholarship, but Dudley chose to accept only the former, giving him the freedom to make a fateful choice. When his football coach told him he couldn't take any science labs because they would interfere with practice, he quit football. Even when the Los Angeles Rams later tried to entice him into a tryout for their team, he "wasn't even tempted." He'd made one of those tough choices that distinguished many of our subjects.

Although he pursued a broad education, he recognized that he would not excel in all areas. "I always have to remind myself that Yo Yo Ma once said, 'I can't sing, but I can play the cello.' You can explore the world, but you don't have to be superior in everything." He remembered a colleague, a distinguished scientist, who never felt comfortable solving quadratic equations, but he did world-class work in organic chemistry. Dudley, like so many of our subjects, didn't beat himself up over what he couldn't do best but instead found those areas that appealed to him. He constantly looked for new associations that could broaden his perspective rather than narrow his vision to a single focus. He wasn't afraid to try new areas simply because he might not shine. Instead, he looked for ways to connect, to see something from a new perspective. Years later, after Dudley received his Nobel Prize for work on colliding molecules in chemistry, he mused that maybe his interest came from those collisions on the sports field.

At Stanford, Dudley felt both the freedom to do as he pleased and the responsibility to become organized. He found a little nook in the library where he did most of his studying, and in that quiet place with no distractions, every morning from nine to twelve, he studied history, science, math, and other intellectual subjects. He could lose himself in ideas and stories, problems and solutions. Because he took a deep approach to these, he became absorbed with every subject, making outlines of what he was learning, connecting dots in one area to the circles and squares in another, and losing track of time. "Some of my friends thought I never studied," he recalled, "but I was just well organized and concentrated intensely."

Within each subject, he learned to ask new kinds of questions that other fields didn't necessarily explore, and he acquired a diverse capacity to solve problems that, in turn, helped him learn deeply in any one field. "Some authorities," he would write many years later, "object to allowing students to sample almost willy-nilly the smorgasbord of courses." But for Dudley, the great virtue of such an education came in learning to question in different kinds of ways. "In such sampling, [we] meet different kinds of questions and wildly diverse criteria for evaluating answers," he explained. With that liberal arts experience, "we learn to challenge evidence and patiently puzzle out our own answers." The liberal art of questioning and measuring answers with "various yardsticks," the scientist concluded, became "essential for scholarly work" and for "meaningful participation in a democratic society."

No one explanation can capture why our subjects developed such broad interests and pursued vigorously that liberal education for the free person. Ability and success alone cannot explain the choices they made. Although curiosity played a central role, so did a sense of purpose, a devotion to some greater cause, and a concern for a just society. They loved beauty in all its forms, often learned as children the power of stories and the excitement of solving puzzles, and they used their college experience to engage and stimulate their minds. They understood education as a developmental process in which they sought to grow the power of their minds, and that too influenced the kind of learning they attempted.

Some pursued that broad and integrated study earlier and more vigorously than did others, and those in our group who pursued it most consistently and extensively exhibited the most impressive accomplishments. Furthermore, while our best students developed broad interests and the capacity to integrate abilities and insights from a wide variety of domains, they ultimately chose a stage upon which to play out their lives and careers. For some, that venue changed from time to time, and for most, it combined activities in unusual ways, but they knew when to focus, to perfect their talents. The decision to specialize didn't mean turning off all those other interests. Rather it meant using everything they had learned to create in one or two primary areas. Most important, they didn't define themselves in terms of the profession they pursued, the contraption they invented, or the song they sang, but instead as creative, curious, compassionate, concerned, and caring human beings, citizens of the world.

# 8

## Making the Hard Choices

Jo Rowling, the woman who created Harry Potter, recently stood before a Harvard graduating class and told them a story from her own life. When she went off to the university to study, she said, her "parents, both of whom came from impoverished backgrounds and neither of whom had been to college," hoped that she would study something "useful," a subject that would earn her a living and keep her out of poverty. They wanted her to pursue "a vocational degree," she explained. "I wanted to study English Literature."

Perhaps after some family bickering, she reached a compromise with them and went to school "to study Modern Language." But that didn't stick. "Hardly had my parents' car rounded the corner at the end of the road than I ditched German and scuttled off down the Classics corridor," she told the graduating seniors.

"I cannot remember telling my parents that I was studying Classics," the author confessed. "They might well have found out for the first time on graduation day. Of all the subjects on this planet, I think they would have been hard put to name one less useful than Greek mythology when it came to securing the keys to an executive bathroom." At the time, Rowling, whose writings eventually made her one of the wealthiest people in the world, simply followed her own passion. Yet that turn down the classics corridor had monumental consequences for her and for millions of her readers and moviegoers.[1]

None of us can, of course, plan to be Jo Rowling and write best-sellers that rival her Harry Potter series, yet a choice of one's major field of study in college plays a huge role in the life of every college student. I can't say that I found many distinct patterns among our subjects. Mary Ann Hopkins was a bit like Rowling, picking Latin on her way to medical school simply because she found it beautiful. Debra Goldson chose social psychology, both because she found it interesting and because she thought it would help her to be a better physician. In both these cases, and in general, our subjects chose their field of study with a purpose, for the sake of beauty, intrigue, fascination, practicality, or whatever.

Picking a major is one in a series of decisions that students make that can have an enormous influence on their academic successes, their growth as human beings, and their lives as creative and productive individuals after college. The trouble is, most of us often don't think much about the choices that really matter.

Which decisions make the biggest difference? If we are to understand what our best college students did that helped them become highly creative and productive people in later life, we must identify those key choices—not so much to see which way they turned, although that can be helpful too, but to see what questions mattered most.

Thus far, I've written little about grades, and virtually nothing about how to make good ones. But I said back in Chapter 1 that, although the general thrust of this book is decidedly not just to help students make the honor roll, eventually I would offer some advice on that quest too. You can, I argued, take a deep approach to your studies and still obtain those high marks. I'd still contend that if getting on the dean's list is a student's primary concern, she or he is less likely to achieve either a deep approach or a creative life. This chapter is the closest I will come to providing that conventional guide to high marks and "academic success." To compose it, I've used both the practices of the amazing people I interviewed and the vast and growing body of research literature on everything from study habits to time management.

This chapter is not, however, some magic book of answers you can follow like a recipe—as if you were baking a cake rather than fashioning a life. It requires deep thought and crucial judgments about a variety of messy problems. It offers food for thought as well as practical procedures you can apply immediately.

Underlying each of the questions we are about to explore lie three key points: First, travel through these areas requires students to change paths from time to time, or even to backtrack and follow a different road when needed. Second, it demands that people accept and even embrace failure, and realize how much they can benefit from falling short. Jo Rowling said it recently: "Failure taught me things about myself that I could have learned no other way." Third, and perhaps most important, students must find a purpose for their education, take control of the process, and believe that they can constantly expand their abilities and achieve.

## What Keeps You Working?

Some years ago, Walter Mischel, a psychologist at Stanford University at the time, concocted a now-famous experiment in which he promised four-year-olds a marshmallow immediately or two of the fluffy treats when he returned from an errand. If they wanted to eat one of the white balls right now, all they had to do was ring a bell, but they would get only one rather than the two they would receive if they waited. He then left the room, leaving them with a plate full of tempting goodies, including the marshmallows, cookies, and pretzel sticks. Some of the children couldn't resist the temptation, and once all the adults left the room they either gorged themselves on the treats or rang the bell instantly. Others, however, resisted, and held out for the greater rewards to come.

In the years following that experiment, Walter and his colleagues started keeping track of the children and their progress through life. Some astounding conclusions emerged from the data they collected. Children who could wait the longest generally grew up to become productive and successful students and adults while those who opted for immediate rather than delayed gratification often had behavioral problems in school, did less well academically, had trouble keeping their friends, and on average compiled SAT scores that were two hundred and ten points lower than those who could wait.

Was there something special about those who could delay gratification, or did they learn some secret technique to keep them from caving in to temptation? Over the last twenty-five years, psychologists have found that children who can resist best find ways to distract themselves from thinking about the marshmallows. They want the treat as much as the others do, but they learn to concentrate on something else rather than focusing on the goodies. Furthermore, the social scientists have discovered that if they can teach kids some mental tricks to turn the enticement into something else in their minds, such as pretending it is just a picture of the tempting treat rather than the real McCoy, they could greatly increase the amount of time the youngsters could wait. "Once you realize," Walter Mischel observed recently, "that will power is just a matter of learning how to control your attention and thoughts, you can really begin to increase it."[2]

For our best students, learning to put aside tempting distractions became part of their plan for getting themselves to work. Their approach frequently paralleled that of Walter's kids who could best delay their gratification. In major part, they decided that they had a purpose for their education and that they were in charge. With that purpose and personal control firmly in mind, they learned to distract themselves toward their studies and away from the party they might attend, the website they could visit, the telephone call they could make, the computer game they could play, or any other enticing diversion. They became so engrossed in their work that they didn't have time to think about what else they might do. But that determination often came also from a mixture of moral commitment, empathy, and compassion, and the role their work might play in that dedication to some higher purpose. Often that meant finding the importance of the overall goal, then zooming in on the details of the task at hand to get started.

Some people told me they had to think about each step in, say, writing a paper, from picking a question to walking to the library. Many of them set deadlines for themselves and held themselves accountable, letting those self-imposed limits distract them from the marshmallows in their lives. They also had to believe that they *could* do something. Whether it was Stephen Colbert finishing a three-year theater program in two, or Neil deGrasse Tyson understanding the heavens, they often kept themselves on task by thinking about the broader rewards of their quest. They let the joys of their own passion for something plus a higher moral commitment drive them through even the most distracting circumstances.

Yet I cannot contend that any one technique worked for everyone. Instead, there is a larger point about their approach that deserves the lion's share of our attention. Their secret came in dedicating themselves to the development of the dynamic power of their own minds and the use of that mind to create a better world, and then exploring what worked, ultimately not depending on anyone else's prescriptions. Instead, they were constantly open to any good approach they encountered in others. Some people, like Tia Fuller, Neil deGrasse Tyson, Dudley Herschbach, and others, did make out a schedule and followed it religiously.[3] Others didn't. Yet they all did what worked for them, sometimes borrowing ideas they learned from others, but never assuming that self-control and delayed gratification came in only one size.

In one of Paul Baker's exercises that Sherry Kafka and others encountered, students thought about some creative work they had done in the past, whether it was baking a pie, writing a story, creating an outfit, solving a math problem, or whatever. They would then examine what it took for them to do that work. What attitudes did they have? Did they control their actions or respond to someone's command? What rituals did they perform, such as making out a schedule or eating ice cream? What did they tell themselves? What did they visualize? Where did they work, for how long, and at what time of day? What did they value? Did they connect the job to some larger purpose? Did they keep constantly in mind the feeling they would have once they had finished, did they focus on each step along the way, or both? How did they feel when they finished the work? Did they enjoy the task, or simply value the results? They had to talk to themselves and to understand their own minds and how they worked, and it was that personal examination that led to the particular practices that drove their labors rather than some tight prescription of activities and procedures.

In recent years, several researchers have looked at the other side of this coin, exploring what causes people to put off tackling a job when they know and believe that they will be better off for finishing it. People in general, and college students in particular, are notorious procrastinators. While that research has explored various aspects of why people delay doing some jobs and what they can do about it, one dominant theme emerges. As Timothy Pychyl, director of the Procrastination Research Group at Carleton University, said, "Procrastination is about not having projects in your life that really reflect your goals."[4] Our subjects found ways to avoid procrastination because they had strong intrinsic motivations and projects that fully reflected their goals.

Common wisdom holds that to break the grip of procrastination we must condemn it in ourselves, rebuking the habit like a stern taskmaster. Yet the studies that Timothy and others have conducted echo and complement a theme we have already explored: forgive yourself. He found that undergraduate psychology students who forgave themselves for putting off their studies on the first examination were less likely to procrastinate on the second exam than were those who beat themselves up over their earlier misdeeds. That kind of forgiveness, however, is not the same as approval. As Kristin Neff has suggested in her concept of self-comfort, forgiveness implies confronting bad behavior, understanding that humans tend to procrastinate, and mindfully searching for ways to overcome it without condemning yourself as a bad person. We found that our best students followed a similar pattern in their thinking. They didn't judge earlier performances but instead focused on what they needed to do to improve.[5]

## What Teachers Should You Choose?

Certain websites can tell you how "hot" or "easy" a professor is, but they offer little insight into whether an instructor fosters deep approaches and achievements in learning. For an earlier book, I studied professors with enormous success in fostering deep learning. To no one's surprise, these master teachers clearly knew their subjects extremely well, and could think deeply about them. But how does a student measure an instructor's knowledge and thinking ability? It is difficult at best. One good way is to look at how the professor assesses students' work. If they use tests that merely require you to memorize information and spit it back, steer clear. That may suggest that the teacher's knowledge and understanding doesn't run deep. Look for people who expect students to develop an understanding and use it to analyze and solve important problems. Based on my studies, the following factors seem to be most important in determining whether the class will provide a good learning experience, assuming that the professor does know her stuff.

1. Is the course built around clearly identifiable questions to be pursued or abilities to be mastered, and does it help students see the importance, beauty, and intrigue of those questions and abilities? Repeatedly, our subjects told us about life-changing courses that had a central question. What is justice? What causes wars? What does it mean to write more effectively and how can I learn to do it? Who has power and how is it exercised? Does evolutionary theory explain why we have different kinds of animals and plants? How do you calculate the area under the curve?

2. Does the course allow students multiple opportunities to engage in those higher order activities in pursuit of those questions or abilities, receive feedback, and then try again before anyone "grades" their work? Or does everything ride on one or two high stakes tests or papers where there is no chance to revise and improve what they have done? In their own intellectual work, professors constantly seek feedback from colleagues, revise their work, and seek more re-

sponses before submitting a paper to a journal, for example. As they do so, none of their colleagues are likely to say, "you're making a C thus far." Instead, they offer substantive comments on how a paper or a line of thinking can be improved long before anyone makes some final judgment about their work. Yet those same people sometimes build courses that fail to offer those opportunities to their students. They teach then test, and the score from each exam lies frozen in the grade book, a permanent record from a single experience. Grades in that type of class reflect various points students have reached in their learning over the semester rather than what they have achieved by the end of the term. There is no sense that the marks might reflect the abilities the students had acquired by the end of the course.

When Derek Bok, the president at Harvard at the time, asked Professor Richard Light to identify those experiences that students found most intellectually satisfying, Light and his colleagues interviewed current and former students. When he published his initial results, the professor reported that those most pleasing courses set high but meaningful standards, goals that were important to students long after the class was over, but they also, as Light once told me, "gave students plenty of opportunity to try, come up short, and try again before anyone put a final grade on their effort."

3. Do students have the opportunity to collaborate with other learners struggling with the same problems, questions, and abilities? Does the instruction foster that collaboration?

4. Does the class encourage speculation, and an opportunity to exercise new skills even before students are well-versed in the discipline? People learn by doing, yet some courses insist that students must simply memorize myriad facts before they can plunge into doing any substantial intellectual, physical, or emotional work. Other

courses will get students involved even before the students know much, helping them to learn as they practice in a nonthreatening but stimulating atmosphere.[6] Those latter classes are like the way most people learn to play the piano. They don't memorize keyboard strokes for months before putting their fingers on the ivories. Aristotle said it best long ago, "For the things we must learn to do before we can do them, we learn by doing them."

5. Does the course challenge existing ways of thinking and seeing the world? People build mental models of the world and then tend to use those paradigms to understand everything they encounter. One of the great traditions of a liberal arts education is that it ideally helps students realize the problems they face in believing whatever they may accept, putting them in situations in which their existing models do not work. Other courses will never challenge anything, and still others will simply expect students to accept a different dogma without questions or reasoning.

6. Does the course expect students to grapple with important questions, mount their own arguments, exchange ideas, accept challenges, and defend their conclusions with evidence and reason?

7. Does the course and professor provide the kind of support that students need as they struggle with important, intriguing, and beautiful questions? This support may take many forms: intellectual, physical, and sometimes even emotional.

8. Do students come to care about the inquiries, the promises and invitations of the course, and about whether their existing paradigms feel challenged and do not work?

9. Do students in the class generally feel in control of their own education, or manipulated by requirements?

10. Do they believe that their work will be considered fairly and hon-

estly and in keeping with standards that are important beyond the class?

11. Does the course encourage and help students to integrate the questions, concepts, and information broadly with other courses and with their understanding of the world?

12. Does the course offer inductive opportunities to learn, moving from specific examples to general principles? Or does it offer only general principles to be memorized and regurgitated?

13. Does the instructor genuinely care about the intellectual, emotional, and ethical well-being of students, and help and encourage them to think about the kind of world they want to help create and live in, and the meaningful philosophy of life they would wish to forge? Is such caring built into the structure of the course? Does the professor model integrity, raise important ethical questions, focus in any way on values, encourage reflection, and help students think about their meaning and purpose in life and the kind of person they want to become? Does he or she foster self-examination, a sense of justice, empathy, and social responsibility? Is the instructor demonstrably interested in helping students become critically thinking, curious, creative, caring, and compassionate individuals? Do the policies and activities of the course reflect those concerns? Has the instructor struggled with her or his own sense of purpose, integrity, and justice, and made contributions that further those aims? Have those struggles been shared with students?

14. Do students believe that their work in the course will matter, that it will make a difference in the world?

15. Does the instructor clearly believe in the students' abilities to grow, to develop the dynamic powers of their minds, or does the teacher assume that abilities come prepackaged, with little or no chance to

improve? Does the instructor have a fixed or flexible view of the intelligence and talent needed in the class?

## What Do You Do When You're Bored?

Some people told me that they never had any highly stimulating teachers, yet they managed to learn deeply and to emerge as adaptive and creative people. They remained active learners, no matter what the instructor did. They formulated big questions, even if the professor didn't. In the midst of a mind-numbing lecture, the active learners speculated about possibilities, applications, and implications. "I always found something of interest," became a common refrain from our subjects. Most important, they explored actively outside of class, reading and thinking, searching and contemplating. "With the Internet, the possibilities are almost endless," one person said. They took control of their own education and remained ultimately responsible for its content and quality.

## How Will You Read?

When you pick up a book or article and run your eyes over words on a page, what happens in your mind? What's going on as you read these pages? "To tell someone to read a book," says David Dunbar, a teacher in the CITYterm program at the Masters School, "is like rolling out soccer balls and asking someone who doesn't know anything about the rules or strategies to go play the game." Reading can take many forms, and how it is done makes a huge difference. We discovered that our students who emerge as highly creative and critically thinking individuals often employ a series of approaches to their reading.

1. They read with deep intentions. Before opening the book, they have questions in mind: What's this all about? What's the point? How does this relate to other subjects? How does this challenge me? They intend to find meaning in the text and to apply it to some problem. Like a detective in search of clues in a murder mystery, they begin scouring the text with questions that lead to more inquiries. They realize that the little lines that we call letters and words are mere symbols, standing for some reality outside the page: an idea, an event, a concept, or something of the sort. They go looking for that meaning that lies behind the page, treating the printed word as a window through which they can see something else.

2. Before beginning the reading, they speculate on what they expect to find, confirming and dismissing those predictions as they go. Good readers invent the book they think they are about to encounter. They imagine questions and possible solutions, and then measure those guesses against what they eventually find on the printed page. Such a practice helps them to make sense of the reading, but it also serves another important purpose. A growing body of evidence strongly suggests that speculating and predicting *before* finding the "correct answer" helps people become adaptive experts, better able to conquer unusual problems.[7] They enjoy taking on the unknown, those cases where the routine procedures don't work. If they have experience in speculating before they "learn," they will likely appreciate how an easy solution that seems so obvious can prove to be so inadequate when compared to what some expert has devised. The next time around, they will be wiser for it, looking for holes in their own thinking. As John Bransford, a learning scientist, put it, "adapting to new situations often involves 'letting go' of previously held ideas and behaviors,"[8] and he and others have discovered that people are most likely to reach that point if they have first specu-

lated about possible solutions before they read what an authority has to say.

3. They examine a book (especially a nonfiction one) or article before they read it, looking through its table of contents for clues about purpose and structure, reading any summary sections first, skimming through headings, and noticing the kinds of evidence and grand conclusions offered. Is it organized inductively or deductively? When was it published? What do I know about the author? Why did she write it? What major questions is he trying to answer? "I often spend thirty to sixty minutes raising questions about a book before reading it," one person told us. Does it have tables and charts? What can they tell you? Is it part of a series? If so, what's the purpose of that series, and how does this book fit into the broader scheme? What do I want to get out of this work? What questions am I trying to answer? Does the book address them directly, or focus on some important tangent of my primary concern? Do I understand the abstract of a scholarly paper before plunging into the body of it? Should I read the discussion before plodding through the experiment?

4. Our best students make connections as they read, relate to bigger questions, pause to contemplate and integrate. They write notes in the margins or jot down ideas and reactions in a notebook. Sometimes they struggle with what questions they want to ask, but those struggles become part of the reading process.

Making connections, especially in science, math, and engineering disciplines, often means visualizing concepts, grappling with ideas, thinking about their implications and applications, asking about evidence in an argument or experiment, looking at procedures but thinking constantly about ideas that lie behind those steps, and applying that emerging understanding to some larger problem.

5. With fictional literature, they connect in a variety of ways. What are the great philosophical questions that this novel or short story raises, if any? How does it help me confront my life and the world in which I live, or the one that I would like to create? They can look at a poem for its beauty and rhythm, but they can also explore any literature as a reflection of a culture or a time and place. They can contemplate its challenge to values and perspectives, or analyze its symbols and metaphors and how they invoke certain thoughts and emotions. Is this the story of a quest? A microcosm of a broader world? Is it like a zoo or museum rather than a journey? How is language used to create certain emotions? Why do I cry or laugh? Or laugh to keep from crying? Does the book help me be more empathetic and compassionate? Does it help me join a different community, and to understand the values and perspectives of the writer? How does it treat space and time, rhythm and movement, silhouette and sound? How do those treatments compare with the way the study of physics, for example, might approach the same subjects, or how my culture approaches them? Does it help me see issues of justice and morality differently? How does it do that? What is unique about the way I will approach this play or novel? Given my background and origins, the soil and people and homes that produced me, why do I respond as I do to the literary conventions that this work employs? When I read an opening line of a great novel like *One Hundred Years of Solitude,* why do certain words conjure up such strong images, mystery, and intrigue: "Many years later, as he faced the firing squad, Colonel Aureliano Buendía was to remember that distant afternoon when his father took him to discover ice."

6. In nonfiction, making connections often means looking first for arguments in the text, recognizing that not every statement rests within an argument but that every argument contains both a con-

clusion and premises offered in support of that conclusion. Sometimes that means recognizing that some conclusions are implied rather than stated, and so are some premises.

When students actively take apart an argument, they can begin to ask questions about those parts. Do the premises support the conclusion (or, as we often say, "does this make sense?")? What alternative ideas can I draw from the same information? What is missing? If I accept the premises, must I accept the conclusion? Or does the evidence make it highly probable? What major concepts does this argument employ, and what assumptions does it make? How is this related to something I've looked at in other classes, and in life?

7. They evaluate the quality and the nature of the evidence. If the evidence comes from inference, does it makes sense to ask from what it is derived? Are there other possible ways to look at the same evidence? If it came from an observation, does it help to find out who did the observing and from what perspective?

8. As active learners, they recognize the kinds of agreements and disagreements that exist between this text and other items they have read and with their own notions. Two people can have different attitudes while entertaining the same beliefs. Or they can believe something different and either agree or disagree in attitude. In historical studies, for example, two scholars can both agree on what caused the United States to become involved in the Second World War but disagree on whether the country should have done so. If the disagreement is strictly about values, no appeals to evidence will likely make a difference. If they are about beliefs, then evidence becomes important. Sometimes conflicting attitudes flow from differences in belief, but not always. As students contemplate these possibilities, their minds become sharper and more systematic.

9. Many of our subjects outline when they read, and later reduce that

initial summary, taking notes on notes on notes. With each step in that reduction, they can begin to judge evidence and conclusions, to poke at the testimonies and generalizations, to notice what concepts are employed, what assumptions have been made, and to think about their implications and applications. Many people keep a dictionary at their side, looking up unfamiliar words, or, better yet, speculate about their possible meaning, deriving definitions from the context, then testing those suppositions once they are able to check the reference book.

10. Our best students engage in all cognitive activities at the same time. They remember, understand, apply, analyze, synthesize, and evaluate as they read. Many college professors, however, organize their courses as if that list of mental activities has to be conquered in order rather than in an integrated fashion. They insist that students memorize large bodies of information before thinking about the data. But the human brain doesn't work that way. If I asked you, for example, to "learn" the following numbers (that is, remember them), you might find it impossible to do: 149162536496481. But if you first realize that they are merely the square of the numbers one through nine ($1 \times 1$ is 1; $2 \times 2$ is 4; $3 \times 3$ is 9, $4 \times 4$ is 16, etc.), they are easy to recite. You must understand before you can remember. If you have applied that comprehension to some consequential problem, it is that much deeper and more meaningful. You can improve your ability to apply if you have taken ideas and information apart and looked at their elements and the relationships among them. You can enhance that capacity to analyze if you have tried to put things back together in new ways. If you have evaluated something with the ideas and information involved, it all becomes more meaningful. (Recall Mary Ann Hopkins and her father, taking apart the family car in the garage. The process is the same, whether it is with

cars or arguments.) When Benjamin Bloom and his colleagues came up with their famous list of activities in which the human brain could engage (recall, understand, apply, analyze, synthesize, and evaluate), there was nothing in that taxonomy that said it had to be conquered in order. Yet many teachers will organize learning as if it does.

11. They read as if they plan to teach. John Bargh and his colleagues discovered long ago that if students merely study as if they are planning to teach, they will remember and understand more. In a now classic experiment, he asked one group of students to study some verbal material for themselves. He instructed others to prepare to teach it to someone else. The second group retained far more, even if they never actually taught anyone.[9] Our best students went far beyond that principle, applying it not just to the memorization of words in a list but to the understanding of ideas, their applications and implications.

At Saint Olaf College in Minnesota, students in large introductory psychology classes discovered the benefits of preparing to teach elementary students some topic from their college class. "Challenging yourself to teach a fairly complex scientific concept to elementary students," one Saint Olaf undergraduate reported, "forces you . . . to understand the concept inside and out, and . . . to be creative in designing ways to teach."[10] It produces elaborative approaches to studying that connect and integrate.

At the University of Virginia, students in Andrew Kaufman's Russian literature class don't just read and discuss *War and Peace;* they take Tolstoy behind bars, preparing seminars for inmates of a juvenile detention facility. The undergraduates go into the Beaumont Juvenile Correction Center, an hour east of the university campus, and help young boys jailed for a variety of offenses. They read Russian literature to grapple with three fundamental questions: Who am I? Why am I here? How should I live? "This class is applied literature," one student concluded. "You're applying it to your life." To get into the course, students must first petition the instructor for admission, taking charge of their own education and joining what Parker Palmer and Andrew Kaufman call a "community of truth," a place where people explore questions and ideas rather than just receive facts. As they battle with some of the deepest questions of our existence and prepare to stimulate that same struggle within young incarcerated males, they learn in ways that profoundly influence how they will subsequently think, act, and feel. As a result, they build deep relationships with the material, one another, and the young people they encounter at Beaumont. "It seemed like everyone was there listening to each other," one student reported. "It goes back to that common ground. We all wanted to be here," another volunteered. "For once, I was actually able to take literature and apply it to a situation. I had almost forgotten that was possible," admitted a third student. "It was very rare to find people commenting just to hear themselves talk," one person observed. "In other classes my main motivation is graduation. Motivation in this class was not to let these guys down. I had to be here to make sure they understand."

These Russian literature students lost sight of the grade and experienced, many for the first time, a focus on understanding deeply. As they prepared not just to explain something to someone else but to stimulate in that person a deep consideration of some important idea, the undergraduates in this class developed their own profound comprehension and appreciation. Few students get an opportunity to teach, and even when they do, it often centers on preparing a presentation rather than fostering a conversation. Yet we heard from people who certainly understood the value of elaborating on their own learning, preparing as if they planned to help someone else learn and exploring the rich variety of ways that they might confront a body of material.

Much the same full-bodied investigation and elaboration takes place in "reading" a lecture. The best students will associate and integrate, interrogate and examine. One trick students use is to take two sets of notes. One records important information and ideas. The other jots down questions, reminders, speculations, implications, applications, and possibilities. Some students will draw a line down the middle of a page, with space on the left for all those inquiries. On the right, they record any information, procedures, concepts, or ideas. And they learn to process and elaborate as they hear something new rather than simply becoming a stenographer trying to "get everything down." Some people take notes in class and then make notes on their notes as soon as possible. "I would buy these 'second sheets,' really cheap yellow paper, and take notes on that in class, and then later make more permanent notes in a spiral notebook," one person reported.

We didn't investigate Isidor Rabi, a Nobel Laureate in physics, but he supposedly once attributed his habit of elaborated learning to his mother. "My mother made me a scientist without ever intending it," he said. While other parents in Brooklyn, where he grew up, asked their children what they learned in school, his mom had a different inquiry every day. "'Izzy,' she would say, 'did you ask a good question today?' That difference—asking good questions—made me become a scientist!"[11]

Only in this context can we understand something that several of the people I interviewed told me. "I didn't really study that much," they said, "although I read a lot." That obviously doesn't mean they never cracked a book. In fact, they spent long hours in the library reading or in the laboratory doing experiments. It means that they didn't depend on last-minute cram sessions or rote review of material, but rather that they constantly elaborated, questioned, explored. They took ideas and arguments apart as they read them. What about this idea or information speaks to me? Is it the line, rhythm, sound, space, or shape? How does it influence my values? Does this make sense? Why? How is it related to something we discussed in another class or some consequential problem? As they read and questioned, probed and contemplated, speculated and evaluated, our best students came to understand and apply, and as they did, they remembered.

## How Will You Study?

Yet there comes a time when students must review material, and how that process unfolds makes an enormous difference. On cold winter days at the University of Minnesota, snow often covers the campus. When spring begins to melt the frozen white blanket, crocuses bloom all across the fading ice, adding little dots of color here and there. Even before green leaves spring from the dormant branches of trees and bushes, the first breath of nonfreezing temperatures prompts students to don their summer garb, perhaps hoping that if they dress for the occasion, they may hasten the arrival of balmy weather. Into this environment in the late 1960s came James Jenkins and Thomas Hyde, and an experiment that would help spark a revolution in thinking about how best to study.

The two psychologists created several groups of students and gave them a list of words to study. They asked some students to notice something rather trivial—whether each word had the letter E in it. They instructed others to rate each item on the list for its "pleasantness." Presumably, those doing the rating would have to think about meaning while the others simply noticed letters. Not surprisingly, the students who did the rating could recall more of the words when tested.[12]

What caught the eye of later psychologists was the simple notion that if students process material actively and meaningfully, they will remember more than they will if they simply repeat it a million times or notice something trivial about it. Over the next forty years, researchers continued to investigate what approaches to study will work best. Scores of writers published guidebooks on how to make good grades based on that research, and Claude Olney, a business professor at Arizona State University, made a small fortune selling cheeky videotapes and DVDs entitled "Where There's a Will, There's an A." Yet most of the conclusions in all that material have several major flaws. For one, those results came from looking at which approaches produce the most recall and the highest grades. They haven't generally investigated which ones support deep learning and creative lives. For another, any of those techniques can be employed in behalf of strategic goals, yet once students focus exclusively or even primarily on getting the A, they are unlikely to become deep learners, adaptive experts, or highly creative people.[13]

Are there some key techniques that will both grow the dynamic power of the mind and support academic success? I think there are, and they are found largely in the approaches that we saw among our best students. Not surprisingly, those ways of doing things have strong support from the research on human learning, yet they require a special rereading of that literature in light of our stories about highly creative people and the vast and growing body of work on deep learning. What does the research tell us about how best to review material?

*Elaborate, elaborate, elaborate.* Associate, associate, associate. Make connections. Ask questions. Evaluate. Play with words in your own mind. Have fun. As Jenkins and Hyde demonstrated, even the somewhat silly notion of rating a word on its "pleasantness" will help. When I introduced their ideas, I set them in the context of snow and winter in Minnesota, greatly increasing the chances that you will remember where they did their original research and even what they concluded. You can think about the rhythm a word conveys, the lines and colors of its meaning. The more associations you make, the greater your chances of recalling it later.

*Develop an understanding before trying to remember.* Recall the number example I mentioned earlier (14916, etc.)? This same principle applies to virtually anything you might try to stuff away in the memory banks. Understanding requires a deep network of associations, and it is those intricate strands of connection that make recalling even possible. I'm currently trying to learn Chinese characters used in writing Mandarin. At first, the task seemed almost impossible, and every guidebook I consulted advised blind memory, repeating them over and over again. Yet I began to make progress only when I started taking them apart, noticing that they often consist of several characters, each with its own meaning. I set about making up stories with them, and learning other tales that native speakers and readers have passed down for generations. The character that means the same thing that the English word "cry" conveys now looks to me like a stick figure of a person with two large eyes, a single tear dripping from the corner of the left one. The character for "forest" consists of three smaller stick drawings of a tree. The one for "good" contains the characters for woman and child.

*Repeat, repeat, repeat.* No matter how much I try to associate, I can remember some characters only after repeated exposure. But how often should I repeat them? Does it pay to repeat endlessly the night before the big examination, or to stretch the same number of repetitions over days and weeks, perhaps spending less total time? Diligent students will often spend hours trying to memorize dates and names, parts of the cell, or other details. Recent research has discovered, however, that some of that traditional process can be a waste of time.

Consider how the brain works. When you encounter something new—let's say a new word—you will begin to forget it almost immediately, and a day later you might not recall it at all. But a second exposure will extend the time you can remember it. And so will a third, a fourth, and so on. Each time you hear it, you can wait a little bit longer before encountering it again and still not forget it. If that next exposure catches your brain just before the word falls out of mind, you can restore its freshness. But what is the ideal space between exposures, both for immediate recall on an examination and for how it will influence the way you will subsequently think, act, and feel?

Although research offers no definitive answers to this question, it seems clear that the empirical studies reinforce the patterns I saw among the people I interviewed. In general, they spaced their repetitions and, most important, studied them in the context of making connections with other things. Several people have tried to work out exactly how long you can go before you need another injection, with the general notion that each time you encounter something, you can go longer and longer before the next exposure. Some popular language learning programs, like Pimsleur, are based in part on this principle. Each time you hear a new word, you will meet it again within a few seconds, but the third instance might be a minute later, the fourth, several minutes on, and the ninth time could be the next day. Computer-assisted flashcards, like SuperMemo and Anki, have even tried to work out algorithms for exactly how long those intervals should be, and some people argue that any more frequent exposure simply wastes time. Although some empirical researchers doubt the evidence, millions of language learners have found great success using carefully spaced repetition techniques. These programs have become increasingly popular among students in translation schools in Europe and second-language learners in China.[14]

All of that suggests that you will benefit most from spacing study over several weeks rather than just massing it right before a big test, although a last-minute brush-up *after* weeks of study could help ensure more accuracy on the examination. Furthermore, that is exactly the pattern that I noticed among our subjects. They read and reviewed constantly, taking notes on their notes and immersing themselves in the material as they went. Dudley Herschbach and others made outlines upon outlines. Tia Fuller began preparing essays, writing out her thoughts repeatedly, using new language and ideas frequently until they became a part of her.

Can you spend too much time reviewing? Probably, especially if all of that time comes massed right before an exam. If you space it out properly over many weeks, you can most likely spend less total time and achieve more then you would in an all-night cram session. Computer programs can help focus your attention on the hard-to-remember items, giving less but still enough time to the items you remember easily.

Yet repetition will pay its greatest rewards if done in the midst of meaningful and elaborated work. Thus, I remember more from my language tapes, in which I'm engaged in conversations that seem authentic, than I do from flipping through flashcards, even though the latter sometimes help polish my skills. I recall characters that I see frequently in interesting passages that I read, rather than those I meet only on the backside of my study cards.

*Testing is better than rehearsing.* A growing body of evidence strongly suggests that if I test myself on that vocabulary, even when I get it wrong, I will learn more than I will simply going over and over the same material. Something happens in the brain when we force it to dig something out of its deepest barrels. The act of searching, trying to recall, and piecing together something builds strong and stable connections that just never emerge from repeating the item again and again. That may be one of the reasons that explaining a concept to someone else helps you to remember what you understand. In that environment, you test your ability to recall. When I listen to my language tapes, I benefit most if I stop the player and try to remember a phrase rather than waiting for the narrator to give me the answer. Humans construct their memories each time they bring them to mind, and those repeated constructions when I test myself make it easier to rebuild them the next time. We heard stories from students who had studied together, quizzing and probing one another, each person taking a turn at teaching the others.

Suppose you begin by just guessing and getting everything wrong. Will that help as much as trying to recall correct answers? Shouldn't you at least study first before attempting to remember something? If you just guess wildly before somebody tells you the right answer, you'll undoubtedly get it wrong, and won't that practice of incorrect information diminish your learning? Quite the contrary, argues some recent research. In experiments at the University of California at Los Angeles, psychologists gave students two different ways to learn some material. Half of them had to guess at a response first before seeing the correct one. The others studied first. So who did better on a subsequent examination? Those who had first generated possible answers, even though they were all wrong, scored significantly higher than the students who had spent their time reviewing the material first. In another experiment, the researchers gave students a scientific article on vision. Half the subjects just read the article, then faced a test on how much of it they remembered. The others took a test *before* reading. Later, they took another exam to see how much they could recall. Even though those who read first had copies of the article that highlighted and italicized all of the material that would be on the exam, and those who speculated first didn't, the speculators did significantly better on the final exam.[15]

*Do you always study in the same spot? Don't.* If you study in different places, that helps create variety, and that rich experience can reinforce what you are learning. When Tia Fuller and others told us they did school work in different places rather than in some favorite nook, that habit reflected the research on learning. Numerous experiments have found that if learners simply study in at least two different places, they are more likely to recall the material. In one of the first such trials, two different groups studied a list of words. Some students returned to the same room twice while their counterparts spent the same amount of time divided between two locations. When asked to recall as many words on the list as possible, those who had moved around did far better. Variety creates rich association, even when those connections form in the background, totally outside of what we are consciously thinking.[16]

*Don't multitask, but do study more than one subject at a time.* That probably sounds like contradictory gibberish, but it's not. Watching television while reading history or playing a computer game while trying to write a paper keeps you from concentrating. Numerous experiments have found that with the exception of a very few routine tasks that we've done repeatedly over many years, the human brain can't really perform two different tasks simultaneously. Thus, we can walk and talk at the same time, but we can't really read a book and watch television simultaneously. Instead, we will, at best, switch constantly between the two, taking twice as long to finish the book and getting less out of it.[17]

Try this experiment. First, write each of the letters from A to Z. Then do the same for the numbers 1 to 26. Next, write the letters and numbers alternately: 1, A, 2, B, and so forth. If you timed both trials, you'd find that alternating between the two tasks takes far longer then doing the numbers and then the letters. Multitasking doesn't work.

But we also have evidence that students remember far better and understand more deeply when they constantly integrate subjects together, even ones as different as chemistry and history. Thus, studying two or more subjects almost simultaneously can help create that integration. That might mean alternating between the two in ways that constantly look for connections, and finding ways to think about one in the context of the other. Dudley Herschbach saw links between research on polymers and the outcome of World War II. The chemistry research allowed the United States to develop artificial rubber at a time when Japan sought to conquer all of the rubber tree–growing areas of southeast Asia.

*Find a quiet place with few if any distractions.* Or maybe two or three of them. Some students believe that they learn best while listening to music, and some may. The research doesn't give us definitive answers, but several studies have found that while introverts and extraverts will both learn less while listening to music, introverts will suffer the most.[18] Other research finds that instrumental music works better than vocals, but both can be distracting. Much of the outcome may depend on you. Once more, examining your own experiences can help guide your decision. You must be honest with yourself, however, and distinguish between what you want to do and what really works.

*Exercise.* Recent years have produced considerable evidence that the brain and learning benefit from regular and steady exercise, adequate and scheduled sleep, and healthy and balanced diets. Studies have found, for example, that regular aerobic exercise can help increase the size of the hippocampus, an area of the brain that contributes to memory.[19] Wendy Suzuki, a professor of neuroscience at New York University, found that students who did aerobic exercise for an hour before listening to a lecture did significantly better than students who didn't.[20] Paul Baker grasped something similar long before the medical research accumulated. Prior to each of those classes in the Integration of Abilities course, students did both vocal and physical exercises.

*Speculate, sometimes wildly, about possible solutions and connections even before you know anything.* When you encounter a math problem or a historical puzzle, begin to suppose this and that, playing with possibilities and developing tentative hypotheses but always recognizing that anything you might conjure out of your imagination has to be tested. Don't just wait for someone to give you the answer.

## How Will You Write?

Just write. A growing body of research tells us that putting words on paper (or a computer screen) can have enormous benefits, especially if you use that exercise to examine yourself, your life, your values, and even your most traumatic experiences. Examples abound in the literature. As I noted in Chapter 3, physics students at the University of Colorado who wrote for fifteen minutes twice a semester on what they valued earned higher marks than their classmates who didn't. In Japan, investigators found that college undergraduates who wrote expressively about some traumatic experience in their lives improved their working memory capacity.[21] At North Carolina State University, social scientists found similar results. Freshmen who wrote about their "thoughts and feelings" upon entering college improved their working memory significantly while those who penned essays on more trivial matters didn't.[22] After decades of exploring the influence of expressive writing, the psychologist James Pennebaker sees even larger benefits. "When people transform their feelings and thoughts about personally upsetting experiences into language," he wrote recently, "their physical and mental health often improves."[23]

"Write out your life story up to now, and write your reactions to everything we do," Paul Baker told his students early in the class. It didn't matter what they used, or even what they wrote. There was no right or wrong way to do it. Write in pencil, he instructed, "or with crayons. Whatever suits you." Most important, examine yourself and how you work. In his second exercise, Baker gave students a word and asked them to write whatever came to mind, to use stream of consciousness, to let their own words flow with no concern about form or the rules of writing.

In both Baker's class and in the psychological experiments, form and grammar rules didn't matter. Expression counted for everything. Writing with no standards in mind had huge benefits. But there comes a time in every student's life when their compositions must follow particular dictates. Honing one's writing skills is a matter of practicing diligently and listening to feedback. Is there anything from the lives and thinking of our subjects that might aid that process?

First, and most fundamentally, our most effective students recognize what's involved. "Learning to write," one person told us, "means joining a new community and accepting its standards." What makes something correct, and something else a mistake? A certain family of readers and writers has come to expect particular forms, and while those ideals vary, none of them emerged arbitrarily. They serve a purpose, worked out over centuries. They help make an essay compelling and clear, logical and persuasive. No language or punctuation is inherently "wrong." It is just different than what a certain community expects.

Second, good reading fosters good writing and vice versa. Like any wise novice, the best students pay attention to the tiniest devices of the masters of the language, recognizing good prose when they see it. Over time, they learn to emulate it. They pay close attention to the rules of language passed down over many generations of readers and writers, respecting the good ideas when they encounter them. Ultimately, however, they are willing to play with convention. They toy with sentences, twisting their parts one way and then another, discovering how the language works, learning what readers will expect, satisfying those needs, but also knowing how and where to employ the right surprise.

Finally, it takes time and dedication to write in ways that other people will want to read. People learn to write in a language by writing and getting feedback on their efforts, and our best students often sought classes that would give them that experience. But they didn't confine their efforts to school. Because they took a deep interest in their ability to think clearly and communicate, they worked on it constantly. Neil deGrasse Tyson, the astrophysicist who has published nine popular books in science and numerous articles, struggled with his writing but admired the clarity and engagement of the prose he read in the *New Yorker* magazine. He set out to capture those same qualities in anything he composed. "I would look at the efficiency of the language and how interesting the juxtaposition of words became, and I would aspire to that," he explained. "It took me ten years before anything I wrote rivaled pieces that appeared in the *New Yorker*."

## Are You Going to Join the Club?

No, I'm not talking about whether to join a Greek fraternity or sorority. Only a handful of our subjects joined a fraternity, sorority, or social club; most didn't. I speak here instead about the decision to join a community of academic learners, with all their rules and expectations, from when you must finish your work to how you can use other people's ideas and language.

When anyone goes to college, they enter a strange new world that has been evolving for centuries. That "club" of academicians has developed its own book of regulations about a variety of matters. Unfortunately, no one has bothered to publish that volume in one place or even to record all of the ordinances in it. Some things are just understood and never explained to students. Going to college can be like arriving at the gates to some mysterious city and being told that you must guess every password that will allow you to travel through the streets. "I figured out very early," Sherry Kafka wisely observed, "that all schools are cultures, and my job was to go into that school and understand how that culture works."[24]

Reading and writing may be treated very differently in physics and math than in an English class. A paper submitted successfully in one might be given a low grade in the other. None of this is to say that the standards of college emerged without rhyme or reason. There is common ground among disciplines, and there are often good reasons why scientists write differently than journalists (although most scientists and academics in general could learn much from the way a good journalist uses language). But sorting it out does present challenges.

Students arrive at the gates of colleges from assorted backgrounds, each with a different level of understanding of the culture that awaits. All have the chance to decide whether they will join the club, play by the rules, or forever remain an outsider. That means learning, among other things, all the rules of citation and attribution, and what it means to plagiarize. The most successful college students found they could do this while still maintaining a strong sense of control over their own education. Let me illustrate further with one of the most important but still controversial aspects of that culture: the requirements on "late work."

Colleges often have rules about when you must do your work. Personally, I think these standards are the most difficult to defend, but most of my colleagues disagree. Great creative work doesn't always conform to some timetable. Yet meeting deadlines sometimes becomes a necessity in our fast-paced society. We think in terms of seconds whereas our distant ancestors, with far less sophisticated ways of measuring time, thought in seasons and years. I frequently tell students that unless you want to make this your life's work, you need to finish it and move on to other projects. I can't give you more time, I say. Only the Angel of Death can do that. If you take more time on this project, you must realize that you are taking time away from the rest of your life.

Sometimes, finishing your work by a certain date becomes important to the integrity of the learning community a student has joined. That was certainly the case in Derrick Bell's law school class at New York University. The whole educational experience depended on students reading each other's work and responding to it. In most cases, however, the deadlines are set arbitrarily. But whether there are reasons for the "due date" or they result from professorial whim, wise students have to decide when to conform, when to move on, and when to challenge—or at least question. Some of our subjects chafed under strict guidelines and had to find teachers who exercised more flexibility. Eliza Noh found one such teacher when she was finishing her honors thesis following her sister's suicide.

A few years ago, at Northwestern University, I was teaching a class on the Cold War. I had asked students to read Mark Danner's heart-wrenching account, *The Massacre at El Mozote*. Danner, a journalist, tells the story of how American-trained troops had entered a small village in El Salvador in December 1981 during the country's civil war and butchered every man, woman, and child, save a few who had crawled in the bushes to escape. Danner had called the event a metaphor for the Cold War, implying that the international conflict was something more than just a struggle between the United States and the Soviet Union. I had asked students to read Danner's account and to ask themselves whether his characterization captured the full meaning of this event.

In the days that followed our initial discussion of the book, Joel, a student in the class, approached me with a special request. He had taken a deep interest in the events of the story, and he wanted to do his term project on what had happened and why. I had invited each student to pursue a historical question, gather evidence, draw conclusions, and then share their work. "You can write an essay advancing your historical argument," I told them. But I always added, half joking, "you can make a film, or write a play. But I'm primarily interested in your research and reasoning abilities." Most students wrote a conventional paper. But not Joel.

He wanted to write a play that would capture what had happened at El Mozote, what it represented in the Cold War, why the Reagan administration had sought to repress any knowledge of the events, and why the American press corps had largely ignored or denied the massacre. To do so, however, he needed to do more research.

I can't do that, he told me, unless I have more time. "I'll need an extension for the class." Because Northwestern, and schools like it, place heavy emphasis on finishing the degree in four years, the dean's office frowned on giving students extensions. But I agreed to Joel's request, and that summer, he did more research and wrote his play. In the fall, he gathered a cast of student actors, lighting technicians, and set and costume designers. He put everyone through a seminar on the Cold War in Central America in the 1980s, rehearsed the cast, and mounted the production for a two-week sold-out run on campus.

But the story didn't end there. The events of El Mozote continued to haunt Joel, and a year later, after he graduated from college, he traveled to El Salvador in search of more insights. He spoke Spanish but also hired an interpreter, and went looking for anyone who could tell him about the civil war in that country. He read through the forensic reports that Argentine researchers had compiled when they dug up more than 300 mutilated bodies, and he found Rufina Amaya, the woman who survived by hiding in the bushes while listening to her nine-year-old son cry out, "Mama, they are killing me."

"That trip to El Salvador had a profound influence on my life," Joel reported later. He stayed for a while in the refugee camp where many of the local peasants had fled during the war. He heard stories of unspeakable horror, including the account of a woman who had lived for several years up in the mountains trying to escape the violence below. She had been carrying her baby son when she was caught in the crossfire between competing groups and had run for miles to escape the violence, only to discover when she finally stopped that her child had been shot through the head. She buried the infant, but "went crazy" and lived for several years high in the mountains, wandering mostly naked and living like an animal. Finally, troops of the Farabundo Martí National Liberation Front (FMLN) found her and brought her back to civilization. Joel met her in a refugee camp where she lived.

After those encounters, Joel reported, "I decided that I wanted to do something to help people and bring a little justice to the world." He entered the University of Arizona law school and a joint program in Latin American studies. When he finished with that work four years later, he had both a law degree and a master's in Latin American studies. After passing the bar, he took a job with the Public Defenders Office, and now brings legal services to the poor. We first met him in Chapter 2. "I can't change the whole system," Joel Feinman observed recently, "but I can help individuals, bringing a little justice into their lives. My trip to law school and to this important work began by reading that book and taking that trip to El Salvador in search of El Mozote."

His work in my class was more than six months past the deadline, but did that really matter?

## What Will Rock Your Boat?

We return to the question that began our discussion and to a central point about success and creativity that our subjects reflect. You don't become creative simply by deciding that you will be creative. You don't become successful by deciding that you will be successful. You don't even focus on yourself. Yes, you do need to develop that conversation with yourself to understand how you operate. But your focus should be on what you want to learn, see, do, and change; what questions you have; what passions drive you—not on your own emotions or desire to be creative. If you focus exclusively on short-term success or on how famous you want to be with your creativity, you are unlikely to achieve success, creativity, or fame. Our subjects found something in the world that interested them more than themselves. Success and creativity—and sometimes fame—emerged as a by-product of full engagement with the problem or task at hand. You have to care about something and let your passion drive your life.

# EPILOGUE

$C$ollege students today face enormous pressures that many of our subjects never endured, or at least not to the same degree. Social, economic, political, and cultural forces compel them to follow a surface or strategic approach to their studies. With the cost of higher education rising and public financial support declining, many students face substantial debts to pay for their education. They often feel pressured to finish school as quickly as possible in order to reduce those debts and begin earning money to pay them back. They emphasize making money over every other goal in life, and fear for their future if they don't. And who could blame them? Many have to take jobs while going to school, reducing their opportunities to follow their own curiosities and take a deep approach. Deep learning requires time, and that's a luxury many believe they cannot afford. Under those circumstances, routine expertise may sound good enough and adaptive expertise far beyond their grasp.

For generations, some students have experienced an educational system that emphasizes surface and strategic learning. Indeed, that emphasis has grown in many places. Societies want to know whether students are learning and if education is a worthwhile investment, and they have imposed standardized tests on teachers and students to find out the answers. Those tests change everything, often encouraging everyone to emphasize rote memorization rather than understanding.

Even in the absence of pressure to achieve on standardized tests, some educators prize surface learning in the mistaken belief that it will suffice for some. "We need some surface learners," a professor told me recently, "who just know how to do the routines of life and their job." He had no sense that understanding might enhance recall or that everyone will face tough questions that require the ability to think and understand. The routine expertise his students acquire in college may quickly become outdated and stale. Pity his students, but they are not alone. All students encounter some educational experience that encourages them to think of learning as simply the ability to remember. Even the best schools often urge students to look for shortcuts. "When I entered college, and even in high school," a student explained, "all my counselors were telling me how to get required courses out of the way."

It takes enormous courage and dedication to take control of your own education and achieve the goals discussed in this book. Yet it is probably the only approach that makes any sense of the college experience, and certainly the one most likely to bring you self-satisfaction. No one can guarantee your long-term success in any sense of that word, but you can equip yourself with the skills for lifelong learning and adaptability, no matter what surprises the future has in store for you. In this book I have offered examples of many people, some from tough circumstances, who have surmounted obstacles and found their chosen life path. Most saw occasional failure or setbacks as events that helped them to understand themselves, seek new opportunities, or refine their goals. You should remember that you too will have time to mess up and recover if you take the right approach to all those disappointments. If you learn to realize the special contributions you can make and develop the capacity to benefit from other people's creations, you can flourish as a curious, creative, and critically thinking individual.

# Notes

# Acknowledgments

# Index

# Notes

### 1.  THE ROOTS OF SUCCESS

1.  All of the Paul Baker quotations appeared in at least one of the following sources: A set of class notes taken in the course in 1962, the recollections of Sherry Kafka and others who took the course, and in a book published in the 1970s that recorded Baker's remarks to his class at that time. Paul Baker, *Integration of Abilities: Exercises for Creative Growth* (New Orleans: Anchorage Press, 1977).

2.  One of the legendary stories is about Fred Smith, who wrote a paper in college that was the genesis of Federal Express, the billion-dollar corporation he founded in Memphis, Tennessee. Legend has it that Smith received a C on the paper, but he claims now that he doesn't remember what grade he received. "Fred Smith on the Birth of FedEx," *Businessweek,* Online Extra, Sept. 20, 2004. Available at http://www.businessweek.com/magazine/content/04_38/b3900032_mz072.htm.

3.  See I. A. Halloun and D. Hestenes, "The Initial Knowledge State of College Physics Students," *American Journal of Physics* 53, no. 11 (1985): 1043–1055.

4.  Michelle Brutlag Hosick, "Growing Power CEO Is NCAA's Theodore Roosevelt Recipient," *NCAA Latest News,* December 1, 2011. http://www.ncaa.org/wps/wcm/connect/public/NCAA/Resources/

Latest+News/2011/November/Growing+Power+CEO+is+NCAAs +Theodore+Roosevelt+recipient.

2. WHAT MAKES AN EXPERT?

1. A. Fransson, "On Qualitative Differences in Learning: IV. Effects of Intrinsic Motivation and Extrinsic Test Anxiety on Process and Outcome," *British Journal of Educational Psychology* 47, no. 3 (1977): 244–257; G. Gibbs, A. Morgan, and E. Taylor, "A Review of the Research of Ference Marton and the Göteborg Group: A Phenomenological Research Perspective on Learning," *Higher Education* 11, no. 2 (1982): 123–145; E. J. Rossum and S. M. Schenk, "The Relationship between Learning Conception, Study Strategy and Learning Outcome," *British Journal of Educational Psychology* 54, no. 1 (1984): 73–83.

2. N. Entwistle, "Strategies of Learning and Studying: Recent Research Findings," *British Journal of Educational Studies* 25, no. 3 (1977): 225–238; F. Marton and R. Säljö, "On Qualitative Differences in Learning: I. Outcome and Process," *British Journal of Educational Psychology* 46, no. 1 (1976): 4–11; F. Martin, D. Hounsell, and N. Entwistle, eds., "The Experience of Learning: Implications for Teaching and Studying in Higher Education," 3rd (Internet) ed. (Edinburgh: University of Edinburgh, Centre for Teaching, Learning and Assessment at the University of Edinburgh," 2005). http:// www.tla.ed.ac.uk/resources/EoL.html.

3. G. Hatano and Y. Oura, "Commentary: Reconceptualizing School Learning Using Insight from Expertise Research," *Educational Researcher* 32, no. 8 (2003): 26–29; T. Martin, K. Rayne, N. J. Kemp, J. Hart, and K. R. Diller, "Teaching for Adaptive Expertise in Biomedical Engineering Ethics," *Science and Engineering Ethics* 11, no. 2 (2005): 257–276; G. Hatano and K. Inagaki, "Two Courses of Expertise," in *Child Development and Education in Japan,* ed. H. Stevenson, J. Azuma, and K. Hakuta, 262–272 (New York: W.H. Freeman, 1986).

4. S. B. Nolen, "Reasons for Studying: Motivational Orientations and Study Strategies," *Cognition and Instruction* 5, no. 4 (1988): 269–287;

S. B. Nolen, "Why Study? How Reasons for Learning Influence Strategy Selection," *Educational Psychology Review (Historical Archive)* 8, no. 4 (1996): 335–355.

5. E. L. Deci, "Effects of Externally Mediated Rewards on Intrinsic Motivation," *Journal of Personality and Social Psychology* 18, no. 1 (1971): 105–115; E. L. Deci, "Intrinsic Motivation, Extrinsic Reinforcement, and Inequity," *Journal of Personality and Social Psychology* 22, no. 1 (1972): 113–120; E. L. Deci and R. M. Ryan, "The Paradox of Achievement: The Harder You Push, the Worse It Gets," in *Improving Academic Achievement,* ed. Joshua Aronson, 61–87. (Boston: Academic Press, 2002). http://www.sciencedirect.com/science/article/ B8651-4P9TW7V-9/2/fa234fce5f4141cc44f495a1ab1487f6.

6. First, they invited twenty-four students to play with a box construction puzzle, a Soma cube. It consisted of seven odd-shaped pieces that could be put together in a variety of ways, including some that would produce a cube. You could actually put them together in millions of different ways, but the trick was to produce a specific shape on any one trial. The students came one by one to a psychology research center, where they encountered this odd but fascinating little game.

The first time they showed up, the volunteers received four drawings and tried to reproduce them using the Soma pieces. After so many minutes, the experimenter left the room and watched each student through a one-way glass from an adjoining area. Experimenters wanted to see how long students would play with the Soma cube entirely on their own, without anyone to watch or encourage them. The latest issues of *Time,* the *New Yorker,* and *Playboy* sat on the desk, offering plenty of temptation to forget the puzzle.

Each student returned a few weeks later, again one at a time, to practice much the same routine, only this time half of the students—let's call them group A—received cash for right answers. Once more, the experimenter left the room for eight minutes. Surely, since they were getting paid, people in group A would use more of that time to practice using the Soma puzzle, and that's exactly what happened. The others didn't know about the money, so they spent about the same amount of time as they had before. However, when each student returned for a third individual session a week later, something strange happened that offers us considerable insight into why school can destroy curiosity and how creative people avoid that fate. The psychologists told the people in group A that they couldn't give them any more money. Meanwhile, those who had never received any payment just showed up and did the puzzle. When the experimenter left the room for eight minutes, the students who had been paid in an earlier session (group A) suddenly lost interest. The amount of time they spent on the puzzle plummeted. Meanwhile, those who had never had any extrinsic rewards kept on playing at their old rate.

7. E. L. Deci and R. Flaste, *Why We Do What We Do: The Dynamics of Personal Autonomy* (New York: G.P. Putnam's Sons, 1995).

8. A. W. Astin, H. S. Astin, and J. A. Lindholm, *Cultivating the Spirit: How College Can Enhance Students' Inner Lives* (San Francisco: Jossey-Bass, 2011), 3.

9. Tucson had emerged as a mission village in the eighteenth century, first as part of colonial Spain, and then as an outpost in northern Mexico. Local people could trace their ancestry to a rich cultural heritage that stretched back for thousands of years along the Santa Cruz River. They sometimes fought violently against the European settlers who came to their area, but over time intermarried with the Spanish newcomers and forged a Hispanic (or Latino) culture out of the unions. In the middle of the nineteenth century, the United States invaded Mexico and took control of the northern half of that country, including much of modern-day Arizona. Five years later, they forced the Mexicans to sell them the area around Tucson because some Americans hoped to run a transcontinental railroad through the region.

By the late twentieth century, many local Hispanics, both those whose families had lived there for centuries and the immigrants who crossed the border from the south, often felt isolated from power, education, and economic opportunities. Spanish-speaking people in Tucson valued tradition and culture, yet frequently found themselves the focus of mean-spirited caricatures that belittled their habits, language, and origins. They were often the targets of hatred and fear. Poverty rates within the Latino community, always high, edged upward as good jobs and education became increasingly difficult to obtain. "Non-Hispanic whites," as the census called them, collectively held most of the political and economic positions, but many of them feared an immigrant invasion from Mexico and sometime confused local Latinos with the people who came from across that border drawn in the nineteenth century.

10. M. E. P. Seligman, *Helplessness: On Depression, Development and Death* (New York: W.H. Freeman, 1975).

### 3. MANAGING YOURSELF

1. I. Halloun and D. Hestenes, "Modeling Instruction in Mechanics," *American Journal of Physics* 55, no. 5 (1987): 455-462; I. A. Halloun and D. Hestenes, "The Initial Knowledge State of College Physics Students," *American Journal of Physics* 53, no. 11 (1985): 1043-1055.

2. W. W. Maddux and A. D. Galinsky, "Cultural Borders and Mental Barriers: The Relationship between Living Abroad and Creativity," *Journal of Personality and Social Psychology* 96, no. 5 (2009): 1047-1061.

3. K. W. Phillips, K. A. Liljenquist, and M. A. Neale, "Is the Pain Worth the Gain? The Advantages and Liabilities of Agreeing with Socially Distinct Newcomers," *Personality and Social Psychology Bulletin* 35, no. 3 (2009): 336-350.

4. The scientific name for the alligator brain is the amygdala, but that isn't as much fun.

5. All of the Langer quotes come from E. J. Langer, *The Power of Mindful Learning* (Reading, MA: Perseus, 1997). For some of Langer's research see L. P. Anglin, M. Pirson, and E. Langer, "Mindful Learn-

ing: A Moderator of Gender Differences in Mathematics Performance," *Journal of Adult Development* 15, no. 3–4 (2008): 132–139; L. L. Delizonna, R. P. Williams, and E. J. Langer, "The Effect of Mindfulness on Heart Rate Control," *Journal of Adult Development* 16, no. 2 (February 2009): 61–65; E. Langer, M. Djikic, M. Pirson, A. Madenci, and R. Donohue, "Believing Is Seeing," *Psychological Science* 21, no. 5 (2010): 661–666; E. Langer, M. Pirson, and L. Delizonna, "The Mindlessness of Social Comparisons," *Psychology of Aesthetics, Creativity, and the Arts* 4, no. 2 (2010): 68–74; E. Langer, T. Russel, and N. Eisenkraft, "Orchestral Performance and the Footprint of Mindfulness," *Psychology of Music* 37, no. 2 (2009): 125–136.

6. E. J. Langer and A. I. Piper, "The Prevention of Mindlessness," *Journal of Personality and Social Psychology* 53, no. 2 (1987): 280.

7. Stanovich quotes come from K. E. Stanovich, *What Intelligence Tests Miss: The Psychology of Rational Thought* (New Haven: Yale University Press, 2009).

8. Drew Westen, *The Political Brain: The Role of Emotion in Deciding the Fate of the Nation* (New York: Public Affairs, 2007).

9. K. E. Stanovich, "Rational and Irrational Thought: The Thinking That IQ Tests Miss," *Scientific American Mind* 20, no. 6 (2009): 34–39.

10. Reacting to the Past, http://reacting.barnard.edu.

11. Stephen Fry, "Learning," interview video and transcript available at http://www.videojug.com/interview/stephen-fry-learning.

12. J. Kounios and M. Beeman, "The Aha! Moment," *Current Directions in Psychological Science* 18, no. 4 (2009): 210–216.

13. For a good discussion of stereotype threat research see C. Steele, *Whistling Vivaldi: And Other Clues to How Stereotypes Affect Us* (New York: W.W. Norton, 2010). See also C. M. Steele and J. Aronson, "Stereotype Threat and the Intellectual Test Performance of African Americans," *Journal of Personality and Social Psychology* 69, no. 5 (1995): 797–811; C. M. Steele, S. J. Spencer, and J. Aronson, "Contending with Group Image: The Psychology of Stereotype and So-

cial Identity Threat," *Advances in Experimental Social Psychology* 34 (2002): 379–440.

14. See J. Aronson, M. J. Lustina, C. Good, K. Keough, C. M. Steele, and J. Brown, "When White Men Can't Do Math: Necessary and Sufficient Factors in Stereotype Threat," *Journal of Experimental Social Psychology* 35 (1999): 29–46.

15. See N. Ambady, M. Shih, A. Kim, and T. L. Pittinsky, "Stereotype Susceptibility in Children: Effects of Identity Activation on Quantitative Performance," *Psychological Science* 12, no. 5 (2001): 385–390; M. Shih, T. L. Pittinsky, and N. Ambady, "Stereotype Susceptibility: Identity Salience and Shifts in Quantitative Performance," *Psychological Science* 10, no. 1 (1999): 80.

16. See L. E. Kost-Smith, S. J. Pollock, N. D. Finkelstein, G. L. Cohen, T. A. Ito, and A. Miyake, "Gender Differences in Physics 1: The Impact of a Self-Affirmation Intervention," in *AIP Conference Proceedings* (2010) 1289: 197.

#### 4. LEARNING HOW TO EMBRACE FAILURE

1. C. S. Dweck, *Mindset: The New Psychology of Success* (New York: Random House, 2007).

2. C. I. Diener and C. S. Dweck, "An Analysis of Learned Helplessness: Continuous Changes in Performance, Strategy, and Achievement Cognitions Following Failure," *Journal of Personality and Social Psychology* 36, no. 5 (1978): 451–462.

3. L. S. Blackwell, K. H. Trzesniewski, and C. S. Dweck, "Implicit Theories of Intelligence Predict Achievement across an Adolescent Transition: A Longitudinal Study and an Intervention," *Child Development* 78, no. 1 (2007): 246–263.

4. M. L. Kamins and C. S. Dweck, "Person versus Process Praise and Criticism: Implications for Contingent Self-worth and Coping," *Developmental Psychology* 35, no. 3 (1999): 835–847.

5. R. Perry, N. Hall, and J. Ruthig, "Perceived (Academic) Control and Scholastic Attainment in Higher Education," *Higher Education:*

*Handbook of Theory and Research* (2005): 363–436; T. L. Haynes, L. M. Daniels, R. H. Stupnisky, R. P. Perry, and S. Hladkyj, "The Effect of Attributional Retraining on Mastery and Performance Motivation among First-Year College Students," *Basic and Applied Social Psychology* 30, no. 3 (2008): 198–207; N. C. Hall, R. P. Perry, J. G. Chipperfield, R. A. Clifton, and T. L. Haynes, "Enhancing Primary and Secondary Control in Achievement Settings Through Writing-Based Attributional Retraining," *Journal of Social and Clinical Psychology* 25, no. 4 (2006): 361–391; N. C. Hall, S. Hladkyj, R. P. Perry, and J. C. Ruthig, "The Role of Attributional Retraining and Elaborative Learning in College Students' Academic Development," *Journal of Social Psychology* 144, no. 6 (2004): 591–612.

6. A. Bandura, "Self-efficacy: Toward a Unifying Theory of Behavioral Change," *Psychological Review* 84, no. 2 (1977): 191–215.

7. J. S. Lawrence and J. Crocker, "Academic Contingencies of Self-Worth Impair Positively and Negatively Stereotyped Students' Performance in Performance-Goal Settings," *Journal of Research in Personality* 43, no. 5 (2009): 868–874; J. Crocker and L. E. Park, "The Costly Pursuit of Self-Esteem," *Psychological Bulletin* 130, no. 3 (2004): 392–414; J. Crocker, A. Canevello, J. G. Breines, and H. Flynn, "Interpersonal Goals and Change in Anxiety and Dysphoria in First-Semester College Students," *Journal of Personality and Social Psychology* 98, no. 6 (2010): 1009–1024.

8. Jeff had read a philosopher named John Searle who had posed a problem that pointed out the difference between understanding and what computers can do. It's a problem that also illustrates the difference between surface and deep learning. Searle had told a story about a fictional man who worked in the "Chinese Room." The room had a desk, lots of paper and pencils, and a huge instruction book. The book gave him detailed instructions on how to manipulate Chinese characters. Some of the instructions said, "draw this line," others, "erase this one," or "move this one over here," and so forth—thousands of detailed, line-by-line instructions like the

kind children might use in putting a three-dimensional dinosaur puzzle together. But not a single word in all of the instructions, written in the man's native English, provided a translation of any of the Chinese characters. He didn't have the foggiest notion what any of them meant.

One day, someone slipped a piece of paper into his office that contained a bunch of Chinese characters on it. In Chinese, it was a story followed by some questions, but the man didn't know that because he didn't understand this foreign language. He picked up the paper, took out his huge rule book, and followed the instructions—change this line, move this character, erase this one, and so forth. Finally, after following the rules one by one for hours, he reached the last instruction. He had produced a whole new set of Chinese characters, but because he didn't know the language, he still had no idea what any of it meant. He slipped his result under the door, and outside a Chinese speaker picked it up and read it. She noted that the paper contained a perfectly written answer, in Chinese, to the questions that had been posed about the story. Someone asked her if those answers came from an intelligent mind that understood the story in Chinese. "Of course," she answered.

But where is that intelligent mind? the philosopher asked. It certainly wasn't in the man who followed the instructions. He had no idea what he was doing, other than blindly following the instructions. That intelligent mind certainly wasn't in the book. It wasn't even in the person who wrote the instructions because that person never saw the story or the questions. Searle's point, of course, was that the man was like a computer that had been programmed to translate Chinese characters, but that computer did not have human intelligence. My point in retelling this thought problem is that surface learning is a lot like the man in the Chinese Room. It might produce correct answers, but it has no human understanding.

9. Charlie is a pseudonym for a composite figure. The students in the

experiment averaged scores in the 35th percentile (that is, on average, 65 percent of students did better) on sixth-grade math tests. Fifty-two percent of them were African American, 45 percent Latino, and 3 percent White or Asian. They came from low-income families with nearly four in five qualifying for free lunch.

10. The researchers had asked all of the teachers to report any students who demonstrated either a decrease or increase in motivation, but the teachers didn't know that students were receiving different experiences or which students were in which group. The teachers identified improved motivation in 27 percent of the students who read the article about how the brain changes, but only in 9 percent of those who read the article on how memory works. Blackwell, Trzesniewski, and Dweck, "Implicit Theories of Intelligence," 256.

## 5. MESSY PROBLEMS

1. Chicago Innocence Project, Mission Statement, available at http://chicagoinnocenceproject.org/mission.

2. "Much of politics," Shawn Armbrust concluded, "has to do with how we treat poverty." The program in which Shawn worked rested on the notion that if poor people could finish high school, they could get a job and avoid dependence on welfare. Many of them had dropped out of school because they needed to make money but had discovered that without a degree they couldn't earn enough to survive. Here were people "desperately trying to improve their lot in life," she remembered, but facing an unkind future. "Once they got the degree and a job they were required to get," she noticed, "the community center babysitting service would end, and there would be no way to take care of their kids, meaning they either had to stop work or abandon their family."

3. S. Armbrust, "Chance and the Exoneration of Anthony Porter," in *The Machinery of Death,* ed. D. Dow and M. Dow, 157–166 (New York: Routledge, 2002), 163.

4. Ibid., 165.

5. All of the Kitchener and King material comes from their website, Reflective Judgment, available at http://www.umich.edu/~refjudg/index.html.

6. *Teaching Teaching & Understanding Understanding,* a short film about teaching at university, part 3; video and transcript available at http://www.daimi.au.dk/~brabrand/short-film/part-3.html.

7. "Biggs' Structure of the Observed Learning Outcome (SOLO) Taxonomy," pamphlet, University of Queensland, n.d.; see also J. B. Biggs and K. F. Collis, *Evaluating the Quality of Learning: The SOLO Taxonomy (Structure of the Observed Learning Outcome)* (New York: Academic Press, 1982).

## 6. ENCOURAGEMENT

1. Kristin Neff, "Epiphany," videotaped interview available at http://www.youtube.com/watch?v=LfMDhZxXSV8&feature=related; see also Kristin Neff, "Epiphany," in *Epiphany: True Stories of Sudden Insight to Inspire, Encourage, and Transform,* ed. E. Ballard, 114–118 (New York: Random House, 2011).

2. N. Branden, *The Six Pillars of Self-Esteem* (New York: Bantam Books, 1994), 5; cited in R. F. Baumeister, J. D. Campbell, J. I. Krueger, and K. D. Vohs, "Does High Self-Esteem Cause Better Performance, Interpersonal Success, Happiness, or Healthier Lifestyles?" *Psychological Science in the Public Interest* 4, no. 1 (2003): 1–44, 3.

3. Ibid.

4. See discussion in J. Crocker and L. E. Park, "The Costly Pursuit of Self-Esteem," *Psychological Bulletin* 130, no. 3 (2004): 392–414.

5. J. S. Lawrence and J. Crocker, "Academic Contingencies of Self-Worth Impair Positively and Negatively Stereotyped Students' Performance in Performance-Goal Settings," *Journal of Research in Personality* 43, no. 5 (2009): 868–874.

6. Ibid., 870.

7. C. M. Steele and J. Aronson, "Stereotype Threat and the Test Performance of Academically Successful African Americans," in *The Black-*

*White Test Score Gap,* ed. C. Jencks and M. Phillips, 401–427 (Washington, DC: Brookings Institution Press, 1998). C. M. Steele, "Thin Ice: Stereotype Threat and Black College Students," *Atlantic* 284 (1999): 44–54.

8. See, for example, S. J. Garlow et al., "Depression, Desperation, and Suicidal Ideation in College Students: Results from the American Foundation for Suicide Prevention College Screening Project at Emory University," *Depression and Anxiety* 25, no. 6 (2008): 482–488; D. Eisenberg et al., "Prevalence and Correlates of Depression, Anxiety, and Suicidality among University Students," *American Journal of Orthopsychiatry* 77, no. 4 (2007): 534–542; D. Eisenberg, E. Golberstein, and J. B. Hunt, "Mental Health and Academic Success in College," *BE Journal of Economic Analysis and Policy* 9, no. 1 (2009), article 40; J. Crocker, A. Canevello, J. G. Breines, and H. Flynn, "Interpersonal Goals and Change in Anxiety and Dysphoria in First-Semester College Students," *Journal of Personality and Social Psychology* 98, no. 6 (2010): 1009–1024; L. N. Dyrbye, M. R. Thomas, and T. D. Shanafelt, "Systematic Review of Depression, Anxiety, and Other Indicators of Psychological Distress among US and Canadian Medical Students," *Academic Medicine* 81, no. 4 (2006): 354–373; J. Klibert et al., "Suicide Proneness in College Students: Relationships with Gender, Procrastination, and Achievement Motivation," *Death Studies* 35, no. 7 (2011): 625–645.

9. Indeed, as Kristin Neff pointed out in a recent newspaper article, "One of the most insidious consequences of the self-esteem movement over the last couple of decades is the narcissism epidemic." One recent study of fifteen thousand college students in the United States found that 65 percent scored higher on measures of narcissism than did their counterparts from an earlier generation. "Not coincidentally," she concluded, "students' average self-esteem levels rose by an even greater margin over the same period." Kristin Neff, "Why We Should Stop Chasing Self-Esteem and Start Developing Self-Compassion," *Huffington Post,* April 6, 2011. Available at http://

www.huffingtonpost.com/kristin-neff/self-compassion_b_843721. html.

10. J. R. Shapiro, S. A. Mistler, and S. L. Neuberg, "Threatened Selves and Differential Prejudice Expression by White and Black Perceivers," *Journal of Experimental Social Psychology* 46, no. 2 (2010): 469–473, 469.

11. J. Crocker and L. E. Park, "The Costly Pursuit of Self-Esteem," *Psychological Bulletin* 130, no. 3 (2004): 392–414, 393.

12. K. Neff, "Self-Compassion: An Alternative Conceptualization of a Healthy Attitude toward Oneself," *Self and Identity* 2, no. 2 (2003): 85–101, 87.

13. K. D. Neff, K. L. Kirkpatrick, and S. S. Rude, "Self-Compassion and Adaptive Psychological Functioning," *Journal of Research in Personality* 41, no. 1 (2007): 139–154, 146.

14. K. D. Neff, Y. P. Hsieh, and K. Dejitterat, "Self-Compassion, Achievement Goals, and Coping with Academic Failure," *Self and Identity* 4, no. 3 (2005): 263–287; K. D. Neff and R. Vonk, "Self-Compassion versus Global Self-Esteem: Two Different Ways of Relating to Oneself," *Journal of Personality* 77, no. 1 (2009): 23–50; K. Neff, *Self-Compassion: Stop Beating Yourself Up and Leave Insecurity Behind* (New York: William Morrow, 2011).

15. E. Cohen, "Push to Achieve Tied to Suicide in Asian-American Women," CNN, May 16, 2007. Available at http://edition.cnn. com/2007/HEALTH/05/16/asian.suicides/index.html.

16. For more discussion, see D. Lester, "Differences in the Epidemiology of Suicide in Asian Americans by Nation of Origin," *OMEGA— Journal of Death and Dying* 29, no. 2 (1994): 89–93.

17. Robert Wood Johnson Foundation website available at http://www. rwjf.org/vulnerablepopulations/product.jsp?id=51208; Friends of the Children website available at http://www.friendsofthechildren. org.

18. Northwestern News, "Undergraduate Humanitarian Honored," *TribLocal Evanston,* May 18, 2010. Available at http://triblocal.com/

evanston/community/stories/2010/05/undergraduate-
humanitarian-honored/.

### 7. CURIOSITY AND ENDLESS EDUCATION

1. Professors and deans sometimes support general education requirements because they want to get their department's offerings
on the mandatory list to protect faculty positions in their area.

2. Department chairs and deans sometimes won't release faculty to
develop and offer interdisciplinary courses because these courses
don't serve the needs of the department.

3. Thanks to the philosopher Tiger Roholt, my colleague, for intro-
ducing me to Taylor's ideas and to the quotations I include here.
Tiger Roholt to author, April 23, 2011.

4. R. Holmes, B. Gan, and T. Madigan, "Richard Taylor Remembered,"
*Philosophy Now* 44 (Jan./Feb. 2004).

5. A. Abbott, "Welcome to the University of Chicago," Aims of Education Address (for the class of 2006), September 26, 2002, Digital
Text International. Available at http://www.ditext.com/abbott/
abbott_aims.html.

6. A. Chrucky, "The Aim of Liberal Education," Sept. 1, 2003, Digital
Text International. Available at http://www.ditext.com/chrucky/
aim.html.

7. Mount Sinai School of Medicine, "Mount Sinai Study Shows that
Humanities Students Perform as Well as Pre-Med Students in Medical School," press release, July 30, 2010. Available at http://www.
mssm.edu/about-us/news-and-events/mount-sinai-study-shows-
that-humanities-students-perform-as-well-as-pre-med-students-in-
medical-school.

### 8. MAKING THE HARD CHOICES

1. J. K. Rowling, "The Fringe Benefits of Failure, and the Importance
of Imagination," speech delivered at Harvard University, June 5,

2008. You can read all of this remarkable speech at http://news. harvard.edu/gazette/story/2008/06/text-of-j-k-rowling-speech/.

2. J. Lehrer, "Don't! The Secret of Self-Control," *New Yorker,* May 18, 2009.

3. One useful way of scheduling is to create a weekly, twenty-four-hour calendar with seven columns and twenty-four rows, so that there is a box for every hour of the week. You can then put into each box the planned activities of that hour. You can also see if you really have time for all the activities of your life, including eating, sleeping, commuting, and so forth.

4. T. Gura, "Procrastinating Again? How to Kick the Habit," *Scientific American,* Dec. 2008.

5. M. J. A. Wohl, T. A. Pychyl, and S. H. Bennett, "I Forgive Myself, Now I Can Study: How Self-Forgiveness for Procrastinating Can Reduce Future Procrastination," *Personality and Individual Differences* 48, no. 7 (2010): 803–808.

6. Examples abound. Chad Richardson, a sociology professor at the University of Texas Pan American, quickly teaches his introductory students how to lead oral interviews, then sends them out to conduct ethnographic research in their own neighborhoods and among their families. As they collect their data, he then helps them understand them in terms of broader sociological principles. Charlie Cannon at the Rhode Island School of Design invites students into an authentic project to tackle some socially and economically significant design issue: for example, what does New York Harbor do with a waste treatment plant?

7. X. Lin, D. L. Schwartz, and J. Bransford, "Intercultural Adaptive Expertise: Explicit and Implicit Lessons from Dr. Hatano," *Human Development* 50, no. 1 (2007): 65–72; T. Martin, K. Rayne, N. Kemp, J. Hart, and K. Diller, "Teaching for Adaptive Expertise in Biomedical Engineering Ethics," *Science and Engineering Ethics* 11, no. 2 (June 1, 2005): 257–276.

8. J. Bransford, "Some Thoughts on Adaptive Expertise," Vanderbilt-Northwestern-Texas-Harvard/MIT Engineering Research Center (VaNTH-ERC), July 9, 2001. Available at www.vanth.org/docs/AdaptiveExpertise.pdf.

9. J. A. Bargh and Y. Schul, "On the Cognitive Benefits of Teaching," *Journal of Educational Psychology* 72, no. 5 (1980): 593-604.

10. G. M. Muir and G. J. van der Linden, "Students Teaching Students: An Experiential Learning Opportunity for Large Introductory Psychology Classes in Collaboration with Local Elementary Schools," *Teaching of Psychology* 36, no. 3 (2009): 169-173, 171.

11. Quoted in Donald Sheff, "'Izzy, Did You Ask a Good Question Today?'" *New York Times,* Letter to the Editor, Jan. 12, 1988.

12. T. S. Hyde and J. J. Jenkins, "Differential Effects of Incidental Tasks on the Organization of Recall of a List of Highly Associated Words," *Journal of Experimental Psychology* 82, no. 3 (1969): 472-481.

13. See Chapter 2 for a discussion of deep, surface, and strategic approaches to learning.

14. N. Györbíró, H. Larkin, and M. Cohen, "Spaced Repetition Tool for Improving Long-term Memory Retention and Recall of Collected Personal Experiences," *Proceedings of the 7th International Conference on Advances in Computer Entertainment Technology* (2010): 124-125.

15. N. Kornell, M. J. Hays, and R. A. Bjork, "Unsuccessful Retrieval Attempts Enhance Subsequent Learning," *Journal of Experimental Psychology: Learning, Memory, and Cognition* 35, no. 4 (2009): 989-998; L. E. Richland, N. Kornell, and L. S. Kao, "The Pretesting Effect: Do Unsuccessful Retrieval Attempts Enhance Learning?" *Journal of Experimental Psychology: Applied* 15, no. 3 (2009): 243-257; N. Kornell, R. A. Bjork, and M. A. Garcia, "Why Tests Appear to Prevent Forgetting: A Distribution-based Bifurcation Model," *Journal of Memory and Language* (2011): 85-97; N. Kornell and R. A. Bjork. "Optimising Self-regulated Study: The Benefits—and Costs—of Dropping Flashcards," *Memory* 16, no. 2 (2008): 125-136; H. L. Roediger and B. Flinn,

"Getting It Wrong: Surprising Tips on How to Learn" *Scientific American,* Oct. 20, 2009.

16. Dudley Herschbach, in contrast, told us that he always studied in the same nook in the library. Find out what works for you, but for a review of some of the research see S. M. Smith and E. Vela, "Environmental Context-Dependent Memory: A Review and Meta-analysis," *Psychonomic Bulletin and Review* 8, no. 2 (2001): 203–220; S. M. Smith, A. Glenberg, and R. A. Bjork, "Environmental Context and Human Memory," *Memory and Cognition* 6, no. 4 (1978): 342–353. For a different finding, see A. Fernandez and A. M. Glenberg, "Changing Environmental Context Does Not Reliably Affect Memory," *Memory and Cognition* 13, no. 4 (1985): 333–345.

17. J. S. Rubinstein, D. E. Meyer, and J. E. Evans, "Executive Control of Cognitive Processes in Task Switching," *Journal of Experimental Psychology: Human Perception and Performance* 27, no. 4 (2001): 763–797.

18. A. Furnham, S. Trew, and I. Sneade, "The Distracting Effects of Vocal and Instrumental Music on the Cognitive Test Performance of Introverts and Extraverts," *Personality and Individual Differences* 27, no. 2 (1999): 381–392; A. Furnham and A. Bradley, "Music While You Work: The Differential Distraction of Background Music on the Cognitive Test Performance of Introverts and Extraverts," *Applied Cognitive Psychology* 11, no. 5 (1997): 445–455.

19. K. I. Erickson et al., "Exercise Training Increases Size of Hippocampus and Improves Memory," *Proceedings of the National Academy of Sciences* 108, no. 7 (Feb. 15, 2011): 3017–3022.

20. E. Mo, "Studying the Link between Exercise and Learning," CNN Health, Apr. 12, 2010. Available at http://thechart.blogs.cnn.com/2010/04/12/studying-the-link-between-exercise-and-learning/.

21. M. Yogo and S. Fujihara, "Working Memory Capacity Can Be Improved by Expressive Writing: A Randomized Experiment in a Japanese Sample," *British Journal of Health Psychology* 13, no. 1 (2008): 77–80.

22. K. Klein and A. Boals, "Expressive Writing Can Increase Working Memory Capacity," *Journal of Experimental Psychology: General* 130, no. 3 (2001): 520–533.

23. J. W. Pennebaker and C. K. Chung, "Expressive Writing, Emotional Upheavals, and Health," in *Oxford Handbook of Health Psychology,* ed. H. S. Friedman (New York: Oxford University Press, 2011).

24. Those cultures do bleed into the neighboring towns, that is, into the high schools and elementary grades, and students do begin to get some taste of them, even in the first grade. But it is only when they arrive in the capital city (college) that they confront the full complexity of this culture—and some of the secrets remain hidden until graduate school.

# ACKNOWLEDGMENTS

The idea for this study and book emerged in 2004 as a result of the publication of my earlier work, *What the Best College Teachers Do*. Two other people also played a significant role in its initiation, execution, and completion. Marsha Bain was there from beginning to end, assisting in every aspect of the research, helping to identify subjects, making contact with them, taking notes on interviews with subjects, formulating conclusions, developing narratives, and helping me explore ideas about the learning biographies of the people we encountered and how their experiences compared with some of the research and theoretical literature on human learning and creativity. A luncheon conversation with my editor, Elizabeth Knoll, in 2007 helped me crystallize my thinking about the project and encouraged me to go forward with it. The financial support that Harvard University Press offered to me was enormously encouraging, even though I subsequently turned it down. As always, Elizabeth provided great suggestions for the manuscript as it emerged. Without her excellent input, the book would be far less accomplished. Kate Brick at Harvard University Press provided some enormously helpful suggestions for the manuscript. She helped make it a significantly better book.

To complete the study and write the book, we depended on the support of many people. My children and their spouses, Tonia Bain and Al Masino, and Marshall Bain and Alice Yuan, offered constant encouragement and provocative suggestions that advanced the whole enterprise. My greatest inspiration came from two future college students, Adam Bain and Nathan Bain, and from all future grandchildren. As I wrote each line, developed each idea, and organized each chapter, I kept constantly in mind how it would play with them in about fifteen years.

I would especially like to thank all of the wonderful people who allowed me to interview them. All of the stories became important in shaping the conclusions of this book, even when I did not use a particular learning biography in the final version. I also want to thank two colleagues, Julie Dalley and Cigdem Talgar, for reading early drafts and offering their suggestions, and Joy Deng for her assistance with endnotes. My staff, Terry Prescott, Denise Slaughter, Benyi Inyama, and Salome Amoussou, gave me the kind of assistance that allowed a busy provost to undertake and finish a project like this one while drinking from the fire hose of responsibilities that fall upon someone in such a position. Finally, thanks to Allen Sessoms, who offered me the job of provost at the University of the District of Columbia in the summer of 2011 but agreed to defer my appointment until January 2012, after I had finished writing the initial draft.

# Index